THE
PASTORAL PROPHET

THE
PASTORAL
PROPHET

MEDITATIONS ON THE BOOK OF JEREMIAH

FOREWORD BY
ROBERT M. HILLER

Steve Kruschel

The Pastoral Prophet

© 2019 Steve Kruschel

Published by:
1517 Publishing
PO Box 54032
Irvine, CA 92619-4032

Publisher's Cataloging-In-Publication Data
(Prepared by The Donohue Group, Inc.)

Names: Kruschel, Steve, author. | Hiller, Robert M., writer of supplementary textual content.
Title: The pastoral prophet : meditations on the Book of Jeremiah / Steve Kruschel ; foreword by Robert M. Hiller.
Description: Irvine, CA : 1517 Publishing, [2020] | Includes bibliographical references.
Identifiers: ISBN 9781945978814 (hardcover) | ISBN 9781945978821 (paperback) | ISBN 9781945978838 (ebook)
Subjects: LCSH: Bible. Jeremiah—Meditations. | Jeremiah (Biblical prophet)—Prayers and devotions. | LCGFT: Meditations.
Classification: LCC BS1525.54 .K78 2020 (print) | LCC BS1525.54 (ebook) | DDC 224/.207—dc23

Printed in the United States of America

Cover art by Brenton Clark Little

Contents

Foreword

Robert M. Hiller

Burnout. Depression. Scandal. These words describe the normal experience of the pastor far too often. It seems that every week I hear about a brother who is taking a leave of absence or see a headline about someone abusing the office of the ministry or witness pastors attacking other pastors in the name of faithfulness.

Pastors are overwhelmed by the demands placed upon them. Temptations for escape abound. The sinful desire to be "liked" replaces the call of Jesus in driving the pastor's words and deeds. It becomes easier to sing the sweet-sounding songs of the culture than to "contend for the faith that was once for all delivered to the saints" (Jude 3 ESV). The ministry is a burden much too heavy to carry. And the clergy are suffering and dying. No wonder so many don't want to enter the ministry.

These trials and temptations are nothing new. Martin Luther spoke of them back in the sixteenth century when lecturing on First Timothy. He said,

> Every theologian has been established as a bishop of the church to bear the troubles of everyone in the church. He stands on the battle line. He is the prime target of all attacks, difficulties, anxieties, disturbances of consciences, temptations and doubts. All these hit the bishop where it hurts. Still greater trials follow. The princes of the world and the very learned seek him out. He is made a spectacle for both devils and angels.[1]

---

[1] Martin Luther, *Lectures on 1 Timothy* (1528), in *Luther's Works*, vol. 28 (St. Louis: Concordia Publishing House, 1973), 219.

In other words, Christ calls a man to the ministry, and the devil puts a hit out on the pastor. So, as Dietrich Bonhoeffer said, "When Christ calls a man, he bids him come and die."[2]

In the midst of such agonizing trials, it is natural for preachers to turn to God's Word for comfort and hope. This is exactly what this book in front of you so graciously does. I'll be honest though, where this book sends you is not initially where I would turn. That is, it sends you to the prophet Jeremiah. In a day and age where the devil attacks and the world weighs heavy on us, Jeremiah's message doesn't bring us the happy, uplifting message we might hope for. And yet, it is exactly Jeremiah's ministry and preaching that we pastors need to hear!

Perhaps better than any other Hebrew prophet, Jeremiah knew the depths of sorrow and angst that come with being a messenger of the Almighty God. God placed his Word in Jeremiah's mouth, and the devil, the world, and flesh went after him. He brought very harsh law to God's rebellious people, and they fought back hard. Jeremiah is mocked, rejected, and given a death sentence, and his sermons are called lies. For goodness' sake, they left him to die in a cistern! And Jeremiah kept preaching. Why?

Why would anyone keep preaching with such a cross to bear? Because of Christ Jesus! The message given to Jeremiah—and the message given to you as a pastor—is a message that is greater than all that the devil, the world, and the flesh can do to us. That little message brings heaven crashing down on the schemes of the devil and gives life and joy and peace. Though these are hidden from us now, for now is the time to bear a cross, they have been won for us by the blood of Jesus Christ. Jesus, "who for the joy that was set before him endured the cross, despising the shame, and is seated at the right hand of the throne of God" (Heb. 12:2 ESV). Jesus is the one who suffered the full brunt of Satan's assaults, the world's temptations, and God's wrath against sin on the cross all to reconcile sinners to God and prepare a place for them in his Father's presence for all of eternity. The resurrection of this crucified God gives us the promise

---

[2] Dietrich Bonhoeffer, *The Cost of Discipleship* (New York: Simon & Schuster, 1995), 99.

that it will last only for the night. Joy will come in the morning of Christ's return! And though all hell fights against our faith, it is only through the preaching of the Word that we will be sustained into life everlasting.

Jeremiah and all preachers are both saved and shaped by this joy that was set before Christ. This joy gets in their hearts and guts, and they cannot stop from preaching it! The trials of the ministry shrink in the presence of this blood-bought joy. "For I consider that the sufferings of this present time are not worth comparing with the glory that is to be revealed to us," wrote Paul (Rom. 8:19 ESV). Christ the crucified is risen so that our preaching is not in vain (1 Cor. 15:20) and will produce faith that leads to everlasting life (Rom. 10:17). The preacher knows the lies that would take this hope away, and he knows he must attack them. His job as a defender of joy and a promiser of hope drives him again and again into the darkness, even though he suffers for the name of Christ.

This is lonely and hard work. No preacher can bear it alone. Every preacher needs a preacher, a voice from outside of himself to put the promises back in his ears and heart. The preacher, like every sinner, is sustained only by the daily giving of God's Word. He needs harsh law to shatter his pride and the sweet gospel to breathe life back into him. With all that he was up against, Jeremiah was sustained by this promise: "They will fight against you, but they shall not prevail against you, for I am with you, declares the Lord, to deliver you" (Jer. 1:19 ESV).

Here is where Pastor Kruschel's book is a great gift for the pastor. He has given us Jeremiah as a preacher of Christ Jesus. As a pastor, he knows exactly what is eating at us, what is chewing us up and spitting us out. He knows firsthand the temptations, sins, and trials we face as pastors. He preaches as Jeremiah, not withholding the law for us in our pride and never for a second letting us go without giving us the blessing of the gospel. Time and again, Pastor Kruschel's words have killed me and brought me back to life. He's fixed my eyes on Jesus and sustained me with the joy of the gospel. Dear preacher, you will find this is the book you need in your trials. It delivers God's Word to sustain you in the ministry.

This is the Word that sustained Jeremiah. It is the same Word that will sustain you. Here is that Word in a nutshell: Dear preacher, you are a sinner who is attacked, who sins, who fails, and who is weak. But what of it? Christ Jesus, who is greater than all of this, has called you to preach his Word. And, he meant it! What is more, the Word you preach is the Word he gives to you, even now. You are forgiven for the sake of his blood. Hear the Word of the Lord, "Do not be afraid of them, for I am with you to deliver you, declares the Lord" (Jer. 1:8 ESV). Amen!

How to Use This Book

"Hear the word of the LORD" (Jeremiah 2:4). The young prophet's voice might have cracked as it spoke these first prophetic words to Jerusalem's elite. As a servant of the Lord, Jeremiah probably wasn't much to look at. No miracles dazzled the crowd. The heavens did not echo the booming voice of the Lord. He was just another prophet with the same old message.

The prophet certainly looked weak. Yet the messages he went on to proclaim found their way into the hearts of countless men and women over the centuries. His words transcend time. Their significance outdistance every map. The hard hand of God's law strikes modern listeners every bit as harshly as it hit Jeremiah's original listeners. God's gospel touches you every bit as personally as it touched his prophet, Jeremiah.

These devotions are meant to help you as a pastor, a teacher, a church leader, and a parishioner as those words of the Lord apply themselves to your life and ministry. As you read through these devotions, you are encouraged to first meditate on the verses of Jeremiah. Then in your personal devotion or with other called workers, read the devotional thoughts based on those verses provided in this book. Appropriate hymn verses form the final prayer for each reading.

Look as Jeremiah holds the mirror of God's law up to your heart. Feel the curb of God's commands bumping you back onto the path of righteousness. Witness God's beautiful gospel message as his prophet speaks it directly to you. And follow that light of God's word as it guides your ministerial walk through the shadows of death and the depths of sadness, and then up to the mountain tops of joy into the selfless pinnacles of praise.

As divisions crack ministerial relationships, as anger rips apart Christians, as grief weighs down called servants, may these devotional words based on the book of Jeremiah give you, your family, your faculty and your congregation the opportunity to be strengthened by God's word. May it offer peace during strife. May it mend the rifts that form in ministry. And may it offer you a daily opportunity to fulfill those words Jeremiah first proclaimed so long ago: "Hear the word of the Lord."

Introduction

> When Jesus came to the region of Caesarea Philippi, he asked his disciples, "Who do people say the Son of Man is?" They replied, "Some say John the Baptist, others say Elijah, and others Jeremiah or one of the prophets." (Matthew 16:13–14)

Perhaps the spiritual scuttlebutt of Jesus' day possessed greater knowledge than we realize. Every comparison the people raised in the gospel of Matthew made at least some sort of scriptural sense. Similarities between Jesus and John the Baptist are understandable. After all, the two were related. Their messages concerning repentance and baptism also sounded synonymous.

Those expecting Elijah's return also mistook Jesus for John the Baptist. Surprisingly, they were not far off. They simply did not realize John had already fulfilled Malachi's prophecy by becoming the Elijah-like prophet destined to prepare the way for the coming Messiah.

Then comes Matthew's final comparison. There were a few people who thought Jesus was the prophet Jeremiah. Do not dismiss their answer as ignorant. These folks were on to something. To compare Jesus to Jeremiah is to understand the seriousness of Jesus' words and the perilous context in which he spoke them.

Both the prophet and the Messiah preached harsh warnings in Jerusalem. Jeremiah prophesied the city's first destruction at the hands of the Babylonians. Jesus warned of her second destruction at the hands of the Romans. The inspired words of both men opposed the religious factions of their day. Each stood before their king, who threatened them with death. Both men lamented over Jerusalem's unrepentant hearts through tears of frustration. Both Jeremiah and Jesus faced opposition and betrayal from their own families and hometowns. In the end, the ministries of both Jeremiah and Jesus finished outside the walls of Jerusalem. The Babylonians had destroyed the city, and Jeremiah's own countrymen dragged him into Egypt. Jesus willingly carried his Roman cross outside the city to suffer and die for the sins of the entire world.

Jeremiah even prophesied many of the details of Jesus' ministry. The gospel of Matthew connects each of these prophecies to Jesus' fulfillment. When King Herod killed every Bethlehem boy two years old and younger, Matthew connected the tragedy to Jeremiah's prophecy (Jeremiah 31:15). When Judas committed suicide, Matthew recorded that the chief priests purchased the field in fulfillment of the prophet (Jeremiah 18:2, 32:6–9). On the Monday of Holy Week, when Jesus accused the money changers of making his house "a den of robbers," he quoted Jeremiah 7:11.

While Jeremiah's ministry often appears as a shadow of Christ's Messianic ministry, it does not mirror it. Jeremiah himself understood this. He often included himself as a fellow guilty party in his list of wicked acts taking place in Judah. He understood his own personal need for redemption. In some of the most beautiful words in all of scripture, Jeremiah looked ahead to the eternally important work of the coming Messiah: "For I will forgive their wickedness and will remember their sins no more" (Jeremiah 31:34).

In reading Jeremiah's words, you soon find out just how similar your ministry might be to his. In fact, meditating on the writings of Jeremiah sends a called worker traveling two and a half millennia into the past to find a modern-day colleague. In many surprising and frightening ways, Jeremiah's ministry compares to the work of today's pastors and teachers. Jeremiah lived in the end times of his people in Jerusalem. He preached that destruction was coming and that the Lord would soon follow. He spiritually grappled with false prophets who were twisting God's message. His kings and officials had no time for his message. National politics ruled his day. He watched the multitudes who had once exhibited faith under the reign of their good king, Josiah, slowly fall away in the years that followed.

Such a volatile, hated ministry perpetually left Jeremiah on a reclusive island of solitude. For years an orchestra of prophets had beautifully sounded the Lord's inspired music through a symphony of law and gospel. By the end of his ministry, Jeremiah seemed to be the last accompanist, playing Judah's last melodic note. His prophetic, monotone music often shifted between the Lord's stern law and Jeremiah's own weeping chant for his people.

The Lord's specific command for Jeremiah never to marry (Jeremiah 16:2) often seemed to compound this tragic loneliness. With only his faithful scribe, Baruch, and a handful of believing Jerusalem officials, Jeremiah cried out the Lord's final words in Jerusalem. Most reverberated off the walls unheeded. If Jerusalem rested on the precipice of destruction like the ancient, tragic city of Troy, then Jeremiah was her Cassandra. His heartfelt pleas and prophecies found only closed ears.

They also incurred retribution.

Jeremiah knew suffering better than any other prophet and perhaps more than any other person. He was called at a younger age than any of his prophetic peers, and the Lord's ordination text for Jeremiah sounded ominous. The Lord explained to his newly minted prophet that he called him to speak "against the kings of Judah, its officials, its priests, and the people of the land" (1:18). And if that was not difficult enough, the Lord added, "They will fight against you" (1:19a).

They certainly did. Jeremiah's own family betrayed him (12:6). His hometown of Anathoth conspired to kill him (11:21). A priest named Pashhur had Jeremiah beaten and placed in the stocks (20:1–2) while the rest of Jerusalem mocked him (20:7). False prophets continually contradicted him (23, 28). His own priests worked against him (29:24–32). Kings threatened him with death (26) and burned the very words of the Lord that Baruch had written down (36). Jeremiah was thrown into prison (37) and then down a cistern (38). King Zedekiah imprisoned him in the courtyard (37:21) while Jerusalem itself finally fell to the Babylonians. Even after the destruction of his city, Jeremiah faced danger. When the Lord told his people to stay put, they decided to pull Jeremiah down into Egypt (43:6). At the end of it all, writers such as Epiphanies, Tertullian, and Jerome recorded a Jewish tradition that describes the Jews stoning their own prophet to death.

Jeremiah's arduous ministry lasted longer than any other prophet's in scripture. Throughout it he was hated, ostracized, labeled a traitor, and considered a spy. For his decades of faithful service, he had to witness the walls of his beloved city of Jerusalem fall. He watched his temple looted and torn down. He saw the fires that burned down the king's palace. In the midst of this rubble, Jeremiah became the weeping prophet we know him to be. His ministry seemed veiled in darkness. Tragedy perpetually pursued him.

No modern minister would wish Jeremiah's life on his worst enemy.

Yet through it all, the book of Jeremiah reveals beauty in realism. Not one account of the prophet's ministry is whitewashed. In Jerusalem's last days, we see a very real prophet struggling against the inner turmoil and thoughts of inadequacy that seize every called worker. He openly argued with the Lord about justice. He fell into despair. And yet, despite the multitude of his hardships, Jeremiah's heart still bled for his people and their salvation.

Weeping though he was, Jeremiah never abdicated. Surrounded by darkness, defiance, and depression, he marched on, fueled by the word of the Lord and strengthened by the Holy Spirit in his prophetic resolve. Jeremiah's ministry stands as the quintessential example of how the light of God's grace shines brightest when the world around descends into its darkest depths. It seems that during history's harshest periods of opposition to the word, the Lord delights to send his greatest servants.

Jeremiah was one such servant. No other inspired tongue slipped as seamlessly between brilliant prose and beautiful poetry. His historical tone rivaled Moses' Egyptian literacy training. His impassioned verses ascend to the heart-moving overtones of the Davidic psalter—raw emotion clothed in the splendor of faith-filled words.

This is ministry, dear fellow called worker. Faithful service in the name of the Lord continues to bring worldly retribution, threats, persecution, false messages, and sometimes even destruction. In this way, Jeremiah's ministry mirrors your ministry. The names and places have changed, but the song remains the same. The Lord's word still stands as the foundation of your faith, the authority of your preaching and teaching, the source of your strength, and the tune to your faithful song of service. There, in the center of it all, stands Christ.

He stood with Jeremiah, too. Through all of it. While his words often sounded harsh, the Lord also whispered to Jeremiah some of scripture's most comforting gospel messages. Already at the beginning of his long, formidable ministry, the Lord made a timeless promise to his called worker:

> "Get yourself ready! Stand up and say to them whatever I command you. Do not be terrified by them, or I will terrify you before them. Today I have made you a fortified city, an iron pillar and a bronze wall to stand against the whole land—against the kings of Judah, its officials, its priests and the people of the land. They will fight against you but will not overcome you, for I am with you and will rescue you," declares the LORD. (1:17–19)

In the final days of Jeremiah's ministry, the Lord reminded his world-weathered prophet of those same promises. The Lord encouraged his faithful servant: "I will build you up and not tear you down; I will plant you and not uproot you" (42:10). And he did.

May these words of God through Jeremiah serve as faithful law and gospel for you and your ministry. May Jeremiah's harsh circumstances remind you to flee to the Lord and his word when similar persecutions come your way. May Jeremiah's God-filled laments help form your pastoral prayers. And may Jeremiah's bleeding heart show you the importance of selfless love in service to Christ and the people he has called you to serve.

Above all, God's ancient promise to Jeremiah remains his everlasting promise to you. In the face of this dark world, in your resistance to the devil's daily temptations, and through your opposition to your own sinful flesh stands God's gospel comfort. It is meant for *you*, dear believer: "'I am with you and will rescue you,' declares the LORD."

"I have put my words in your mouth"

Jeremiah 1:1–10

Even from a young age, Jeremiah seemed destined for the ministry. As the son of Hilkiah, a priest in the territory of Benjamin, Jeremiah must have been familiar with the joys and struggles a family experiences when serving the Lord. It seems ministry was their family heritage. The village of Anathoth was the home town of Abiathar, who was the high priest during the reign of King David.

David was long gone by Jeremiah's day. But a David-like king named Josiah was sitting on the throne. As a faithful king, Josiah had once again ushered in good days for Judah. An older Jeremiah may have looked back on them fondly.

Then, all at once, those gloriously free younger days were gone. The word of the Lord came to Jeremiah. This was such a memorable experience for a prophet that the year was seared into his memory: the thirteenth year of the reign of the good king, Josiah. Looking back on the occasion, Jeremiah also writes the ending date of his ministry in Judah: the eleventh year of Zedekiah, son of Josiah, king of Judah. Through the lens of hindsight Jeremiah briefly shows us just how far his people had fallen spiritually. In the span of his forty-year ministry, one of the longest of any prophet, Jeremiah had witnessed his people go from reformation to desolation. A ministry that began soon after Josiah's cleansing of the temple and rediscovery of God's word would eventually give way to the destruction of the temple and the godless captivity of God's people.

It was quite a period in which Jeremiah served! Looked at positively, Jeremiah witnessed some of most important years in Judah's entire history. Negatively, Jeremiah witnessed Judah's spiritual fall from grace and the physical fall of his people.

Knowing all that was going to happen over the course of the next forty years, the Lord did something we certainly would not have. He came to a young man named Jeremiah and prepared him to minister. The Lord's first words to Jeremiah may have been some of the most comforting he ever told his prophet:

> Before I formed you in the womb I knew you,
> before you were born I set you apart;
> I appointed you as a prophet to the nations.

What comforting words to hear from our omnipotent, omniscient, and omnipresent Lord! From eternity the Lord knew all about Jeremiah. He foresaw everything Jeremiah would experience. He understood the trials Jeremiah would face. He formed Jeremiah for this calling.

Just imagine, the omnipotent, eternal God taking the time to carefully craft his small prophet. How can someone so large, so holy, so unknowable reach down and gently call a sinful man to serve him? The answer, as is so often the case, is love. The Lord *loved* Jeremiah. That love expressed itself in the very creation of Jeremiah. The Lord set Jeremiah apart. The Lord appointed him to be a prophet. Perhaps young Jeremiah even saw God's undeserved grace pouring out through these initial words of the Lord.

The task itself would be considerable. "I appointed you as a prophet to the nations." Most of God's prophets stayed within the confines of the kingdom, with a few notable exceptions. No such borders would shut in Jeremiah. Chapter 25 lists Egypt, Uz, the Philistines, Edom, Moab, Ammon, the coastlands across the sea, Arabia, the kings of Zimri, Elam and Media, the kings of the north, and "all the kingdoms on the face of the earth" as places to which the Lord sent Jeremiah. It is as true today as it was in Jeremiah's day. The word of the Lord continues to spread as the Lord sends out his followers to every country and kingdom.

You are part of that call, too. You have been sent out by the Lord to speak his word with care and boldness, as Jeremiah did. Perhaps, like Jeremiah, you come from a family with a heritage of public ministry. Perhaps you also grew up in a household of pastors and teachers. Perhaps, like Jeremiah, you dedicated yourself to serving in the public ministry from your youngest days.

Or perhaps you are nothing like Jeremiah, growing up in a family that was once distant from the Lord. Perhaps you came to ministry later in life. Maybe your family and relatives don't approve of your work for the Lord. This, too, is similar to Jeremiah's experience.

How can one react to these deep and meaningful words of the Lord when they fall on one small, sinful individual? Jeremiah responds with his first words to the Lord: "'Alas, Sovereign LORD,' I said, 'I do not know how to speak; I am too young.'" Indeed, he was! Jeremiah may have been the youngest prophet called to serve the Lord in the Old Testament. How could this young boy possibly carry out God's important task of ministering to Judah? How could such a young child live "as a prophet to the nations"?

Jeremiah's youthful reluctance toward ministry sounds eerily similar to Moses' aged objections at the burning bush. Neither thought they could speak the way God needed them to speak. Yet both went on to be listed among the greatest preachers in the history of Christendom. Both were pretty good inspired writers, too. Moses' words from the Lord formed the first five books of the Bible! Jeremiah's words from the Lord created the longest book of the Bible!

Of course, the Lord doesn't explain all of that to Jeremiah at this point. Instead, he meets the objection headlong. "Do not say, 'I am only too young.' You must go to everyone I send you to and say whatever I command you." And Jeremiah would say those words—whether they were law or gospel.

Yet he remained understandably afraid. Who wouldn't be? God's law can stir up very powerful and angry emotions in people. In fact, this word of the Lord would produce persecution throughout Jeremiah's ministry. So the Lord reminded him, "Do not be afraid of them, for I am with you and will rescue you."

Those words of the Lord probably would have been enough. But in his love, the Lord followed them with one of his most loving actions. "Then the LORD reached out his hand and touched my mouth and said to me, 'Now, I have put my words in your mouth.

See, today I appoint you over nations and kingdoms to uproot and tear down, to destroy and overthrow, to build and to plant.'"

The *Lord himself* touched Jeremiah's mouth! The very fact that Jeremiah survived this experience illustrated God's grace. When the Lord called the prophet Isaiah, a burning coal was brought to his mouth by one of the seraphim. Here the Lord touched Jeremiah *with his own hand!* Jeremiah's words would be God's words. The Lord would accomplish the uprooting, the tearing down, the destruction, and the overthrowing. And the Lord would also take care of the building and planting. The touch of the hand of the Lord became an extraordinary event in Jeremiah's life and ministry. From now on the two would be woven together.

What about you? I doubt the hand of the Lord physically touched your mouth when you were called to serve him. No voice from heaven boomed from the sky to send you forth. And yet you have probably had doubts similar to those Jeremiah shared with the Lord. You are not the greatest speaker in Christendom. You cannot teach as well as the greatest teachers. An admonition of these truths is not evidence of any shortcoming in how God knit you together. It is a confession of sin. Every prophet, judge, priest, king, pastor, and teacher has possessed sinful shortcomings. We are all daily plagued by a sinful nature that cries out with Jeremiah, "I'm not capable— find someone else!" We all have fallen into the ditches on either side of the road of righteousness. At times we have exemplified prideful arrogance. At other times, we lived in hopeless ministerial despair.

The presence of the Lord and his call shines a glorious light on these filthy marks of ours. We stand ready to be ruined. But like Jeremiah, we hear the word of the Lord lovingly say, "Do not be afraid." What can take away this fear of eternal punishment for sin? What enables us to stand in the presence of such powerful perfection? It is the very Savior we are privileged to proclaim. The sins Jesus has forgiven include ministerial shortcomings, too. Because these sins manifest themselves daily in your ministry, this confession of sins must also remain a daily exercise. The absolution that follows is the daily reminder of God's grace. That grace motivates your ministry on his behalf.

We give ourselves too much credit when we think that the gospel ministry stands and falls because of our own strengths and weaknesses. The word stands powerful by itself! And yet in his infinite love, the Lord has chosen to use us, sinful human beings, to carry that powerful message. The word of the Lord remains ever powerful, even when you are not. What a comforting message for the struggling called worker!

The Lord also promises to give you the gifts necessary to accomplish your task. Just look at Jeremiah! The boy who was unable to preach was touched by the hand of God! He was appropriately prepared. The Lord touches you through his word, too. He has equipped you for serving him. No excuses remain. No wallowing self-pity should be allowed to lurk under your guise of humility.

This makes all the difference in the Lord's ministry. Your daily confession and absolution of sins stands as a constant reminder of God's grace. That very grace brought you to serve the Lord. And if the Lord has accomplished all of this for you, of course he will stand with you always—through persecution and joy alike. The comfort the Lord shared with Jeremiah so many years ago still remains a powerful comfort for any servant in the church. In the face of anger and bitter disputes, in the presence of persecution and hatred, your Savior calls *you* by name. "'Do not be afraid of them, for I am with you and will rescue you,' declares the LORD."

Prayer

"Dear Lord, to your true servants give The grace to you alone to live.
Set free from sin to serve you, Lord, They go to share your living Word,
The gospel message to proclaim That all may know your saving name."
   Amen.

—*Christian Worship* 542:1[1]

---

[1] Commission on Worship of the Wisconsin Evangelical Lutheran Synod, *Christian Worship: A Lutheran Hymnal* (Milwaukee: Northwestern Publishing House, 1993). Hereafter abbreviated as *CW*.

"I am with you and will rescue you"

Jeremiah 1:11–19

Seasons of hope can quickly turn ominous. After Adam and Eve fell into sin in the garden of Eden, God's tree of life changed from a harmless source of fruit to a dangerous eternal device. Years later, the very water that Noah's world perhaps initially welcomed became a world-covering deluge that washed away the wicked.

In his first vision to the young prophet Jeremiah, the Lord turned a season of hope into an ominous warning. He showed Jeremiah "the branch of an almond tree." Jeremiah wasn't the only one watching in this vision. The Lord also was "watching" to see the fulfillment of this vision. This Hebrew word for "watching" sounds similar to the Hebrew word for "almond tree." The Lord's play on words here is purposeful. As the Israelites watched for the blossoms of the almond tree to indicate the arrival of spring, so the Lord was watching the almond tree "to see that [his] word is fulfilled."

While Jeremiah contemplates the "watching" of the Lord, another vision quickly arrives. A boiling pot in the north is tilted toward Jeremiah and his people. The meaning of this vision would be even more ominous. "From the north disaster will be poured out on all who live in the land." The next words of the Lord sounded treasonous. Foreign kings would enter Jerusalem, toppling David's great and ancient seat to set up their own thrones.

Clearly, for Jeremiah and the kingdom of Judah, the hopeful, rejuvenating sight of the almond tree would soon become an apocalyptic sign. The storms of spring would not compare to this coming squall of destruction. The harsh reality was that the people of Judah

deserved the entire tempest. The people of Judah lived their wickedness by burning incense to other gods. They had been unfaithful to
their Lord, their husband, through their spiritual adultery.

None of these actions made any sense. One of sin's greatest
temptations is its logical appearance. However, at their core trespasses always remain illogical. The people of Judah were now "worshiping what their hands have made." The thing formed cannot
stand greater than the one who forms it. Our sinful nature deeply
desires to be greater, wiser, and more powerful than he who formed
us. When these desires apprehend us, we need to be reminded that
we are not greater than our God.

This danger can subtly creep in to the mind of the called worker,
too. As sinners, we can be very adept at turning the hopeful blessings and messages of the Lord into ominous devices of sin. Humanly
speaking, turning God's perfect, eternal hope into a law message can
appear very effective. After all, guilt can drive sinners to follow laws
too. What a temptation for a pastor or teacher to change God's gospel message of hope into an ominous warning of law! Results may
follow, but the motivation becomes all wrong. Martin Luther knew
this as well as anyone. Plagued by a guilty conscience, Martin Luther
was driven to extreme lengths in his efforts to make himself right
with God. But because Luther took God's law seriously, he soon realized that none of his works could ever earn him the eternal hope he
so desperately desired. "Or else" does not get us to heaven. Turning
God's gospel hope into an ominous warning doesn't either.

Miraculously, the Lord accomplishes the opposite. Only Jesus
can change an ominous, torturous cross into a sure and certain hope
of forgiveness and eternal life. Who in the Roman world would
have ever envisioned a day when their bloodiest, most frightening
instrument of death would become the most cherished symbol for
Christians? At the cross, the ominous became auspicious. A generation before Jeremiah became a prophet, the prophet Isaiah compared
every ominous aspect of Jesus' suffering with the beautiful result it
would bring about:

> He was pierced for our transgressions,
> he was crushed for our iniquities;

the punishment that brought us peace was on him,
and by his wounds we are healed. (Isaiah 53:5)

While Jeremiah was probably familiar with Isaiah's gospel prophecy, there would be no gospel for God's people in Jeremiah's message on this day. Instead we see a boy prophet who was perhaps scared to share this extensive law message. Who wouldn't be apprehensive? Jeremiah's first message from the Lord was pure law. The Lord was watching, and he didn't like the idolatry he saw. The Lord was summoning foreign invaders to surround Jerusalem. As the Lord's worker, there would be no probation period for Jeremiah. People were going to hate him and his message already in the first days of his ministry. What pastor would preach such harsh law in his first sermon? What teacher would share such harsh words in her first parent-teacher meeting? The law has always been difficult to share boldly.

Jeremiah must have been apprehensive. The Lord needed to spur him on or he might never have shared his first prophecy. "Get yourself ready! Stand up and say to them whatever I command you." It would be good for every called worker to recall those words before a difficult meeting where God's law will have to be shared.

So how can we get ourselves ready? Daily preparation for ministry comes through our own reading of God's word. We need to hear that same law convict us before we can hear the gospel heal us. A healthy prayer life with our Father in heaven also remains a necessity. Our Father in heaven gave his own Son to save us. Surely he will answer our every prayer according to his good will.

Fear is a powerful emotion. It can hijack a well-prepared Christian and convince us to bury our talent or to cover the light of the gospel. Jeremiah knew those fears well. He knew his own people would hate this message and hate him for sharing it. He needed to hear a strong reminder of God's love. "Do not be terrified by them, or I will terrify you before them." If Jeremiah wanted to be scared, then God would make him scared. But he didn't need to be.

The Lord then went on to share some of the most comforting words he would ever speak to a prophet. No doubt Jeremiah held on to them throughout his ministry. "Today I have made you a fortified city, an iron pillar and a bronze wall." He would certainly need the fortitude of iron and bronze. Jeremiah was about "to stand against the whole land—against the kings of Judah, its officials, its priests and the people of the land."

Previous prophets usually had the luxury of living among other prophets. These previous messengers of God could lean on the faithfulness of the priests of the temple. The most blessed prophets even had the support of faithful kings. Not Jeremiah. He would stand as an enemy to his own kings (Jeremiah 36), his own officials (36:19, 26; 38:4), and even his own priests (26:7–9)! False prophets would plague him most of his ministry (14, 23, 28). And even his own friends (11:21) and family (12:6) would reject him.

What hope could there be for this young, scared, and hated prophet? What hope is there for the modern-day minister of the gospel who sometimes stands against his own leaders, community pastors, friends, family, and culture? How can we endure when the Christian churches of our communities band together in refuting our scriptural foundation? Other schools attract more students with their surplus of funding and endless extracurricular activities. Divisions within our church always seem one argument away. Feelings get hurt instantly. People leave the congregation in a rage and run your name through the mud in your community on their way out. Perhaps even threats of death have come your way because of your position and the message you share.

"They will fight against you but will not overcome you."

What a message for Jeremiah to hear at his commissioning! Were those words similar to what you heard when you were ordained or installed? Perhaps not. But maybe they should have been shared. God was up front about the persecutions Jeremiah would face. So was Jesus with his disciples. Early in their tutelage, Jesus warned them before he sent them out, "Brother will betray brother to death, and a father his child; children will rebel against their parents and have them put to death. All men will hate you because of me, but he who stands firm to the end will be saved" (Matthew 10:21–22).

Even in the face of these possible persecutions, the Lord's message remains the same: "Get yourself ready! Stand up and say to them whatever I command you." Don't feel sorry for yourself. Fellow servants throughout the kingdom are undergoing the same persecutions. Jeremiah suffered, too.

So what sustained this suffering prophet? What held him together when strife threatened to rip him apart? At the end of the beginning, the Lord gives a loving, gospel reminder for his Jeremiah to hold all his days: "'They will fight against you but will not overcome you, for I am with you and will rescue you,' declares the LORD" (Jeremiah 1:19). And he did.

Remember those words. Your Lord is speaking them to you, too. The almighty fortress that protected Jeremiah throughout the most perilous ministry of them all stands fast around you too. An iron pillar keeps you immovable. A bronze wall holds you firm when the flood of persecution washes all around you. On seven different occasions the Lord reminded Jeremiah, "Do not be afraid" (1:8; 30:10; 40:9; 42:11; 46:27; 46:28; 51:46). He daily reminds you of the same. "'They will fight against you but will not overcome you, for I am with you and will rescue you,' declares the LORD."

Prayer

"Why should cross and trial grieve me?
Christ is near With his cheer; Never will he leave me.
Who can rob me of the heaven
That God's Son For me won When his life was given?" Amen.

—CW 428:1

"The devotion of your youth"

Jeremiah 2:3–5

No sooner had Jeremiah been called by the Lord and warned of a difficult ministry than he was given the word of the Lord to speak to his people. The thrill of his new role as the prophet of the Lord may have still fluttered through his heart. No doubt Jeremiah was both ready and willing to fulfill his God-given role on behalf of his people. Perhaps he could picture it all unfolding: a blessed message from the Lord related eloquently to a grateful people.

"The word of the LORD came to me: 'Go and proclaim in the hearing of Jerusalem.'" Jeremiah's first message as a prophet of the Lord would be to the inhabitants of Jerusalem. What an honor! Every prophet dreamed of such an audience, in Judah's great city, under the faithful King Josiah!

Then came the message. The Lord compares his relationship with his people to a marriage. He is the groom, and the Israelites are his bride. He had brought them up out of Egypt "through a land not sown" and into a fertile land. Then "disaster overtook them." God's people had strayed. "They followed worthless idols and became worthless themselves."

So the Lord brings a charge against the people of Jerusalem and their children. Spiritual rebellion had become so commonplace that it was no longer questioned. God's people had done something no other nation had. They changed their gods! "Has a nation ever changed its gods?" the Lord asks rhetorically. And his reaction becomes far more perilous: "Be appalled at this, you heavens, and shudder with great horror."

This was the first of Jeremiah's many messages as a prophet of the Lord. All at once the grand stage of Jerusalem most would seek became a source of turmoil. The people who witnessed Josiah's reforms had never truly reformed their hearts. If he didn't realize it before, Jeremiah certainly knew now that his would not be an easy ministry with sweet-sounding words laid before a grateful people.

But to be honest, no ministry consists solely of honey-filled words spoken to perfect people. What would be the point if that were the case? Think back to your first preconceptions as a pastor or teacher in the opening days of your ministry. Perhaps you were ready to light the world on fire with the perfect sermon and the best lessons. Your people would love you and praise you.

Then, all at once, the honeymoon was over. The sermons weren't perfect, and there weren't as many parishioners coming to hear them. The meticulously planned lessons needed to be changed when parents started complaining. When you yearned for recognition, everyone seemed to have forgotten that your church even existed.

Like in Jeremiah's ministry, the most difficult task that ends a called worker's honeymoon period the quickest is the preaching of the law. We know our people will balk at hearing about their sins and the punishment they deserve. We dread sharing the law with the couple that we just found out is living together. We probably don't look forward to meeting with the parent that always takes her child's side of the argument rather than yours.

That is when the devil loves to enter your ministry. When your honey-sweet words turn bitter, the devil makes temptation taste sweet. He convinces you to keep your mouth shut. He has you overlook the law to extend your ministry's honeymoon period a little further.

But the married couple that refuses to address its problems in favor of an extended honeymoon will fall much harder later on. Complications need to be talked about. Communication, even difficult communication, needs to continue between husband and wife.

This is precisely what the Lord was doing through his young prophet, Jeremiah. He couldn't overlook the unfaithfulness of his bride. He had to address her adultery. And it was the Lord's love that led him to speak those sobering words of law.

"My people have committed two sins: They have forsaken me, the spring of living water, and have dug their own cisterns, broken cisterns that cannot hold water." The marriage metaphor now becomes a cistern simile. God's people had refused the life-giving water of his word and exchanged it for worthless, waterless cisterns.

Jesus once stopped at a Samaritan well to give this living water to a Samaritan woman. "Everyone who drinks this water will be thirsty again, but whoever drinks the water I give them will never thirst" (John 4:13–14). So many of Jesus' own people refused his life-giving water. Yet this foreign adulteress drank from Jesus and faithfully pointed her village his way.

Old Testament Jerusalem refused. "Have you not brought this on yourselves by forsaking the Lord your God when he led you in the way?" Jeremiah's difficult first sermon now became even more poignant. The people had only themselves to blame for their spiritual dehydration.

Yet the worst indictment of them all comes at the end of the sermon: "In vain I punished your people; they did not respond to correction." There is no worse accusation than this. Solomon preached these same words three hundred years before Jeremiah, "Mockers resent correction, so they avoid the wise" (Proverbs 15:12). God's people epitomized denial. To their dying breath, they claimed, "I am innocent; he is not angry with me." Like an adulterous wife in denial about her unfaithfulness Jerusalem continued to think she was in the right.

In Jeremiah's first sermon, the Lord called his people idolaters, worthless, detestable, backsliding sinners, prostitutes, vile, corrupt, confused she-camels, thieves, and people who do all the evil they can. This was quite a first sermon for the young prophet to preach to the citizens of Jerusalem! Humanly speaking, it would only get worse from there. The sermons would become even more pointed. Jeremiah's actions would continue to embody strong warnings of the coming wrath of God.

The Lord doesn't expect you to use that same firebrand way of speaking, but he does expect you to appropriately preach the law in every sermon. The Lord expects his teachers to discipline justly rather than to appease for parental peace and praise. Lord willing, those words of the law will cut to the heart and lead to repentance.

That is when you have the God-given privilege of sharing his gospel, centered on the death and resurrection of Jesus.

We don't hear those words in Jeremiah's sermon because true repentance never came from these people. They rejected the law, and therefore God could not give them his gospel at this moment.

Your ministerial honeymoon won't last forever. But that isn't a bad thing. No married couple lives in honeymooned bliss forever. The sooner the difficult problems come, the sooner husband and wife began to grow closer to each other. The same is true in ministry. Whether you are preaching law and gospel or counseling or teaching or disciplining, may Paul's words to Timothy guide you in your Jeremiah-like ministry: "Do your best to present yourself to God as one approved, a workman who does not need to be ashamed and who correctly handles the word of truth" (2 Timothy 2:15).

Prayer

"Preach you the Word and plant it home To those who like or like it not,
The Word that shall endure and stand When flow'rs and mortals are
    forgot . . .
Preach you the Word and plant it home And never faint; the Harvest-Lord
Who gave the sower seed to sow Will watch and tend his planted Word."
    Amen.

                                                    —CW 544:1, 5

"I am your husband"

Jeremiah 3:6–4:4

Does the Lord bless the marriage bond when he knows it will be broken? The Lord answered that question in the ministry of the prophet Hosea. Back before the Assyrian Empire scattered the northern kingdom to the four winds, the Lord gave the prophet Hosea one of the strangest commands he ever gave to one of his prophets. As far as we know, these were the *very first words* the Lord told to Hosea, and they must have been shocking: "When the LORD began to speak through Hosea, the LORD said to him, 'Go, marry a promiscuous woman and have children with her" (Hosea 1:2a). I suppose one could call this an arranged marriage of the worst kind. Hosea was commanded to marry a woman who had been unfaithful.

Hosea didn't ask any questions, but we probably would have. Why? Why have a prophet of the Lord marry an adulterous woman named Gomer? The Lord's answer is that sometimes words can only say so much. It was time for God's prophet to *live* God's word. Here is what that message meant: "The land is guilty of the vilest adultery in departing from the Lord" (Hosea 1:2b).

No surprise there. The people of Israel had been wandering away from the Lord for generations. But the picture here is not simply a wandering away. This time the illustration is even harsher—perhaps the harshest, most sobering illustration in scripture. A faithful prophet marries an unfaithful woman. And Israel was not the faithful husband in this illustration. They were the unfaithful wife.

Now, over one hundred years after Hosea, the Lord uses that same illustration to refer to Israel's sister, the southern kingdom of Judah. The Lord's words through Jeremiah are very similar to the Lord's words through Hosea in the twilight years of Israel. In many ways Hosea was the Jeremiah of the northern kingdom. He lived God's parables. He spoke harshly against the adulterous sins of God's people. And while Jeremiah was told not to get married as a living sermon to his people, Hosea was told to marry an unfaithful woman as an example of God's love. Both men spoke to their respective people at the end of their kingdoms. And most of all, the Lord gave both men amazing gospel words to share with those who had remained faithful.

Through Jeremiah the Lord speaks to Judah about unfaithful Israel. As adulterous as she was, Judah was even worse. Judah had the benefit of seeing Israel's example and the punishment they incurred because of their actions. Judah was falling into the same adulterous sins—knowing full well what had happened to her "sister" Israel.

In the context of adultery, the Lord tells his wife, Judah, "I gave faithless Israel her certificate of divorce and sent her away because of all her adulteries." Yet Judah had been worse. She acted as though she was returning to the Lord, under King Josiah's reformation, but that return was "only in pretense."

C. S. Lewis once wrote, "As long as he doesn't convert it into action, it does not matter how much a man thinks about his repentance."[1] The people of Judah may have thought a lot about repentance. The priests must have discussed it. Perhaps even the false prophets referred to repentance at times. Yet there was no genuine repentance in the hearts of the people. Most of Judah had become like the Pharisees of Jesus' day, who were "like whitewashed tombs, which look beautiful on the outside but on the inside are full of the bones of the dead and everything unclean" (Matthew 23:27).

Perhaps as a pastor you have encountered this type of man. He and his wife are having marital problems, and they continue to come to you for counseling. The husband has been unfaithful to his wife but promises that those types of actions are now in the past. He says all the right things. The first few times you met with the couple,

---

[1] C. S. Lewis, *The Screwtape Letters* (New York: Simon & Schuster, 1996), 57.

he may have persuaded you. But all the while, his knowing wife remained unconvinced. She knew him for who he really is. And sure enough, initially, to your surprise, he eventually does cheat again. His outward actions and words did not match what was in his heart.

First-year pastors can often be blindsided by those outward actions of others. "I never saw that coming!" they admit. Experienced pastors react in much more jaded ways. They have seen everything and have learned to expect the worst. This also can be a danger to the counseling practices of their ministries as they assumes the worst in a married couple's strife, which may impair their desire to serve as their counselor.

Teachers can also feel blindsided by the actions of students and their parents. Young teachers cannot understand why the parents are not perfectly helping their children at home. Broken families and poor choices are a curious conundrum to teachers in their early years. On the other hand, teachers who have "been around the block" have learned to expect the worst. "Don't assume the child will get help at home," they say from weathered experience. But this can also be a danger. Soon the parents begin to fulfill the low bar set by the unimpressed teacher.

The Lord also could have been jaded by sin. Throwing up his arms in frustration, he could have simply cried out, "What's the point!" He could have expected nothing from his king, his priests, his prophets, and his people. But the only time the Lord asks, "What's the point?" is to further strengthen the believers who hear him ask the question.

Jeremiah was that listening believer. He didn't hear the words of a God who had given up. He heard the pleading cries of a loving husband: "Return, faithless Israel . . . I will frown on you no longer, for I am merciful . . . I will not be angry forever."

As always, words were not enough. Out of his grace and love, the Lord promised to do the unthinkable. He would receive his formerly unfaithful people back. This was the poignant message God's people had not heard for over a hundred years. Back then the prophet Hosea's wife had once again been unfaithful. She had committed adultery, and Hosea had every right to give her a certificate of divorce. Instead the Lord gave a most shocking command to Hosea:

"The LORD said to me, 'Go, show your love to your wife again, though she is loved by another man and is an adulteress'" (Hosea 3:1a).

This could not have been an easy command for Hosea to follow. The situation was actually made worse because of who his wife ran back to. Hosea would have to *pay* to receive his wife back. And yet, even after all of the sadness of betrayal between husband and wife, Hosea took his returning wife into his arms and lovingly told her the most tender words he had ever spoken: "You are to live with me many days; you must not be a prostitute or be intimate with any man, and I will behave the same way toward you" (Hosea 3:3). God has a special word for this beautiful picture. It is called *reconciliation.*

To effectively preach and teach these words to your people, you need to understand something about yourself. You have betrayed your Lord through the temptations you have given yourself to. You have been that unfaithful spouse. And like with the kingdoms of Israel and Judah, like with Hosea's unfaithful wife, Gomer, the Lord would have every right to give us a certificate of divorce and send us away forever. But he doesn't send you away. He lovingly calls you to repent and return. "If you, Israel, will return, then return to me."

Jeremiah did this. After the Lord pleaded for the return of his bride, Judah, Jeremiah gave a beautiful response of faith. His personal repentance culminated with the words of verse 25, "Let us lie down in our shame, and let our disgrace cover us. We have sinned against the LORD our God, both we and our ancestors; from our youth till this day we have not obeyed the LORD our God." The only way Jeremiah could preach repentance was by faithfully repenting of his own sins.

The called worker needs to repent daily, too. After taking time with personal devotion in God's word, the repentance of sins and the reminder of the absolution allow for a servant of the Lord to effectively encourage their members to do the same. The phrase "those who can't do, teach" is dangerously inaccurate. Only those who repent themselves can properly encourage their fellow brothers and sisters to do the same.

Through daily repentance and the study of your Lord's word, you yourself become part of the fulfillment of the Lord's promise through his prophet Jeremiah. "Then I will give you shepherds after my own heart, who will lead you with knowledge and understanding." You don't need to be a blissfully ignorant shepherd anymore, nor do you need to be negatively grizzled, waiting for disappointment around every turn. Simply be a faithful shepherd after God's own heart.

Prayer

"Send, O Lord, your Holy Spirit
On your servants now, we pray;
Let them all be faithful shepherds
That no lamb is led astray.
Your pure teaching to proclaim,
To adore your holy name,
And to feed your lambs, dear Savior,
Make their aim and sole endeavor." Amen.

—*CW* 545:1

"Wash the evil from your heart"

Jeremiah 4:5–31

Søren Kierkegaard was a Danish philosopher known for his religious writings, poetry, and insights into the human character. He once wrote, "There are two ways to be fooled. One is to believe what isn't true; the other is to refuse to believe what is true."[1] There was no truer description for Jeremiah's Judah than that. The Lord sent prophet after prophet to plead with his people to repent and return. God's own people consistently and defiantly refused to be his people.

But there was to be no spiritual void. Many exotic gods took the place of the one, true God. These gods appealed to the people because they said nothing. These gods did not keep the people from the sins they wanted to commit. Quite the contrary, these gods silently approved of every sinful desire.

The prophets were worse. The false prophets had taken the place of the Lord's true prophets. They told the people sweet-sounding messages of peace and freedom. They supported the worship of false gods and spoke for the idols that could not speak for themselves.

God's people had been fooled *twice*. The devil had lured them away from the loving arms of the true God and drew them into the jaws of the false ones. In the end, the Lord gave his people exactly what they wanted. Jeremiah saw the tragedy unfold before his very eyes, "Alas, Sovereign LORD! How completely you have deceived

---

[1] Søren Kierkegaard, *Works of Love* (New York: Harper Perennial, 1962), 23.

this people and Jerusalem by saying, 'You will have peace,' when the sword is at our throats.'"

The Lord does that sometimes. When his patience finally runs out, when a people has so thoroughly and vigorously rejected him, he hands them over to the sins they crave so much. Paul reminded the Thessalonians that it remains the same today: "They perish because they refused to love the truth and so be saved. For this reason God sends them a powerful delusion so that they will believe the lie" (2 Thessalonians 2:10–11).

Then will come the disaster they refused to believe would ever arrive. The city of Dan in the far north will serve as the first warning beacon, sounding the trumpet. As the sounds of church bells echo throughout the town at the death of someone famous, so the bells in Dan would ring in the coming onslaught from the north. The false priests who aided unbelief "will be horrified." The false prophets who lured the people away from the Lord like pied pipers "will be appalled." Indeed, they should have been.

The disaster from the north reads like a lost transmission from the future. One can almost picture Jeremiah and the people gathered, listening together like people sitting around a radio. The sounds and cries that came through must have stirred strong emotions. "Sound the trumpet throughout the land!" calls one from the future conquest. "Gather together! Let us flee to the fortified cities!" others cry out.

The details of the coming terror must have been frightening. The Lord was releasing "A lion . . . out of his lair." This lion of Babylon, King Nebuchadnezzar, would indeed be "a destroyer of nations." He would be God's handpicked destroyer, sent against God's own people.

Jeremiah faithfully relayed all of these earth-shaking prophecies to the people. Perhaps he expected the obvious question from the people: "What should we do?" And even though it seemed as though no one listened to the warning, the Lord answered the question that his people should have asked in the first place. "Jerusalem, wash the evil from your heart and be saved. How long will you harbor wicked thoughts?" Judah's blood was not just on her hands. Her wickedness continued to originate from her heart and mind. Jesus often pleaded with the people of Jerusalem with similar words: "What comes out of a person is what defiles them. For it is from within, out of a person's heart, that evil thoughts come" (Mark 7:20–21). But no one listened.

The Lord's passionate response holds nothing back. "My people are fools; they do not know me. They are senseless children; they have no understanding. They are skilled in doing evil; they know not how to do good." They were twofold fools, rejecting truth and believing lies. One disaster would follow another; ruined hearts would give way to ruined homes.

It is at this moment that the Lord opens his heart to reveal his intense anguish over the cataclysmic situation his people faced. One can almost hear the break in his saddened voice and see the tears streaming down his face. "Oh, my anguish, my anguish!" The Lord felt every bit of this punishment: "I writhe in pain. Oh, the agony of my heart!"

The agony of the daughter of Zion would be just as intense. Crying like a woman in labor, she will grasp for breath. As one being murdered, she will reach out her hands in prayer to the Lord. This emotion between the Lord and his people becomes palpable throughout the book of Jeremiah.

The scene becomes even more poignant when we view these pains and anguished feelings pouring out of the heart of God himself on the cross in Jerusalem. He also would cry out under the eternal punishment for sin. He also would "writhe in pain" and experience agony in his heart. His life would be given over to murderers, too.

How can a pastor adequately relay the tears of our Lord that Jeremiah reveals for us here? How can a teacher reveal the raw emotion expressed between those dying in Jerusalem, their Lord painfully allowing it to happen, and their Savior who would ultimately take it all upon himself? There is no perfectly relatable way to delineate these emotions. We will always fall sinfully short of sharing God's perfect message with those who called us.

This is when we remember to get out of the way and point to Christ on the cross. Don't just talk *about* our Savior's sacrifice but *show* it through his word. Show the spiritual cataclysm for what it is. Reveal to you listeners how their eternal lives hung in the balance. Remind yourself every day that you should have been inside the walls of Jerusalem on her worst day. Express how the Lord reached out his loving arms and took the words out of your mouth: "Alas! I am fainting; my life is given over to murderers."

Then exemplify the thankful heart. Christ's heart experienced pain and agony to free yours from the depths of sin. And watch as the Holy Spirit enables your heart to overflow with faithful words and actions. Graciously sing the words of a fellow sinner, David, who understood the depths of forgiveness: "The eyes of the Lord are on those who fear him, on those whose hope is in his unfailing love, to deliver them from death and keep them alive" (Psalm 33:18–19).

His eyes have always been on you. Point other eyes heavenward, even as disasters befall our world and suffering envelops our families. When this earthly storm subsides and the heavens part, your risen Savior Jesus will bring you in to his presence to see him face-to-face. No more pain, no more separation, no more battle cry, no more tears . . . just Jesus.

Prayer

"The Church's one foundation Is Jesus Christ, her Lord;
She is his new creation By water and the Word.
From heav'n he came and sought her To be his holy bride;
With his own blood he bought her, And for her life he died.

"Mid toil and tribulation And tumult of her war
She waits the consummation Of peace forevermore
Till with the vision glorious Her longing eyes are blest
And the great Church victorious Shall be the Church at rest." Amen.

—*CW* 538:1, 5

"Why should I forgive you?"

Jeremiah 5

Why does the Lord so often ask his servants to go and find out information when he already knows everything? The investigation is never for the Lord. It is for the sake of his servants. Now Jeremiah joins the ranks of so many Old Testament individuals who were told to investigate for God. The Lord sends Jeremiah among the people to seek out the honest and the truthful. Fervently the prophet walked up and down Jerusalem's corridors, searching through squares, speaking with women gathering water and striking up conversation with men conducting business.

Humanly speaking, these were still the good days of Jeremiah's ministry. While he had been rejected by his family and hometown, Jerusalem had not yet turned against the prophet. Jeremiah could still walk unopposed through the city watching her people and listening to their public lives.

More hung in the balance than anyone knew. The Lord himself had told Jeremiah, "If you can find but one person who deals honestly and seeks the truth, I will forgive this city." It did not take Jeremiah very long to find the impenitent, those people struck by the Lord only to make "their faces harder than stone." These people had committed the ultimate sin: they had refused to repent.

Jeremiah thought the explanation lay in the demographics. "These are only the poor; they are the foolish, for they do not know the way of the Lord, the requirements of their God." Yes, these people were foolish, but perhaps that was low-level ignorance. So Jeremiah goes to those who should know better. Those high-ranking officials could not hide behind ignorance. "But with one accord they too had broken off the yoke and torn off the bonds."

The refusal to repent transcended socioeconomic barriers. To borrow a scriptural axiom, the citizens of Jerusalem, from the king on the throne to the lowest slave girl, refused to repent. After his spiritual tour of the city even Jeremiah had to admit "their rebellion is great and their backslidings many."

The investigation had revealed a complete spiritual rebellion in Jerusalem. And it all led the Lord to ask a question no soul on earth would ever want to hear. In fact, this might be the most frightening question asked in all of scripture: "Why should I forgive you?"

Jerusalem had no good answer. Of course, that did not stop God's people from coming up with their own misguided solutions. Some thought they had forgiveness coming by virtue of the fact that they belonged to God's chosen people. Others thought they did not even need forgiveness. Some, like the false prophets and wicked priests, thought their position precluded them from punishment.

Jerusalem's answers were all incorrect. So the Lord's question remained: "Why should I forgive you?" At this point God listed the fruit of Jeremiah's investigation of the people. Their children had sworn by other gods. The adults were committing adultery both spiritually and physically. Although they had been blessed by the Lord like "well-fed, lusty stallions" they acted like stubborn donkeys, refusing to acknowledge the true God who had given it all to them.

"Should I not punish them for this?" the Lord asks rhetorically. And punishment was coming. Once again the Lord reminds the people that the enemy from the north would succeed in burning through Jerusalem's walls like a consuming fire. Harvests will be devoured, spelling disaster for God's people. No fortified city will be able to save them.

It was all because the called workers of Jerusalem had completely failed those they were called to serve. "The prophets prophesy lies, the priests rule by their own authority." And wouldn't you know it, these actions were met with enthusiasm among the people: "My people love it this way."

Is this still the case today? It seems that the days when pastors could command unquestioning authority are long gone. A century ago, pastors could tell their people how to live and most would acquiesce. Teachers could discipline however they liked and the parents would always follow suit. Clearly this is no longer the case. But perhaps that is for the best. Such authority placed into a sinful individual's hands carries perhaps too many opportunities for sinful pride to wreak havoc.

Abraham Lincoln knew a thing or two about the dangers of power placed in sinful hands. He once wrote: "Nearly all men can stand adversity, but if you want to test a man's character give him power."[1] There are times when pastors or teachers are tempted to use their position to garner popularity by making others happy. When this gets in the way of God's word, the ministerial situation becomes as dangerous as the prophets of Jeremiah's day.

Even if you do not serve in an authoritarian ministry, temptations abound. Seeing your community living like Jeremiah's Jerusalem might tempt you to let them walk down their path to destruction, never giving them a second glance. These are the thoughts of a battle-hardened heart that no longer thinks true repentance is possible. Solomon once warned against withholding God's good word from the people: "Do not withhold good from those to whom it is due, when it is in your power to act" (Proverbs 3:27).

These temptations can strike teachers, too. How tempting it is to give up on the rebellious child and have him sent to another school for the smallest infraction! Or perhaps your temptation is more subtle, as you simply "wait out" a troubled child to finish out the year so you can "move him up" to bother another teacher. If you can't beat 'em, graduate 'em.

So what makes us different from the prophets and priests of Jerusalem? We still sinfully exert our power when we can. We still give up on the people of our community because of who they are or because of their socioeconomic status. We are called workers, but we still sin.

The difference has been laid out throughout these first chapters of Jeremiah. It is repentance. Faithful workers of the Lord are not perfect servants. They are repentant servants.

---

[1] *Williamsburg Journal-Tribune*, March 26, 1931, page 2, column 4.

The priests and prophets of Jerusalem refused to repent so the Lord asked them an ominous question: "What will you do in the end?" That question still gives perspective today. Point your flock to the end of all things, because that is the only place that will show everything for what it really is. The stuff of this world we love so much will be gone. The money collected will be of no use. All the friends I gained by giving up on parts of God's word will not be able to save me. The end will reveal what really matters—faith in our Savior, Jesus.

Thanks be to Jesus, who has taken away our prideful sins, our apathetic trespasses and our incendiary iniquities. Thanks be to the Holy Spirit, who gives us the willingness of our new man to not give up on our calling but enables us to speak the truth in love to our people, our children, our families, and our community.

So the Lord's frightening question remains: "Why should I forgive you?" You know the answer. He came to be one of us. He came to be punished for every one of our sins. He came to be completely washed over by death. He came to take life back and give it to you.

Why should God forgive you? Because of Jesus. What will you do in the end? Trust in Christ, who will be there in the end to take you home forever.

Prayer

"'As surely as I live,' God said, 'I would not have the sinner dead,
But that he turn from error's ways, Repent, and live through endless days.'

"To us, therefore, Christ gave command: 'Go forth and preach in ev'ry land;
Bestow on all my pard'ning grace Who will repent of sinful ways.'" Amen.

—*CW* 308:1–2

"As though it were not serious"

Jeremiah 6

The greatest physician the world had ever seen had a table prepared for himself in the presence of his enemies. It was a great banquet. Everyone who was anyone had been invited. But so had everyone who was no one. The high society did their best to look down on the "unworthy." These people were sinners and needed to be reminded of it.

Surprisingly, Jesus was sitting in the midst of these "sinners." Apparently he needed to be reminded of who his banquet company really was. The Pharisees and teachers of the law were all too happy to tell him. "Why do you eat and drink with tax collectors and sinners?" (Luke 5:30).

The room had the physical appearance of a grand meal, but the spiritual situation looked far more like an infirmary. See the room through the eyes of the surgeon seated with the wounded and the picture becomes much clearer. Those lowly sinners had come looking for the surgeon they so desperately needed. But there were others who had come almost by accident. If they had wounds, they were so minuscule that they could treat them on their own. In fact, these were the ones pointing out just how mangled the others were.

No one present saw the room properly. So all at once Jesus turned on the lights. "It is not the healthy who need a doctor, but the sick" (Luke 5:31). You can almost see Luke smile as he wrote those words of Jesus. One doctor recording the prognosis of another.

Those who understood their own spiritual wounds also knew that they needed the surgeon. The sick had come to be healed. Sadly, many of the sick thought they were healthy. Many of the sinners thought they were righteous. "I have not come to call the righteous, but sinners to repentance" (Luke 5:32).

In Jeremiah 6 the Lord gives a similar diagnosis of the people of Jerusalem. He compares their wickedness and oppression to "sickness and wounds." This was the type of spiritual disease that ended in painful, agonizing death. If left alone, this wound would fester and get infected until finally death would come almost as a relief.

The Lord always compares sin to something memorably disastrous. In this case, the fallout from this sin, the punishment of the Lord, was unforgettable. "Pour it out on the children in the street and on the young men gathered together; both husband and wife will be caught in it, and the old, those weighed down with years."

Jerusalem's prophets and priests had made matters worse. Like witch-doctors they treated these serious spiritual wounds with made-up medicine. "They dress the wound of my people as though it were not serious." An uneducated, ignorant doctor soon becomes a threat to the lives of everyone he treats. Usually the medical community will not stand for such a shoddy, selfish worker in their midst.

Yet Jerusalem had been happy with their spiritual doctors for decades. Their priestly physicians made the people think that their wounds were not very severe. Their prophetic surgeons refused to admit that anyone needed any sort of spiritual operation. "'Peace, peace,' they say, when there is no peace." These are relieving messages to hear in the waiting room. But if the doctor's nice-sounding prognosis proves to be false, he is far worse than the doctor willing to give the cold, hard truth. A deadly diagnosis is difficult for anyone to deal with. But an erroneously good diagnosis is far more dangerous.

Everything about these false priests and prophets looked legitimate. The priests still had the people offering sacrifices. The prophets seemed to faithfully proclaim messages. Yet it was all a sham, a Band-Aid on a mortal wound. The appearance of praise can be far from actual worship. "Your burnt offerings are not acceptable; your sacrifices do not please me."

What continued to frustrate the Lord was the fact that he had blessed Jerusalem with some of the most wonderful spiritual doctors. Men like Obadiah, Isaiah, Jeremiah, and Ezekiel all served as some of the greatest surgeons of sin the world has ever seen. Jerusalem was a regular Mayo Clinic of God's word. But the people preferred their back-alley medicine with its sweet taste accompanied by an oblivious message. We can almost hear the frustration of the Lord in his words when he says "I appointed watchmen over you and said, 'Listen to the sound of the trumpet!' But you said, 'We will not listen.'"

As awful of a situation as this was in Jerusalem, it is not hard to understand how they arrived at that point. Who wants to hear the sad message of a dire diagnosis? Who wants to go through years of spiritual treatment that can be pervasively painful? Slowly, subtly a different sort of doctor had arrived in Jerusalem. Originally, he set up shop in back alleys and the dark recesses. But by the time of Jeremiah's ministry, this devilish doctor had businesses on every main street in Jerusalem. Now nearly all the people were hooked on the good-feeling, opioid-like medicine Satan was selling.

Did you notice in all of this that the Lord seemed to weep most over the loss of Jerusalem's spiritual doctors? They had sold their souls to promote the devil's drug, and the people went with them. The temptation still exists for spiritual leaders today. It is far easier to downplay the wounds of sin to our members because the real prognosis would offend them. What if we actually gave it to them? They might leave the church in a fit of rage!

So the devil tempts you to look the other way when you find out about the couple living together. You give no prognosis to the member who has taken communion at another church of a different denomination. You act as if you didn't hear the child taking God's name in vain on the playground because it is easier not to have that conversation. You don't tell the parents all the struggles that happened during the school day because if they find out then you might look like a bad teacher.

We have stood silent as our fellow patients refuse to admit their wounds, their sins. The Pharisees and teachers in Jesus' midst thought they were the healthy ones. They couldn't have had a more incorrect self-diagnosis. Those tax collectors and sinners knew exactly who they were. Just as importantly, they knew exactly who Jesus was.

As a spiritual doctor, you need to see yourself the way Jesus sees you. You are not "the righteous" because nobody is "the righteous" apart from Christ. You are one of the "sinners" who needs to see the importance of repentance. That is your Great Physician's prognosis.

Understanding your own dire situation also helps you to understand how best to give that prognosis to the spiritually wounded among you.

Jesus is not the type of doctor to leave you with a deadly examination. He has your medicine. And unlike the sugar pills of false prophets and pathetic priests, high-society Pharisees and teachers, Jesus' medicine is real. And it is everlasting. "Surely he took up our pain and bore our suffering" (Isaiah 53:4).

In this way, Jerusalem's greatest human physician had the greatest message their people could ever hear. And it comes straight from their Lord: "Nevertheless, I will bring health and healing to it; I will heal my people and will let them enjoy abundant peace and security" (Jeremiah 33:6).

You have been called to be a doctor of souls. See the room the way your Savior viewed it. It isn't a feast for the righteous but an infirmary for the spiritually sick. The Lord installed you to work in that sad, sometimes disgusting environment. But what a privilege it is! Your great physician will enable you to give that cold, hard spiritual diagnosis of sin. Your heavenly doctor will continue to give you and your patients of the medicine of the gospel. It is sweeter than honey. It lasts into eternity. And it is yours, and theirs, by grace.

Prayer

"When sinners see their lost condition
And feel the pressing load of sin
And Jesus comes on his blest mission
To heal the sin-sick heart within,
All grief must flee before his grace,
And joy divine will take its place." Amen.

—CW 32:1

"The temple of the Lord"

Jeremiah 7:1–29

Venue matters. Mom and pop stores and billion-dollar companies may not have much in common, but they do agree on the age-old mantra: "Location, location, location." Even social media and online shopping have had to come to grips with the importance of venue. People need a location in which to gather, speak, share, and argue.

The difficulty with location is that time always seems to pass it by. The Roman forum was once the bustling center of the grand Roman Empire. Now grass grows through her ancient streets. Phoenician trade once covered the Mediterranean Sea with thousands of ships sailing from ports like Tyre and Carthage. But the ships sank long ago, and the ports have become deserted. Those changes seem to come more quickly every year. Today's venues can change as quickly as webpages. The quaint physical gatherings of old have been replaced with new digital meeting spaces.

But something gets lost when the physical gathering gives way to the video and audio of the computer. To say "I was there" means more than simply "I saw it happen." It is to say "I experienced it first-hand with others." And even if those "others" were strangers, you have shared something with them. Now you will always have that physical event in common. The location doesn't just matter for the sake of the event. It matters for the people experiencing it. Venue matters.

Venue matters to the Lord, too. For the first time in Jeremiah's ministry, the Lord places his prophet at the gate of the temple. What an honor to preach to the people of Israel at their most prestigious gate! To join the likes of prophets and priests who spoke among those hallowed halls may have been more than Jeremiah could have ever dreamed. This was *the temple* of the Lord! This was the center of Judah's world. This was the place psalmists longingly sang about: "Your altar, LORD Almighty, My King and my God. Blessed are those who dwell in your house!" (Psalm 84:3–4).

And that was the problem. The temple had become such a fixture in Judah's culture that it seemed eternal. Ask someone near the temple during Jeremiah's ministry: "Could anyone destroy the temple of the Lord?" and their emphatic answer would be a resounding "No! The Lord would never allow that to happen."

Soon Judah perceived long-lasting to mean eternity. Proximity to such an eternal relic came to mean safety. The temple had became a holy good luck charm, and the closer a person lived to it, the better his chances were for survival. Perhaps even Jeremiah had harbored those thoughts of comfort in proximity to the venue of the Lord. As always, the message the Lord had his prophet speak was for the prophet as well as for the people.

"Do not trust in deceptive words and say, 'This is the temple of the LORD, the temple of the LORD, the temple of the LORD!'" The very presence of the temple had given God's people a false sense of security. They no longer lived according to Josiah's reformation. The Lord needed to remind his people of the covenant he had made with them hundreds of years earlier:

> If you really change your ways and your actions and deal with each other justly, if you do not oppress the foreigner, the fatherless or the widow and do not shed innocent blood in this place, and if you do not follow other gods to your own harm, then I will let you live in this place, in the land I gave your ancestors for ever and ever

Venue mattered for this message. At the gate of the very temple, in which God's people trusted so much, Jeremiah points out that their hearts were not with the Lord. "Will you steal, murder, commit adultery and perjury, burn incense to Baal and follow other gods you have not known, and then come and stand before me in this house, which bears my Name, and say, 'We are safe!'" You can't have it both ways with the Lord.

A lesson in venue was needed. The Lord points Jeremiah and the people to Shiloh, the place of peace originally meant to be the location of the tabernacle. The Lord digs up the memories of Shiloh in the minds of his people not to reminisce better times, but to warn of the punishment coming for similar sins. "Therefore, what I did to Shiloh I will now do to the house that bears my Name, the temple you trust in, the place I gave to you and your ancestors."

That place of peace had become a Jewish ground zero. Shiloh was now used as a synonym of disaster. The message was as clear as the historical event. Act as your forefathers did and Shiloh becomes Judah. Learn from your forefathers and the peace that Shiloh was meant to symbolize becomes Judah's.

King Josiah tirelessly worked toward this goal of lasting peace with God. His reformation was to bring God's people back into their covenant relationship with God himself. It was a success . . . on the surface. 2 Kings 22–23 and 2 Chronicles 34–35 paint a wildly successful picture of Josiah's reformation. However, Jeremiah describes the lack of spiritual depth among his people during Josiah's reign.

Now the Lord's words become as harsh as the illustration of Shiloh. Most surprisingly, God tells his prophet "do not pray for this people." Instead, he points Jeremiah to children gathering wood and women kneading dough for a Babylonian goddess and fathers lighting the fire. Judah's failure had become familial as fathers led entire families away from the Lord. These fallen families may be the saddest picture of the Old Testament. Family ministry in Jerusalem had become so misguided that these families were willing to tirelessly work for false gods.

In response to these heathen parents leading their children into sin, the Lord promised the strongest kind of punishment. To all of this idol worship and sacrifice, to all of this defiant superstition, the Lord Almighty, the God of Israel, says: "Go ahead." This remains the harshest earthly punishment God could ever give. God's people had hardened their hearts so often that God was now hardening them himself, much like he had done with Pharaoh almost a millennium earlier in Egypt. Beware when the Lord gives you what your sinful nature wants!

At the end of his sermon, the Lord finally tells Jeremiah the reaction he will receive. "When you tell them all this, they will not listen to you; when you call to them, they will not answer." How was the prophet supposed to react to that? Jeremiah may have been tempted to get angry with his people's stiff-necked ways. Perhaps he was tempted to give up in despair, wondering what the point of all of this was. To his credit, we hear no reaction from Jeremiah at this point. Silence may have been the best response.

How do you feel in your ministry when no one seems to be listening? The called worker can be tempted to give in to sinful, inappropriate anger that makes the situation worse. Human anger always pushes people further away.

The other extreme may be even more tempting—to give up. What's the point when no one shows up to hear God's word? Why continue when no one seems to be listening? These results happen so often in the ministry that depression has become a constant danger for servants of the Lord.

Either extreme, anger or depression, ultimately sets us up for another temptation. It is the temptation of venue. Our people do not seem to be listening, so we pour ourselves in to something else at some other venue. Or we place the emphasis on the venue itself rather than on the people. "Even if the people are not showing up, the church building will always continue." That is what the people of Jerusalem erroneously thought.

This temptation makes the instrument the focus rather than the one playing it. Through these words of Jeremiah the Lord warns us: don't make an instrument like the church or the school building the end in itself. Don't hang the violin on a wall to revere it. What a sad fate for such a beautiful instrument! Violins are not meant to be looked at. They are meant to be played! If such an instrument could talk, wouldn't it say the same thing?

Judah continued to revere the instrument of the temple rather than use it to God's glory. The venue had become their salvation while the God to whom it pointed was forgotten. No wonder they had no use for Jeremiah's words. The temple still stood. Their perceived "safety by proximity" remained.

So what was the point of Jeremiah's temple-gate sermon? The point was for the Lord to lovingly give his people chance after chance. Had it been up to us, we might have given up. We are still tempted to give up. Yet those decisions are not up to the prophet or the called worker. Like Jeremiah, we faithfully speak the word and leave the results to the Lord. When the day comes for that word to be taken away, the Lord will do so in his perfect timing. The decision to take away God's word is never ours to make.

Perhaps that time for the Lord to take away his word is coming more quickly than we realize. Jeremiah's warnings sound so very modern, don't they? "Truth has perished." From fake news to false advertising to the growing amount of rumors and erroneous opinions, truth continues its swift exodus from our modern world.

What an opportunity for those called by Christ! You are sent out like Jeremiah to a world where truth has perished, armed with the everlasting truth of God's word, guided by your Savior Jesus, who is Truth himself. It is that truth we continue to gather around as we physically and spiritually encourage one another. Thank your Lord daily, who has gathered your flock around you. You need their physical presence more than they need you.

Venue matters. It doesn't matter because God is local or because certain spaces stand on holier ground. Venue matters when God's word stands at its center, when God's people gather to hear that word. Sometimes they will yearn to hear more. Other times they won't listen at all. Either way, as the Lord's called worker, you get to faithfully share that truth as an instrument of the Lord. And like it was for Jeremiah, that is enough for you, too.

Prayer

"Speak, O Lord, as we come to you
To receive the food of your Holy Word.
Take your truth, plant it deep in us;
Shape and fashion us in your likeness
That the light of Christ might be seen today
In our acts of love and our deeds of faith.
Speak, O Lord, and fulfill in us
All your purposes for your glory." Amen.

—*CWS* 735:1[1]

---

[1] Commission on Worship of the Wisconsin Evangelical Lutheran Synod, (Milwaukee: Northwestern Publishing House, 2008). Hereafter cited as *CWS*.

"An end to the sounds of joy"

Jeremiah 7:30–8:3

The Lord never shies away from calling things what they really are. He calls the devil the "father of lies" (John 8:44) because that is who he is and that is what he does. When his people act stiff-necked, the Lord labels them "foolish." When Judah celebrates their idolatry, the Lord describes the scene as though it precedes a funeral.

When it came to describing the despicable practices of idolatry in Jerusalem, the Lord did not hold back. "They have set up their detestable idols in the house that bears my Name and have defiled it." Setting up idols in God's temple would have been bad enough. But Judah was guilty of greater sins. "They have built the high places of Topheth in the Valley of Ben Hinnom to burn their sons and daughters in the fire."

This type of pagan revelry, this form of guiltless slaughter of children by burning them alive, almost seems too awful to be true. Even the Lord admits this was "something I did not command, nor did it enter my mind." What does that say about Judah's sin if even the Lord did not want it to enter his mind?

At this point Bible critics will hold up a finger to the Lord himself, reminding him that he commanded Abraham to sacrifice his son, Isaac. In an effort to call the Lord's commands what they really are, they believe themselves to be successfully undermining them. These critics may pride themselves on their logic, yet their objection shows surprisingly little of it.

Differences abound between the Valley of Ben Hinnom and Mount Moriah. The burning of children for the false gods was meant to be a human act that earned dependable weather, a good crop or a healthy family. It was punishing others to win something for oneself.

Now look at God's command to Abraham. He was to sacrifice his son while armed with the promise that through Isaac would come a nation, and eventually the blessing of the Savior. The book of Hebrews brings us briefly into the mind of Abraham at this point, "Abraham reasoned that God could even raise the dead" (Hebrews 11:19). This was not a deed done to earn heaven at the expense of Isaac. It was an opportunity for Abraham to live his already saving faith by his actions. It was the ultimate test of trust.

Bible critics are encouraged to read to the end of the account. The father is about to accomplish the most painful task of his life. His boy is tied to the wood. He raises the knife. The father holds his breath. Then the knife comes down—only for Abraham to hear the gracious, yielding words of the Lord, "Abraham! Abraham!" (Genesis 22:11).

God called him by name. Never once did the false gods in the Valley of Ben Hinnom call out to stop the fathers from throwing their sons into the fire. "Do not lay a hand on the boy" (Genesis 22:12) the *true* God commands Abraham. The test was over. But a sacrifice still needed to be made. And wouldn't you know it, at that very moment, "Abraham looked up and there in a thicket he saw a ram caught by its horns. He went over and took the ram and sacrificed it as a burnt offering instead of his son" (Genesis 22:13).

On that most memorable day for Abraham and Isaac, ultimate trust in the Lord was shown. The awful event ended with a most beautiful lesson: the Lord will provide. "So Abraham called that place The LORD Will Provide. And to this day it is said, 'On the mountain of the LORD it will be provided'" (Genesis 22:14).

What had the Valley of Ben Hinnom doled out to anyone but the guilt of child murder and the lifetime of despair that followed the dark deed? To those standing on the outside, Ben Hinnom might look like Mount Moriah. But to those who trust in the Lord as Abraham did, the two places could not be more different.

The Lord needed his people to see these false gods for what they were. And because of their actions, they needed to understand the coming punishment for what it really would be. Just as Judah had committed their atrocities in the Valley of Ben Hinnom, so the Lord changes the name to the "Valley of Slaughter." Jerusalem's streets will become desolate and her people will be destroyed in the valley. The birds will pick their flesh. The sun will dry their bones.

Those will be the people who get off easy. The people of Judah who are banished into exile will have it far worse. "Wherever I banish them, all the survivors of this evil nation will prefer death to life, declares the Lord Almighty" (Jeremiah 8:3).

It is difficult to talk about Judah's saddening actions, isn't it? Sermons rarely touch on the sacrifice of children. Sunday school lessons certainly do not discuss such descriptive sins. We might even be tempted to avoid reading about it at all. When the Lord calls something what it really is, it is almost too much for us.

Ministry is filled with those awful sins. A guilt-stricken teenager will come to you admitting that she aborted her unborn baby. Is that any different from the selfish sins described of Judah in these verses? So how do you react? Will you angrily send her out? Will you despise her because of her sinful actions? No. You are called to give this repentant girl what Jesus has given you: forgiveness. Yes, forgiveness—even for this.

Unconscionable sins find their way into the school room, too. What will you do when you notice bruises on a child in places that could not have been an accident? Will feelings of anger at parents and friends lead you to lash out at them and drive them away? Or will you ignore what you saw, making up an excuse to do nothing? No. You lovingly speak to the child. Then you lovingly speak to the parents, and if need be, to the appropriate social service people.

Deal with sin the way the Lord deals with it—call it what it is. That includes your own sins as well. The outright sinfulness of our people may shock us at times. But are we capable of anything less? What if the people you have been called to serve knew your every sinful thought? What if they heard every word you said about them? What if they saw your actions you tried so hard to keep secret from the world?

First look at the sinful inclinations of your own heart. Then nothing about your members will surprise you. We are all sinners capable of indescribable thoughts, words, and actions. Yet where most of Judah remained different from you and your congregation and your school is what comes *after* those sins. Jerusalem refused to repent. We have the privilege of repenting daily. We are to return to the living well of our baptism, being comforted by the sure prom-ises of the forgiveness of sins, our new life in Christ, and the heaven he has won for us. Abraham held on to those promises even more strongly than the knife in his hand.

After weeks of struggle, or months or years, you can still hold firmly to those promises of sins forgiven. Then you can firmly give them to the sinners around you. Their sins couldn't be any worse than yours in the eyes of the Lord. And if your sins remain forgiven, so are theirs. Share that message of eternal relief with your neighbors. They might be struggling with more guilt than you realize. Give the promise of forgiveness to your family members you have not spoken with for a while. Unless they repent, your loved ones are facing a worse punishment than Judah. The day may come when they "will prefer death to life." Show them the life they have beyond death. It is the gift from the Resurrection and the Life himself.

The Lord never shies away from calling things what they really are. He has called you a sinner. He has called you doomed to hell. Now, because of Christ's death for your sins, your Lord calls you who you really are: his dearly loved child.

Prayer

"God's own child, I gladly say it: I am baptized into Christ!
He, because I could not pay it, Gave my full redemption price.
Do I need earth's treasures many? I have one worth more than any
That brought me salvation free, Lasting to eternity!

"Sin, disturb my soul no longer: I am baptized into Christ!
I have comfort even stronger: Jesus' cleansing sacrifice.
Should a guilty conscience seize me Since my baptism did release me
In a dear forgiving flood, Sprinkling me with Jesus blood." Amen.

—*CWS* 737:1–2

"My Comforter in sorrow"

Jeremiah 8:4–9:6

> Say to them, "This is what the LORD says: When people fall down, do they not get up? When someone turns away, do they not return? Why then have these people turned away? Why does Jerusalem always turn away?"

The word *frustration* hardly begins to describe the tone of the Lord's words here. His long-suffering voice had been so calm for so long that when his grievances trumpet through Jerusalem, they seem to echo through the souls of men. "Why does Jerusalem always turn away?"

It all starts with that age old question: Why? If there was ever an English word that was meant to get to the very bottom of the affair, this word *why* is it. Have you ever had a child ask you why? If you have, you know just how deep the word digs. Eventually, the question *why* methodically walks from something simple like trees and eventually brings you to leaves, then to the science of growth, and then to the creation of vegetation and finally to, it always seems, God himself.

Now God himself asks the question to cut to the heart of Jerusalem's impenitence. "Why does Jerusalem always turn away?" I bet you have asked that question, too. The Old Testament can seem like a veritable "how to" of impenitence. Perhaps in your own frustration you have also asked, "Why does Jerusalem always turn away?"

Of course, you know why. In this case, the simple answer also happens to be the right answer. Jerusalem always turned away because of sin. But let's use that annoying interrogative *why* to dig further. Why did Israel always turn away because of sin? To ask the question of Israel is to ask the question of yourself. Why do we always fall back into our sins the way God's people did? That is where the digging starts to hurt.

A group of sociologists at Stanford who study human behavior asked a very similar question. They performed a scientific study to answer the question of why people do bad things.[1] Throughout their research, the group noted that after people do something good, they tend to compensate by doing something bad. Sociologists call this finding "moral licensing."

To be clear, scientific study cannot be a savior for sin. But research like this Stanford study can help us better understand our sinful failings and predispositions. And it certainly sheds light on Jerusalem's preference for backsliding. Just look at what happened in the days of Jeremiah. King Josiah had come to the throne. By the power of God, he reformed Jerusalem by repairing the temple, rediscovering the scriptures, and including the people with their repentant sacrificing. These actions were all God-pleasing.

Then came Jerusalem's "moral licensing." As a kingdom, Judah had collectively returned to the Lord. Now, in their minds, they had leeway to act the way they wanted all over again. The Dr. Jekyll of Judah's faithful actions had now, once again, given way to the Edward Hyde of their sinful lusts.

If you are familiar with Robert Louis Stevenson's *Strange Case of Dr. Jekyll and Mr. Hyde*, you know Dr. Jekyll's reason for turning into Mr. Hyde. Becoming the grotesquely evil Mr. Hyde allowed Dr. Jekyll to act on his deep-seated urges without incurring the ire of his Victorian community. Hyde offered Jekyll a moral license to do whatever he wanted. If you know the story then you will recall that Jekyll's attempt at moral licensing though Hyde ends in self-destruction.

Stevenson got it right. Moral licensing always leads to self-destruction. Look no further than Jerusalem for proof. They

---

[1] Anna C. Merritt, Daniel A. Effron, and Benoît Monin, *Moral Self-Licensing: When Being Good Frees Us to Be Bad* (Stanford University, Social and Personality Psychology Compass 4/5, 2010), 344–357.

attempted to separate the Dr. Jekyll of their godly religious duties from the Mr. Hyde of their secret worship of their false gods. Their hearts had become a house divided. Now the Lord tells his people through Jeremiah that such a house cannot hope to stand.

The Lord's punishment for such blatant moralizing would be swift and severe. Those who think they are wise by living this way "will be put to shame." They will be the very people who are "dismayed and trapped." Their rejection of the Lord would mean the loss of "their wives to other men and their fields to new owners."

The priests and prophets who led the charge will lose the most. "Prophets and priests alike, all practice deceit." They were the ones falsely encouraging their people's defiant turn to false gods, crying out all the while, "Peace, peace!" But there was to be no peace.

All of these harsh warnings build up to the poetic justice of verse 20: "The harvest is past, the summer has ended, and we are not saved." Such are the consequences of moral licensing.

Children can seem especially prone to the temptation of moral licensing, even if they do not understand the concept. Have you noticed that once you compliment a child for doing something right, the child turns around and disobeys? The response of the parent often is, "Well, that's what I get for complimenting him."

Called workers can be even worse at moral licensing. Think of all the good you do for others throughout your day! You give God's word to shut-ins. You faithfully teach the catechism to students. You write beautiful sermons. You put together well-thought-out lessons. On Sunday morning, you are privileged to baptize and distribute the Lord's Supper and speak the words of absolution. These are all wonderful tasks the Lord bestows on you purely out of his grace.

Then come the devil's deceptively logical temptations. "You did all this good. Now do something for yourself." And we give in. "Certainly the list of good will outweigh my few bad things I do, right? I can occasionally use the wrong words as long as I use the right words *most* of the time. I can give in to my secret, Hyde-like sins as long as people usually see me living my good-looking Dr. Jekyll life."

Once again, the Lord illustrates the consequences of moral licensing through Jerusalem. They wanted balm for their diseased sin. They replaced the Lord's gospel healing with false dressings on their wounds. Such defiance led Jeremiah to become the "weeping prophet" we know him to be. "Oh, that my head were a spring of water and my eyes a fountain of tears! I would weep day and night for the slain of my people."

Beware of those who encourage you to offset faithful good works with sinful lust. Even your friends may bring the deception to you with logical-sounding words. But there is no logic to sin. And any friend who would entice you in this way is really not a friend.

Find true friends. Look for those in ministry who can help you to avoid your pet sins. Maybe that is your spouse or a fellow called worker or a close family member. The Lord has given you these people to aid you in your fight against temptation's backsliding. Turn back together to the word of the Lord when you find yourself frustratingly asking, "Why do I always turn away?"

The God-pleasing reaction to faithful service in your ministry is not moral licensing. It is a soul that returns to the Lord in true repentance. It is a thankful heart that desires to live its thanks for the Lord. It is the genuine tears shed for those members and students who continue to struggle with backsliding in sin. It is the strong and effective prayers of you, a righteous person, on behalf of your people offered up to the Lord daily.

Through Christ, you have a license to live for the Lord—to forgive, to serve, and to give him all glory.

Prayer

"Jesus sinners does receive; Oh, may all this saying ponder
Who in sin's delusions live And from God and heaven wander.
Here is hope for all who grieve Jesus sinners does receive.

"We deserve but grief and shame, Yet his words, rich grace revealing,
Pardon, peace, and life proclaim; Here their ills have perfect healing
Who with humble hearts believe Jesus sinners does receive." Amen.

—*CW* 304:1–2

"Their tongue is a deadly arrow"

Jeremiah 9:7–22

"Not many of you should become teachers." That is how James begins his narrative on the tongue. We might call it "terse teacher talk." But his language had to be strong. Here's why: "Because you know that we who teach will be judged more strictly" (James 3:1). The task of teaching God's word remains so vitally important that the teacher must be completely trustworthy. A teacher cannot be immature in his faith. A teacher must not be sinfully attached to her worldly things and opinions.

Yet there is one small thing that becomes a big stumbling block to this honorable calling of teacher. It has ended ministries so quickly that the called worker was left wondering what happened. It is simultaneously the teacher's greatest tool and his biggest source for sin. It is the tongue.

James strongly warns teachers against misusing their words: "All kinds of animals, birds, reptiles and sea creatures are being tamed and have been tamed by mankind, but no man can tame the tongue. It is a restless evil, full of deadly poison" (James 3:7–8). Words of gossip drip deadly poison into the ears of others. Heated arguments burn vitriol into the hearts of brothers and sisters in the ministry. And at the end of the day, the little rudder has once again steered your ministerial ship off course. Had more people heard what you said, your ministry might have ended.

So it was with the teachers in Jerusalem. "Their tongue is a deadly arrow; it speaks deceitfully," Jeremiah writes. But it was even worse than that. Their words didn't just manifest the sinful thoughts of their minds or the sinful emotions from their hearts. "With their mouths they all speak cordially to their neighbors, but in their hearts they set traps for them."

Jerusalem echoed with the "song of the sirens." According to Greek mythology, the sirens were a dangerous group of sea nymphs who would sing to sailors as they passed by their island. The women appeared so enticing and their song sounded so beautiful that the sailors could not help but turn toward the women. In so doing, their boats crashed upon the rocks. Their sweet-sounding words produced a horrific death.

In Jeremiah's day those sweet words sounded from Jerusalem's most notable teachers to her lowest students. Everyone looked like they had tamed their tongue. People spoke nicely. Individuals exchanged kind words. But it was all a trap.

The Lord desperately wanted to forgive his people for misusing their tongues. Sadly, their mouths refused to repent. So it became time to use the tongue of his prophet, Jeremiah, to echo his powerful word. "I will make Jerusalem a heap of ruins, a haunt of jackals; and I will lay waste the towns of Judah so no one can live there."

Judah could not talk their way out of their fate. So they sealed themselves inside the stout confines of their capital city. They thought that even the Lord would not carry out his punishment and destroy his beloved people. Their sinful perceptions led them to believe death itself could not conquer the kingdom of Judah.

Edgar Allan Poe's "The Masque of the Red Death" paints a similar picture. The short story describes Prince Prospero as he amasses his people within the confines of his impenetrable castle. The "Red Death" was sweeping through Europe and had killed half of his people. The disease was memorably marked by "The scarlet stains upon the body and especially upon the face of the victim."[1]

But in the midst of death's reign, Prospero remained happy. He had built his massive fortress. He reveled in the safety he thought was his. And to illustrate his perceived security, he threw a masquerade ball. As the nobles celebrated, a guest dressed as the "Red Death"

---

[1] Edgar Allan Poe, "The Masque of the Red Death," *The Works of Edgar Allan Poe* (Beelzebub Classics, 2018), Location 6455.

appeared, walking through the rooms of the abbey. Prince Prospero discovered the man and angrily commanded him to be seized and hanged. But no one could lay a hand on this guest. He stalked from one room to another. Wherever he walked, death followed.

The story culminates with Prince Prospero himself succumbing to the very death he thought he had forever avoided. Soon the crowd inside the abbey fell dead around him. No one, not even Prince Prospero, could wall themselves off from the "Red Death." Poe writes, "He had come like a thief in the night."

The walls of Jerusalem appeared just as safe as Prospero's. But the ominous words of the Lord's punishment stalked through the high walls and thick gates. Those words would not be idle, nor would they become a sweet-sounding trap. They would mark Jerusalem's deserved punishment. "Death has climbed in through our windows and entered our fortresses." The halls of Jerusalem would someday stand as dead and dormant as Prospero's abbey. "Dead bodies will lie like dung on the open field."

How could a Jerusalem father protect himself and his family from such an end? How does the called worker keep the souls entrusted to him from seeing such a fate? The schools of Jeremiah's day are long gone. The Christian churches across Europe where adults and children once faithfully heard God's word now stand silent.

So how does your church and school avoid such a fate? How do you protect yourself from that stalking Red Death? Surprisingly, the answer is the tongue. Use the instrument of your small, fallible tongue to speak God's eternal, powerful word. Use your mouth to repent of your sins every day in your personal devotions and together with your people in the divine service. Use your words to speak what actually matters. Like Jeremiah found out, those words from the Lord can cut to the heart. That doesn't mean we refuse to say them, although the devil's nagging temptation for you will be to keep silent. He knows the word works, and he will do whatever it takes to silence your tongue from speaking it. He will use embarrassment and worry and anger to manipulate your words. And often he will succeed.

Still, the word of the Lord stands above the tempter and above every temptation. The word of the Lord, both law and gospel, remains living and active. By the power of the Holy Spirit, we boldly speak those law and gospel words faithfully. In the face of such power, even the devil cannot stand. As Martin Luther memorably affirmed, "One little word can fell him."[2]

"Not many of you should become teachers." Let James' words ring in your ears as you stand in your classroom. Your calling remains a special honor, even when your students appear less than honorable. Your calling remains exclusive, even when your situation feels inferior. Such an honor does not fall on you because of your importance, but because the Lord has graciously blessed you the gifts and abilities to succeed in the place to which you were called.

Do not let your words undermine the Lord's calling. Instead, use them to your Lord's glory. Pray in his name when joy comes and when sadness hits. Praise his name with the words you speak to others, whether in church or in the classroom or in private. And give your God thanks, as you recall all of his mercies for you, which are new every morning. "Gracious words are a honeycomb, sweet to the soul and healing to the bones" (Proverbs 16:24).

Prayer

"Teach us, Lord, full obedience, Holy reverence, true humility.
Test our thoughts and our attitudes In the radiance of your purity.
Cause our faith to rise, cause our eyes to see Your majestic love and authority.
Words of pow'r that can never fail, Let their truth prevail over unbelief."
    Amen.

—CWS 735:2

---

[2] Wisconsin Evangelical Lutheran Synod, *Christian Worship*, "A Mighty Fortress Is Our God" (Milwaukee: Northwestern Publishing House, 1993), 200.

"The understanding to know me"

Jeremiah 9:23-26

C. S. Lewis once wrote: "Pride . . . is the mother of all sins, and the original sin of Lucifer . . . I am an instrument strung but preferring to play itself because it thinks it knows the tune better than the Musician."[1]

Sinful pride leads to the dangerous sin of boasting. Boasting itself remains so dangerous because it is so easy to do. And that which is easy is usually also prevalent. It shouldn't surprise us then that boasting is prevalent on a grand scale throughout scripture. Pharaoh boasted of his strength even in the face of God's powerful plagues. The tax collector at the temple in Jesus' day boasted of his own perceived perfection *right in God's house*. These overt examples can be so jarring that even an unbeliever would raise an eyebrow.

Surprisingly, boasting can be subtle, too. We all have that tendency to think we are superior to those around us. Professor David Myers memorably called this "The Lake Wobegon Effect." Garrison Keihlor often described the fictional city of Lake Wobegon, Minnesota, as a place "where all the women are strong, all the men are good-looking, and all the children are above average."

This is the subtle side of boasting. Psychologists call this "Lake Wobegon Effect" an overestimation in one's abilities. We all think we are smarter than the average person. We all think we are stronger

---

[1] Edited by Walter Hooper, *The Collected Letters of C. S. Lewis Volume 1: Family Letters 1905–1931* (New York: HarperCollins, 2009), 675.

physically, emotionally, and spiritually than most. To one degree or another, we all suffer from this "illusory superiority."

The sinful nature takes this one step further. It is not enough to think of oneself as superior. We also feel the need to boast about this superiority. And while the psychological terms might sound modern, there is nothing new about boasting. The Lord heard this same boasting in the days of Jeremiah pouring forth from the mouths of his own people. "This is what the LORD says: 'Let not the wise boast of their wisdom or the strong boast of their strength or the rich boast of their riches.'"

Pastors and teachers are expected to stand above the overt boasting the Lord describes through Jeremiah. But we have to admit that we are not always very good at avoiding it. We love to promote our own wisdom. It would be enough for a pastor to explain a Hebrew word or phrase in a sermon, but there is certain self-gratification in blowing the congregation away by detailing the process of study and the hours that it took to find that nugget of information. The teacher shares new information every day with her students. But there is a temptation to turn those lessons into a focus on the wisdom of the teacher rather than on the learning of the student.

This type of boasting pulls the called worker into the subtle shift from a selfless humility to a selfish inward focus. And Satan knows that these subtle shifts can eventually turn into seismic shifts of "illusory superiority." Such self-perceptions slowly undermine the Lord's ministry. The servant who lacks humility runs the risk of no longer being a faithful, effective servant for the Lord. Solomon knew that as well as anyone. He wrote: "Let someone else praise you, and not your own mouth; an outsider, and not your own lips" (Proverbs 27:2).

Boasting in strength can be just as dangerous as boasting in wisdom. We can all agree that the church is not a weight room. Spiritual shepherds are not usually flexing physical muscles in an effort to impress their flock. But strong called workers are tempted in a far greater way to boast of their spiritual strength to one another. Circuit meetings can become a sharing of grievances among pastors, resulting in some attempting to prove their ministerial sufferings to be far worse than any Christian martyr. Teachers, too, are tempted to boast in their ability to weather the stormiest child who would be lost if not for the teacher's masterful devotion to appropriate discipline.

To be sure, there is a fitting time for pastors and teachers to share their struggles. And we certainly need to encourage one another through God's word in those moments. But a called worker should be aware of the fine line that still exists between helpful sharing and boastful recounting. We should ask ourselves why we are sharing our struggles. Is it to garner sympathy or to receive helpful, ministerial advice and encouragement?

Even riches can be a source of boasting among called workers. This might not be a boasting of one's own riches. After all, you probably did not enter the ministry expecting an exorbitant paycheck. Yet a comparison often exists between churches and ministries. It can be easy for the pastors and teachers of richer congregations to boast in their members' deep pockets. It can be easier still for pastors and teachers of struggling congregations to complain about their annual shortfall and the stipulations and strains those shortcomings cause.

Boasting in wisdom, in strength, and in riches all stand at odds with the humble attitude our Lord expects. The humble called worker does not boast in himself, or in what she has done. And we all must admit that we have fallen far short of perfect humility. Our boasting has, at times, undone the ministry given to us. Punishment should be sent our way as it was sent to those Jeremiah listed: "Egypt, Judah, Edom, Ammon, Moab and all who live in the wilderness in distant places."

Our sinful nature wants to avoid this punishment by pointing to our own physical and spiritual connections. It cries out: "Remember, my family has always belonged to the church. I'm safe from destruction" and "I'm a minister of the gospel—a called worker. I have everything in hand." Yet by nature, we stood with those physically uncircumcised nations and those spiritually uncircumcised Israelites.

Jeremiah's words from the Lord must have come as quite a shock to the original recipients. To label "the whole house of Israel" as "uncircumcised in heart" remained akin to declaring them unbelievers headed to hell. Israel's spiritual boasting carried eternal consequences.

Yet there can be appropriate boasting. "Let the one who boasts boast about this: that they have the understanding to know me." Appropriate boasting always points to the Lord. The apostle Paul used Jeremiah's words to state this truth to the Corinthians. "God chose the lowly things of this world and the despised things—and the things that are not—to nullify the things that are, so that no one may boast before him" (1 Corinthians 1:28–29).

By the grace of God, you stand as a called worker who epitomizes this truth. In choosing the foolish things of this world and the weak things and the despised things, God chose you. You represent the power of God as he works his perfect will through you, an imperfect servant. What a comfort that is! The Holy Christian Church does not stand or fall on your actions. God's word might look foolish to the world, but it shames the wise. You might look weak, but God's word stands powerfully on its own. When it does, it shames the strong. You may be looked down upon, despised, or rejected by others because of the word you preach and teach. Yet your strength remains in the Lord. After all, "It is because of him that you are in Christ Jesus" (1 Corinthians 1:30a).

Your Lord, the Savior you share, continues to exercise kindness, justice, and righteousness on earth. He continues to display his delight in using you. Don't boast in yourself. You are simply an instrument of the Lord. Boast in the One who can play such a beautiful ministerial melody through such an imperfect instrument.

Prayer

"Your love and grace alone avail
To blot out my transgression.
The best and holiest deeds must fail
To break sin's dread oppression.
Before you none can boasting stand,
But all must fear your strict demand
And live alone by mercy." Amen.

—CW 305:2

"There is no one like you"

Jeremiah 10:1-16

One of the devil's most dangerous illusions is his attempt to convince us that the battle between good and evil is a close contest. He bolsters his deception through the logic. Movies and books add emotion to the illusion, displaying powerful stories of the dualistic battle. Usually in the end, those on the side of good just barely prevail. Sometimes even evil prevails.

Dualism has occasionally worked its way in to the Christian Church, too. C. S. Lewis understood the appeal of dualism to the Christian mind. He wrote, "I personally think that next to Christianity Dualism is the manliest and most sensible creed on the market. But it has a catch in it."[1] The catch, he goes on to explain, is that dualism assumes the powers of good and evil have existed from eternity.

Can you see why this plays into the devil's favor? If he can't convince the world that he doesn't exist, the next best thing is to convince the world that he has *always* existed. Satan wants the world to view him the way he would like to view himself . . . as God.

Then the devil adds another dangerous piece to his illusory puzzle. It is the lie he tells the world, and especially believers, that he is more powerful than God himself. It sounds ridiculous when you view the lie standing outside of the illusion. But when you live in the midst of the world, surrounded by enemies, it looks all too real.

---

[1] C. S. Lewis, *Mere Christianity* (New York: Macmillan Publishing Company, 1997), 33.

One of the greatest examples of this illusion came on the summit of Mount Carmel during the ministry of the prophet Elijah. King Ahab and his wicked queen, Jezebel, had hunted down and murdered so many of the prophets of the Lord. The situation had become so dire that a man named Obadiah had hidden one hundred of the Lord's prophets in two caves.

Then, on one of the most frightening occasions in Elijah's life, Ahab had personally hunted him down, too. Surprisingly, Ahab's purpose was not murder . . . at least not yet. Initially, he simply wanted to berate the prophet. "Is that you, you troubler of Israel?" (1 Kings 18:17). Indeed it was. Now came the prophet's proposition to Israel's idolatrous king. "Summon the people from all over Israel to meet me on Mount Carmel. And bring the four hundred and fifty prophets of Baal and the four hundred prophets of Asherah, who eat at Jezebel's table" (1 Kings 18:19).

The ensuing faceoff first appeared like a satanic illusion. There were so many prophets of Baal and Asherah—almost a thousand! And there, all by himself on the other side of this contest, stood the prophet Elijah. He was the sole representative of the one true God. Even the people refused to back him up. Then Elijah addressed the crowd on the mountain: "If the LORD is God, follow him; but if Baal is God, follow him" (1 Kings 18:21). They responded with silence.

It was time for the showdown. The prophets prepared the altars. They killed the sacrificial bulls. Then the prophets of Baal began calling. But they were only met with silence. Although the prophets themselves made a bunch of noise, "There was no response; no one answered" (1 Kings 18:26).

There is nothing quite like the ironic silence of an idol. A century and a half after the prophet Elijah, the prophet Jeremiah was still desperately pointing that out to his people of Jerusalem. "For the practices of the peoples are worthless." He described the ludicrous practices of his people, cutting wood, crafting the form, and adorning it with gold. Their gods were made by humans. "Their idols cannot speak."

Baal was just as silent on Mount Carmel. The illusion was breaking. How much the devil must have wanted to use his power to give some sort of sign! If only he could make some sound, or offer some sort of fire or project a sign in the sky, then he could have bolstered his illusion. But even the devil was forced to be silent by the true God, who remains infinitely more powerful than he.

Then it was Elijah's turn. While the illusion of Satanic power was silently shattering on the mountain, Elijah had his altar doused with water three times. The lighting of his altar fire would be no fluke. Then he prayed to the God who always hears and always answers. "Answer me, LORD, answer me, so these people will know that you, LORD, are God, and that you are turning their hearts back again" (1 Kings 18:37).

All at once the silence was broken. "Then the fire of the LORD fell and burned up the sacrifice, the wood, the stones and the soil, and also licked up the water in the trench" (1 Kings 18:38). The illusion was destroyed. And those onlookers who were mute before could no longer keep silent. "They fell prostrate and cried, 'The LORD—he is God! The LORD—he is God!'" (1 Kings 18:39).

The same powerful Lord could no longer keep silent in Jerusalem. Jeremiah's sermon picks up where Elijah's sacrifice left off. "No one is like you, LORD; you are great, and your name is mighty in power." Believers see evidence of God's power everywhere. "When he thunders, the waters in the heavens roar; he makes clouds rise from the ends of the earth. He sends lightning with the rain and brings out the wind from his storehouses."

So why was Jerusalem still tempted to believe the illusion? Why are we? Why do the powers of this world still look stronger? Why does the devil often seem victorious? Because the illusion looks so real. Those in power smother the weak. The boastful still yell louder than the humble. And in our darker moments of depression, we start to question the very power of God. Even if we don't question God's power, we want to question God's love. How could our loving God *not* show his power? Why does God seem so . . . silent?

There was exactly one occasion on earth when God the Father remained completely silent. It was when his Son was on the cross. As Jesus suffered our hell, his enemies all looked victorious. The Jewish rulers had gotten what they wanted. The Romans were able to show their power at a time when Jews were streaming into Jerusalem by the thousands for the Passover. And the happiest of them all was the devil.

Over the course of thousands of years, the devil had tried to put an end to that first gospel promise God made against him in the garden of Eden. Satan had turned so many away. On multiple occasions, he nearly wiped out David's family line. But all of it was to no avail. Until Calvary. There Satan had finally gotten what he wanted—Jesus, the Son of God, crucified and killed.

Finally, the illusion appeared to become the reality. Dualism had triumphed. Satan looked to be more powerful than God himself. And it all seemed to be such a fitting revenge. Once on Mount Carmel Satan had been outdone. Now he appeared to have won on another mountain.

Then the voice of God himself broke the silence. Jesus, the Son of God, cried out, "It is finished!" All at once the illusion of Satan's victory was shattered forever. He had not won the victory over God. He had not crushed the Seed's head. He had only struck his foot, and now in turn Satan's own head had been crushed.

Satan had convinced himself of his own illusion. He thought his rebellion in the beginning could be justified if he defeated Christ in a show of power. He couldn't. Nor would he ever. And just in case the devil was in denial about his defeat at Calvary, Jesus descended straight into the bowels of hell to declare his victory over the old evil foe.

Your salvation is no illusion. Your forgiveness stands as an eternal fact. Even the devil cannot undo it. Instead, he continues to promote the illusion of his own power in this world. In your shadowy moments when sin threatens to eclipse your heart, or when the world appears as though it is about to drown you in sadness and despair and pain, flee to Christ. Look to the cross, which has forever shattered the devil's illusion. Then, as a servant of Christ, point those entrusted to your care to that illusion-shattering cross. Remind them of God's real power shown at Mount Carmel. Remind them of Jesus' real death at Mount Calvary. And remind them of their real, eternal salvation in Mount Zion.

Don't believe the illusion. Idols forever remain silent. The devil forever remains defeated. "He who is the Portion of Jacob is not like these, for he is the Maker of all things, including Israel, the people of his inheritance—the LORD Almighty is his name."

Prayer

"Jesus, send your angel legions
When the foe would us enslave.
Hold us fast when sin assaults us;
Come then, Lord, your people save.
Overthrow at last the dragon;
Send him to his fiery grave." Amen.

—CWS 726:6

"A man's life is not his own"

Jeremiah 10:17–25

The week had been a tumultuous one, and it was still only Thursday night. It all began with Jesus peacefully riding into Jerusalem on Palm Sunday. The week continued with his preaching and teaching on Monday and Tuesday, and perhaps Wednesday also. Then Thursday swept in with its Passover preparations. Jesus humbly washed his disciples' feet. Soon enough Jesus and his disciples were reclining at the table, prepared to partake in history's last Passover meal. The wine was poured. The bitter herbs were served. The unleavened bread was placed on the table.

Then, at the end of this final Passover celebration, Jesus began a new meal. Taking the bread, he broke it and gave it to his disciples. He told them to eat it because it was also his body. Then he took the cup of wine and passed it to each of them. It was also his blood, he said. They drank it for the forgiveness of sins.

After two of the most important meals in history, Jesus and his disciples walked to the garden of Gethsemane. No one expected anything out of the ordinary to happen—save for Jesus and Judas. Judas had already gone to bring the captors to arrest Jesus. Jesus was now deliberately walking to the place where Judas expected to find him.

In a matter of minutes, the peaceful night of the Passover would surrender to the horrors of unjustified capture and execution. The coming punishment of hell that belonged both to everyone who had ever lived and also to those who had yet to live would be thrust upon Jesus. Soon the ancient promise first declared in the garden of Eden would finally be fulfilled as the Seed would crush the serpent.

But Jesus had given himself a little time. The Orchestrator of the world, of history, of time and space had allowed himself a few hours with his disciples in a garden. The greatest spiritual storm the world would ever witness was approaching. We can almost hear the wind picking up, the storm clouds mounting, and the thunder rumbling in the distance.

This storm seemed to be coming at the worst possible time. Thousands had streamed into Jerusalem. The Romans were on high alert for any sort of riot or public disturbance. Jesus' disciples remained clueless. This was not for lack of teaching from their Teacher. He had warned them of the coming weather, but they refused to believe such a spiritual storm was possible.

At the center of this storm was Jesus. The Calm in the middle of the storm "looked toward heaven and prayed" (John 17:1). How could he? Knowing everything that was coming, how could Jesus just stand there and pray? To the world the scene seems absurd. Perhaps even to our logical minds it seems curious.

But listen to the words of Jesus in the prayers he prayed before his death: "Now, Father, glorify me in your presence" (John 17:5). He is praying about glory as he looks forward to his execution. "I have given them your word and the world has hated them" (John 17:14). He is praying about his disciples. He knows they will face physical deaths similar to his for the Word. "My prayer is not that you take them out of the world but that you protect them from the evil one" (John 17:15). Now he is asking that the disciples remain in the world, protected from their real enemy, the devil—not their physical, worldly enemies. "My prayer is not for them alone. I pray also for those who will believe in me through their message, that all of them may be one" (John 17:20–21). Did you catch that? Jesus just prayed for *you* with the cross in view.

These words of Jesus' high priestly prayer stand as the quintessential example of the power and effectiveness of a righteous man's prayer. God himself prayed for the very sinners who sentenced him to the cross. Had that awful storm been approaching us, we would have turned inward, felt sorry for ourselves, or even attempted an escape. Not Jesus. He prayed.

A storm had been forming as the prophet Jeremiah stood in Jerusalem. This was the type of storm that could not be weathered by battening down the hatches. No amount of hunkering down could save the citizens of Jerusalem from the thundering punishment the Lord was sending. "Gather up your belongings to leave the land, you who live under siege." Distress was coming. Captivity would follow.

But the second half of Jeremiah chapter 10 is not just another prophecy of impending doom. The Lord also explains his "why." He tells his people what led to the incurable sickness of their defiant sin. "The shepherds are senseless and do not inquire of the Lord; so they do not prosper and all their flock is scattered."

Jerusalem's pastors and teachers had stopped inquiring of the Lord. Their senselessness gave rise to the audacity of self-promotion and made-up spiritual lessons. When teachers go off the rails, what hope is there for their students? Or to use Jeremiah's imagery, what hope do the sheep have when their shepherd abandons them?

These warnings transcend time. You now stand as a shepherd to those who called you. Your students follow as your flock. Your members gather around you to hear God's word purely taught and faithfully expounded. And God has fully equipped you to fulfill your important calling.

But what have you been doing when the spiritual winds begin to swirl? We just saw the powerful example of our Savior praying for those entrusted to him, even as he faced hell itself. Have you been faithfully inquiring of the Lord in such moments? Has your ministerial prayer life humbly requested the good of the souls entrusted to your care?

The honest answer is no. The prayers we raise up to the Lord during the storms of our lives often remain self-focused. "Lord, help me get out of this one with my ministry intact!" These were not the words we heard in Jesus' high priestly prayer. He prayed that *the Father* would be glorified. He prayed that his *disciples* be strengthened. He prayed for *you*.

When Jeremiah saw the storms of punishment swirling, he did what we would expect him to do as Jerusalem's last faithful teacher. He prayed. And just listen to the beautiful words of his prayer: "LORD, I know that people's lives are not their own; it is not for them to direct their steps." That might just be the greatest definition of prayer. It is the admonition of helplessness. It is the epitome of hope in the true God. Prayer is the great request to "correct me, Lord, but only with justice—not in your anger, lest you reduce me to nothing." And more importantly, prayer is that great request for the Lord to watch over those around me.

This was Jesus' prayer. It can be your prayer, too. As a servant of the Lord, you have been given the glorious task of praying for those entrusted to you. Pray for them by name. Remember their struggles that they shared with you the other day so that you know what to ask the Lord for on their behalf. Remember that beautiful phrase that Jeremiah's Jerusalem had forgotten: "Thy will be done."

The devil seethes when he hears those words. In his attempt to remove us from God, he continues to try and sever our communication with him. One effective tactic Satan uses to carry his mission out is distraction. He convinces us that we can be successfully busy in ministry by not "wasting our time" in prayer. He then proceeds to lead us into other wastes of time that *look* efficient under the guise of good intentions. Yet the truth remains that apart from prayer, and apart from time in God's word, your ministry would be undone.

May Christ continue to keep your prayer life strong and active. May he remind you, as a called shepherd, of the importance of daily prayers that include praise, repentance, and thanksgiving. May he help you to pray for others. And last of all, if there is time, may he help you to pray for yourself, too.

Prayer

"Grace taught my soul to pray And made my eyes o'erflow;
His grace has kept me to this day And will not let me go.

"Grace all our work shall crown Through everlasting days;
The heav'nly home God gives his own Shall echo with our praise." Amen.

—*CW* 381:4–5

"A conspiracy among the people"

Jeremiah 11:1-17

A conspiracy was afoot in Judah. Secret plans and hidden worship took place in the dark recesses of the hearts of God's people. The reformation of Josiah had not been that long ago, yet a godly visitor to Jerusalem would hardly notice there had ever been one. Josiah had changed the outward appearance of Judah, but he had not changed the people's hearts.

By the time Jeremiah wrote the words of chapter 11, Jehoiakim was king of Judah. While he was the second son of Josiah, he was nothing like his father. After Josiah's death, Pharaoh Neco had actually made Jehoiakim king of Judah. When the pharaoh was defeated by the Babylonians in the Battle of Carchemish in 605 BC, Jerusalem was besieged. Understanding which way the wind was blowing, Jehoiakim changed allegiances to Nebuchadnezzar and the rising power of the Babylonian Empire.

If allegiances remained fluid for Judah's king, how much more for her people! Political allies and spiritual faithfulness all were means to an end. That end was self-preservation. The Lord calls this laissez-faire attitude what it really is: "You, Judah, have as many gods as you have towns; and the altars you have set up to burn incense to that shameful god Baal are as many as the streets of Jerusalem."

No longer did God's people bring their prayers to the true God. Instead, they were "covering their bases" by praying to many gods and burning incense to Baal. Although this approach to faith is a cynical one, we occasionally see it among our own members. The brother in faith who is undergoing an important surgery calls upon all of his friends and family to pray for him—even those of other religions. When asked to explain why, he simply says, "Well, pastor, I'm just trying to cover my bases." This was the Judean approach to religion: "The more the better—one of them has to be right!"

The school family occasionally operates in a similar way. Some parents move their children from one school to another based upon what their young child wants. This seems to make worldly sense. However, the child who changes schools every year (or every semester) is done a disservice by her parents. She has no educational foundation. And she is especially running the risk of having no biblical foundation in God's word. The parents just want to "cover their bases" while the child receives far less than if she had remained in one place, hearing God's word.

This warning wasn't just for the average Judean. The priests were also at spiritual fault. To mark the importance of this warning, the Lord's words turn from prose to poetry: "What is my beloved doing in my temple as she, with many others, works out her evil schemes? Can consecrated meat avert your punishment?"

The very priests charged with continuing Josiah's reformation were instead leading God's people further astray. This isn't just an ancient threat. After Martin Luther died in 1548, the Lutheran Reformation appeared as though it would fizzle out. The Catholic Church delighted in the thought that Luther's Reformation might be so short that those who were alive to see it begin would live to see it end.

But it didn't. The Lutheran Reformation succeeded through the men who came after Luther. These men continued Luther's return to the word through preaching and teaching. With each generation, the roots of the word grew further down in the German families. Today we can thank our Lord for this great heritage that has now been passed on down to us.

Sadly, this was not the case in Jehoiakim's Judah. The very priests who were supposed to continue Josiah's reformation were now educating the people in offering to false gods. These men thought the magnificence of the temple could protect their "evil schemes" and their consecrated meat could fend off God's punishment. They would soon find out that outward works cannot protect a godless heart from God's wrath. Jeremiah tells them as much: "The LORD

Almighty, who planted you, has decreed disaster for you, because the people of both Israel and Judah have done evil and aroused my anger by burning incense to Baal." So serious was God's punishment that he changed from poetry back to prose. The verse would have stood out as an indicting summary at the end of the chapter.

It is possible that at this point the prophet Jeremiah was ready to pray on behalf of his people. How could he not? Like Abraham praying for the believers in Sodom and Gomorrah, Jeremiah was ready to request that the Lord put off his punishment. In response, the Lord speaks one of his most surprising commands to Jeremiah: "Do not pray for this people or offer any plea or petition for them, because I will not listen when they call to me in the time of their distress."

At this point we might ask: "Isn't our God a God of love? Doesn't he promise to patiently wait for his people to return to him?" The simple answer comes from the timing of the situation. The Lord had shown patience for hundreds of years. He had patiently sent his prophets to bring his people back to him. He sent his last good king, Josiah, to reform his people. By the day Jeremiah spoke these words, the people would only call to God in the midst of a life-threatening disaster. By then it would be too late.

The objections of unbelievers on the Last Day will sound like the cries of unbelieving Judah. When the Lord returns, everyone will be gathered before him. Those who believe in him will rise to live, and those who rejected him will cry out for mercy. But it will be too late.

The actions of Jerusalem's priests offer a stark warning to called workers today. The devil looks to tempt you with the trust others place in you by virtue of your calling. By the grace of God, many will believe everything you say because you are the pastor. By God's grace, the children of your classroom will take your lessons as God's truth. How wonderful when that happens!

Yet the devil methodically entices you to abuse your position through the guise of infallibility. Just as most of your members take your scriptural exposition at face value, they will take your opinions on adiaphora as hard and fast commands of God as well. The temptation is to mandate matters the Bible calls adiaphora (those things that are neither commanded nor forbidden). In many ways, this is what the Pharisees did in Jesus' day. They were revered by the people and used their high positions to make hard and fast rules that went beyond what God had commanded. That temptation still threatens pastors today.

The teacher who is always right in the eyes of her students can fall prey to this temptation also. What happens when a student asks a question that the teacher cannot answer? The temptation is to keep the appearance of infallibility by giving a firm answer, even if it is the wrong answer. One of the best lessons a teacher can illustrate for her students is understanding when to admit "I don't know." She can then follow that lesson by showing her students that we all continue to learn and grow in knowledge and understanding.

In both cases the *appearance* of the called worker has taken the place of humble service of those entrusted to their care. The gaze has turned inward when it should have remained, as always, on those the worker has been called to serve.

Jesus perfectly executed this in his ministry. Notice in the gospels that he did not spend most of his sermons and lessons telling people: "Hey, I'm God—so listen up!" While he certainly told the people who he is, he spent most of his ministry teaching the people with authority, using the Holy Spirit to create and strengthen faith through his word. We are privileged to do the same. The Holy Christian Church does not stand or fall on the appearance of our knowledge as called workers. It stands on the word of Christ. Faithfully share that word, trusting in its power and authority, as Jeremiah did, even in the face of anger and persecution.

Prayer

"When all their labor seems in vain, Revive their sinking hopes again;
And when success crowns what they do, Oh, keep them humble, Lord, and
   true
Until before your judgment seat They lay their trophies at your feet." Amen.
—*CW* 542:3

"A gentle lamb led to the slaughter"

Jeremiah 11:18–23

"Blessed are you when people insult you, persecute you and falsely say all kinds of evil against you because of me. Rejoice and be glad, because great is your reward in heaven, for in the same way they persecuted the prophets who were before you" (Matthew 5:11–12).

Was Jeremiah the prophet Jesus was thinking about when he spoke those words at the beginning of his Sermon on the Mount? It certainly seems so. By this point in his ministry, Jeremiah had started facing various persecutions. People were now secretly plotting against the prophet. They were saying all kinds of evil against Jeremiah because of the message the Lord told him to share.

What was worse was the location where all this was taking place. The "men of Anathoth" were Jeremiah's own relatives. They may have included the members of Jeremiah's own immediate family! This hometown of priests from which Jeremiah came were acting more like a Philistine city might respond toward a prophet of the Lord. Perhaps that is why Jeremiah didn't see their wrath coming.

On his own, Jeremiah had no way of knowing what these people were planning. How could he? These plots of death were fomented within the minds of his extended family and discussed behind his back. Looking back on the situation, Jeremiah uses strong, emotional imagery to paint the picture for the reader: "I had been like a gentle lamb led to the slaughter; I did not realize that they had plotted against me."

Considering the words of those plotting against Jeremiah, perhaps the prophet wasn't exaggerating. Jeremiah's kindred enemies were saying these words to one another: "Let us destroy the tree and its fruit; let us cut him off from the land of the living, that his name be remembered no more." These men of Anathoth were devising destruction for Jeremiah, cutting him off in an effort to rid themselves of this fruit of the word they were receiving.

This seems to be a rather curious way for a town to rid themselves of God's word, and yet it happens all the time in scripture—especially in the ministry of the prophet Jeremiah. Kings will not like the prophet's message from the Lord, so they will persecute the prophet and burn his words. Priests will not want to hear the Lord's reprimand, so they will lock up Jeremiah and warn him never to preach again. And at this point in Jeremiah's ministry, we see his own family plot to kill him because of the words he speaks.

Jesus warned us this would happen. In a beautiful reminder of the origin of our ministry, Jesus says to his disciples, "Whoever listens to you listens to me; whoever rejects you rejects me" (Luke 10:16). Although it would have been very easy for Jeremiah to take this plot personally (how could he not?), the words of his family show their true intent. They wished to rid Anathoth of God's words of law. Sinfully, they thought this could only be possible by ridding themselves of the very prophet who spoke those words.

What can a called servant of the word possibly say in circumstances like these? A servant can say exactly what Jeremiah said. "But you, LORD Almighty, who judge righteously and test the heart and mind, let me see your vengeance on them, for to you I have committed my cause."

Somewhat surprisingly, Jeremiah asked the Lord to punish his family of foes. Perhaps even more astonishingly, the Lord promises to carry out Jeremiah's request! Those very men of Anathoth saying to Jeremiah, "Do not prophesy in the name of the LORD or you will die by our hands" would see punishment from the Lord. "Their young men will die by the sword, their sons and daughters by famine." In fact, the Lord states, "Not even a remnant will be left to them."

Jeremiah's hometown faced punishment for their rejection of the word of the Lord. Jeremiah himself was safe because he continued to trust in that word of the Lord, even when it brought him persecution and plots of death. Although Jeremiah did not see this plot coming, he should have. The Lord was not kidding when he foretold these persecutions at Jeremiah's commissioning:

> "Today I have made you a fortified city, an iron pillar and a bronze wall to stand against the whole land—against the kings of Judah, its officials, its priests and the people of the land. They will fight against you but will not overcome you, for I am with you and will rescue you," declares the LORD. (Jeremiah 1:18–19)

Have you had a "Jeremiah moment" in your ministry? Have you had to make a choice between faith and family? Almost all of us have extended family that hold to beliefs that differ from what God's Word states. Perhaps, like Jeremiah, those relatives—or even immediate family members—have turned their backs on you. Perhaps, like Jeremiah, those who were once close to you have now turned on you.

It is always difficult to lose a loved one. Yet it is far more difficult to lose a loved one spiritually. As always, Jesus is very straightforward with his warnings of the family divisions faith can cause. As Jesus was sending out his disciples to preach as Jeremiah did, he warned them: "Brother will betray brother to death, and a father his child; children will rebel against their parents and have them put to death. You will be hated by everyone because of me, but he who stands firm to the end will be saved" (Matthew 10:21–22).

By the grace of God, we see Jeremiah made the difficult choice to hold to the Lord's word rather than giving up his faith for his family. We have not always been so faithful. We can all think back to times when we avoided the subject of religion around our family and friends in an effort to keep them close. Perhaps we have even been suspect of certain biblical doctrines because our brothers and sisters disagree with them.

If you have not experienced family strife because of faith in Christ, thank the Lord! But remember that your members experience this often. More now than ever before, the students entrusted to your care come to school from spiritually broken homes. In some ways, our people are further on the front lines in their battle of faith than we are. Many of them have had more "Jeremiah moments" than we ever will. And like us, there have been times when they have compromised their faith for their family.

So what can the pastor do to help his front-line members when the battlefield sits in their own homes? What can the teacher say to the children who are silenced by their families when they boldly share their faith? Point them to Christ. Look at the Lamb of God who, even more than Jeremiah, was led like a lamb to the slaughter. Consider your Savior, who knew every plot against him, from his own family trying to take charge of him to his disciples trying to keep him from the cross to the spiritual and secular leaders of his people successfully sentencing him to death.

Yes, God eventually used the Babylonians to bring his promised punishment upon the men of Anathoth. Yet in a greater way, God himself took our promised punishment of hell upon himself at the cross. Jesus allowed himself to be cut off from the land of the living. Yet wonderfully, when his enemies thought the name of *Jesus* would be remembered no more, they could not have been more wrong. The very name *Jesus* now stands synonymous with "resurrection" and "eternal life." By the faith the Holy Spirit has given you, the name *Jesus* remains your strength and your song.

The devil, the world, and our own sinful nature will continue to fight against us. Those ancient enemies will attempt to turn our own loved ones against us. Like Jeremiah, stand firm in Christ to the end. Encourage your people in their fight against these enemies with the life-giving word of the gospel. Daily remember what Jesus prophesied: "You will be hated by everyone because of me." Don't be surprised by that hatred. Instead, look to Christ, who also daily reminds you that "the one who stands firm to the end will be saved" (Matthew 10:21–22).

Prayer

"Lord, gather all your children, Wherever they may be,
And lead them on to heaven To live eternally
With you, our loving Father, And Christ, our brother dear,
Whose Spirit guards and gives me The joy to persevere." Amen.

—CW 557:5

"I would speak with you about your justice"

Jeremiah 12

"Why does the way of the wicked prosper?" Jeremiah asks the Lord. I suppose it is the opposite of another often-asked question: "Why do bad things happen to good people?" Jeremiah will get to that question, too. But first, he asks, "Why do good things happen to bad people?"

Just by asking the question, Jeremiah is in good company. Job was a God-fearing man who had experienced unimaginable loss. As he struggled with that loss, he also looked to the wicked and asked, "Why do the wicked live on, growing old and increasing in power?" (Job 21:7). Job, whose home had collapsed on all of his children, took his complaint even further:

> They see their children established around them,
> their offspring before their eyes.
> Their homes are safe and free from fear;
> the rod of God is not on them. (Job 21:8–9)

Everyone else looked prosperous and happy to Job—especially the unbelieving world. So Job concluded,

> They sing to the music of timbrel and lyre;
> they make merry to the sound of the pipe.
> They spend their years in prosperity
> and go down to the grave in peace. (Job 21:12–13)

And worst of all, Job saw that the wicked prospered: "Yet they say to God, 'Leave us alone!'" (Job 21:14).

In Psalm 73, Asaph also admitted his Job-like thoughts: "I envied the arrogant when I saw the prosperity of the wicked" (Psalm 73:3). Asaph's envious eyes led him to another, far more dangerous thought: "Surely in vain I have kept my heart pure and have washed my hands in innocence" (Psalm 73:13).

We hear the words of Job and Asaph underneath Jeremiah's argument. He expresses the same concern for true, righteous justice. Jeremiah even sounds humble in how he brings it to the Lord's attention: "You are always righteous, O LORD, when I bring a case before you. Yet I would speak with you about your justice."

Jeremiah took issue with how the Lord planted the wicked in prosperity. These people didn't look overtly wicked. After all, even Jeremiah admits to the Lord, "You are always on their lips." But Jeremiah knew there was nothing behind those words. The Lord remained "far from their hearts." Interestingly, we see yet again that the sweeping reforms of the good King Josiah only changed Judah's outward appearance. The hearts of most in Judah remained far from the Lord. And Jeremiah had had enough of them.

When was the last time you took issue with God's justice? It probably was not that long ago—perhaps even today. Why do the wicked always seem to prosper? Rich men and women turn their backs on God, mocking his followers and appearing on the surface to be blessed for it. Many pastors who call themselves "Christian" have sold the truth of the gospel for a nice-sounding social message only to be rewarded with thousands of members in their community churches. The teachers who do not take a hard line with their students, who have given up on the difficult parts of education, are praised by parents, while the faithful teachers are now often hounded for their faithfulness by the very parents who should be supporting them. It all leads us to ask Jeremiah's one-word question all over again: "Why?"

The Lord's answer to Jeremiah can best be described as tough love. "If you have raced with men on foot and they have worn you out, how can you compete with horses?" the Lord asks. He is telling Jeremiah, and all called workers, that worse things are coming. If you cannot handle this first minor appearance of injustice, how will you ever be able to withstand the far worse injustices in the future?

This answer would have been a hard pill to swallow for Jeremiah. His own family and hometown had turned against him, going so far as to plot his death. Perhaps any believer would have taken the opportunity to ask the Lord about his justice after that. The people who wanted Jeremiah dead seem to be living it up! Where is the justice in that?

Justice was coming. However, it wouldn't come upon the wicked when Jeremiah wanted it to. Justice and judgment approached in the Lord's time. "I will forsake my house, abandon my inheritance." Judah's situation would get worse before it got better. "Many shepherds will ruin my vineyard and trample down my field." This would happen throughout Jeremiah's ministry. The men who were supposed to shepherd God's people instead trampled his ground and led his sheep astray. Jeremiah would incur the wrath of these false shepherds on many occasions. In those days he would witness with stark clarity just how minor this first appearance of injustice really was.

So will we. The Lord has a way of giving us the overall spiritual perspective. Those instances of injustice we see in our ministry feel like the worst wrongs we could ever grapple with. Yet more will come. Some will be far worse. And through all of it, the Lord is preparing you for those occasions, just as he was getting Jeremiah ready for the persecutions and hardships and heartache that would come his way throughout his ministry.

Justice is coming . . . in the Lord's time. The punishment prescribed in the law will be brought on those who reject the Lord. "It is mine to avenge; I will repay. In due time their foot will slip; their day of disaster is near and their doom rushes upon them" (Deuteronomy 32:35). The pastor who has given up the truth of God's word for a surplus of members will not succeed forever. Mega-churches seem to be fading as people realize that show has replaced substance. Teachers who would rather garner praise from parents instead of caring for their students may not last long.

It seemed Jeremiah was facing the prospect of what God had promised him when he was called. He was indeed starting to stand "against the whole land—against the kings of Judah, its officials, its priests and the people of the land" (Jeremiah 1:18). Jeremiah had hoped to see God "uproot and tear down . . . destroy and overthrow" (Jeremiah 1:10). The Lord's answer made it clear that his punishment was coming, but not on that day.

Of all the men and women of the Old Testament, Jeremiah might be the man we can most identify with in our twenty-first-century ministry. He isn't conquering kingdoms. He isn't reforming the world. He is faithfully preaching and unfairly persecuted for it. He is a man who asks that very modern question: Why?

We ask that question all the time. But it can be aggravating when we realize that God rarely answers it. In Alfred Tennyson's famous poem "The Charge of the Light Brigade," a brigade charges into the enemy in the midst of the Crimean War. The charge of six hundred men on horseback seems gloriously heroic . . . at first. "Forward, the Light Brigade!" the commander cried. But the charge was doomed from the beginning. "Cannon to right of them, Cannon to left of them, Cannon in front of them Volleyed and thundered; Stormed at with shot and shell." They had ridden into certain death. "While horse and hero fell. They that had fought so well Came through the jaws of Death."

What becomes most prominent in the poem is the question that is *not* asked. While riding in to certain death, not one man asked "Why?" These were soldiers bound to carry out their orders. "Theirs not to make reply, Theirs not to reason why, Theirs but to do and die. Into the valley of Death Rode the six hundred."

We find ourselves in the midst of a spiritual battle. At times it feels as though the enemy has won. Parts of the battle appear to be doomed. We might as well be rushing the devil's surrounding cannons. It is precisely at those moments when our Lord reminds us of the big picture. Ministry is more than just one small spiritual battle. It is a series of battles within our spiritual war against our enemies: the devil, the world, and our sinful nature. We are not here to reason why God commands what he does. We are to trust that he has figured it all out, because he has.

Jeremiah's ministry would eventually end on the spiritual battlefield. I suppose all of ours do. Tennyson's famous poem "The Charge of the Light Brigade" ends with the big picture. Although the men had courageously fought and died, he asks: "When can their glory fade?" These men would be remembered for their unquestioning sacrifice.

We can ask that question of faithful believers, too. When can their glory fade? It won't, because of the salvation that is theirs, and ours, through our Savior, Jesus. Your Lord has everything worked out. You don't need to question why.

> Yours is to preach, to teach, to forgive.
> And after death, in Christ, to live.

Prayer

"My God has all things in his keeping; He is my ever-faithful friend.
He gives me laughter after weeping, And all his ways in blessings end.
His love endures eternally: What pleases God, that pleases me." Amen.

—CW 414:4

"Hear and pay attention"

Jeremiah 13

Effective teachers are like best-selling authors. They don't dictate to their students what they ought to learn. They show them. Engaging authors take their readers on a walk through beautiful scenes and point to their characters with clever, detailed imagery. An effective teacher can go even further. While a writer can appeal to imagination, a teacher gets to fortify a student's imagination by touching the senses.

Do you remember reading about the periodic table as a student? Maybe not. But do you remember the day your science teacher dropped potassium in water? If you saw it happen, you would remember the scene as the solid material plopped into the water and promptly burst into flames. Any good teacher will tell you that to make a lesson take hold in the minds of your students, you need to reach as many senses as possible.

The Lord is the ultimate teacher. As his people continue to get unruly in the days of Jeremiah, he attempts to capture their attention through object lessons. He touches as many of their senses as possible to make the truth stick in their minds and memories.

So the command came from the Lord to Jeremiah, "Go and buy a linen belt and put it around your waist, but do not let it touch water." That might sound like a strange command to us, but the Old Testament context can help us understand some of the meaning that Jeremiah would have readily realized. The priestly garments were linen. Jeremiah's linen belt was an especially significant piece of clothing. The belt represented God's once-close relationship with his people. Having Jeremiah use a priestly garment showed that God expected holiness from his people.

Then came God's strange command. "Take the belt you bought and are wearing around your waist, and go now to Perath and hide it there in a crevice in the rocks." We don't know exactly where Perath is. It could be near the modern Wadi Farah, which isn't too far from Jerusalem, or it could be referring to the Euphrates River. If the latter was the location, then this was quite a journey for Jeremiah to travel to hide a belt.

Later, the Lord told Jeremiah to retrieve the belt again. "Now it was ruined and completely useless." That was the point. The people of Judah were once like a beautiful belt. They were bound to the Lord. But now, because they refused to listen, they "will be like this belt—completely useless!"

We are never told that Jeremiah actually shared this message with the people. Perhaps he did, or perhaps the message was for him alone. After all, it was Jeremiah who bought the belt, buried it, retrieved it, and found it useless. Sometimes God does that for pastors and teachers. God uses lessons and reminders and encouragements specifically for you.

The next illustration was certainly meant for all of Judah. The Lord told them through his prophet, "Every wineskin should be filled with wine." This word of the Lord sounds laughably simplistic. And that is the reaction the Lord expected! "If they say to you, 'Don't we know that every wineskin should be filled with wine?'" Judah's expected response has now become defiant ridicule combined with drunkenness. "I am going to fill with drunkenness all who live in this land, including the kings who sit on David's throne, the priests, the prophets and all those living in Jerusalem."

This spiritual drunkenness will completely turn them against one another. "I will smash them one against the other, parents and children alike, declares the LORD." This fallout from Judah's spiritual drunkenness is a sobering message. "I will allow no pity or mercy or compassion to keep me from destroying them." Many times in the past, Israel stood on the precipice of disaster, only to be saved at the last minute by their loving Lord. From Egypt to the wilderness, to the conquest of Canaan to the Assyrian siege of Jerusalem God's pity, mercy, and compassion led him to save his often-thankless people.

But this would not happen forever. Jeremiah probably wrote these words during the reign of King Jehoiakim, which meant the city of Jerusalem had only fifteen to twenty years left before it would be destroyed. No one in Jeremiah's day thought that was possible. Jerusalem had become so spiritually drunk that it didn't even realize what was happening.

As this drunken stupor slowly led God's people to drift further away from him, the Lord continues his message with a wake-up call: "Hear and pay attention!" Destruction was coming. So was darkness. "Give glory to the LORD your God before he brings the darkness, before your feet stumble on the darkening hills." The fires of sacrifice, the candle flames in the homes of Jerusalem will all be snuffed out. Even the king and the queen mother would not be safe from this coming darkness. Captivity was coming from the north, and no political ally could save Jerusalem from the Babylonian menace, King Nebuchadnezzar.

During the siege of Jerusalem and all throughout captivity, God's people will ask a question we often ask: "Why has this happened to me?" It is natural to ask, "Why?" We like to make connections in our lives between causes and effects. But we are not always adept at honestly seeing the causes. "What did I do to deserve this?" The question comes with a tinge of anger. The implication in our question is that we *never* do anything to deserve the consequences that come our way. Pride and arrogance had led Judah to believe their sins were not important. They didn't believe their consequences could be real.

Our sins can seem just as inconsequential to us. We ask, "Do silent sins have consequences?" Satan tempts us to think of our sins as the metaphorical tree falling in the secluded forest. If no one hears it, does it really make a sound? God answers with a booming "Yes!" And the called worker does well to remember the reality of sin and its damning consequences.

This is why it is so important for the pastor to face the altar and speak the confession of sins with his congregation. He and his flock need to remember that he is not above them. They have *together* become like one who is unclean. *Together* they need forgiveness in

Christ. And while the pastor speaks the words of absolution, they are really the words of Christ. They are for the pastor as much as they are for his congregation.

The Lord remains the ultimate teacher. He knows how to impact every sense we have. He should; after all, he created them. He created us. Using a linen belt to show what sin does is a memorable lesson. Using wine might be even more impactful. Wine touches every sense. You can hear it being poured. You smell it when it is close. You see the red color. You touch it to your lips right before you taste it in your mouth. No wonder the Lord chose to use wine as one of the earthly elements in the sacrament of the Lord's Supper. The blood of Jesus purifies us from every sin. That wine, which is also Jesus' blood, makes us *remember* that. It helps us fulfill the command of the sacrament: "Do this in remembrance of me."

Do you remember the first time you were given Holy Communion? As you sat toward the front of the church, you perhaps heard the wine poured. You saw your pastor hold his hands over the elements as he spoke the words of institution. As you came forward, you could smell the strong aroma of those fermented grapes. Then, touching the cup to your lips, you tasted it.

The scene isn't easy to forget. And that is the point. The Lord doesn't just *tell* you to remember that he is good. He says, "*Taste* and *see* that the Lord is good." And in that way our unapproachable, unseen Lord of the universe makes himself approachable, seen, and remembered.

Prayer

"Here, O my Lord, I see you face to face;
Here would I touch and handle things unseen,
Here grasp with firmer hand eternal grace,
And all my weariness upon you lean." Amen.

—*CW* 315:1

"Savior in times of distress"

Jeremiah 14

There was once a rich miser who buried his gold in a secret place. Every day he journeyed back to the hidden spot to dig it up and count it. One day, a thief observed this man traveling to the secret place and digging up his hidden treasure. After the miser left, the thief dug up the treasure and took it.

The next day, the miser arrived to dig up the treasure. When he realized it had been stolen and replaced with a rock, he cried and tore his hair. A passerby noticed the sad miser and asked what happened. The miser explained that the gold he came to dig up every day was now stolen. The passerby then asked, "Why didn't you keep it safe at your house so you could use it to buy what you needed?" The miser scoffed, "I never touched the gold! I only came to look at it, not to spend it!" So the passerby took a rock and threw it in to the hole. "If that is all you did," he said, "then cover up that stone. It is worth just as much as that rock."

Aesop wrote that. It was one of his famous fables, and this was the moral he attached to it: "A possession is worth no more than the use we make of it." For years the people of Judah acted like that miser. They received rainfall and good harvests and never considered where those blessings came from. They assumed their safety and success would continue whether they gave credit to the Lord or not.

Then came the famine. This lack of rain became so disastrous that Jeremiah remarked "even the doe in the field deserts her newborn fawn because there is no grass." The wild donkeys panted like jackals and their eyesight failed due to the lack of pasture.

It was even worse for the people of Judah. The rich sent their servants for water, perhaps even to their secret cisterns, but they found none. The dry, cracked ground stood as a symbol of this disastrous drought. It also defined Judah's spiritual situation, although you wouldn't have known it to look at them. In response to these hard times, the people of Judah fasted and offered even more sacrifices.

But these were merely motions. The Lord saw the hearts of his people. He knew they were not truly repentant. In verse 10 the Lord memorably assesses the spiritual situation among his people.

This is what the LORD says about this people:

> "They greatly love to wander;
> they do not restrain their feet.
> So the LORD does not accept them;
> he will now remember their wickedness
> and punish them for their sins."

Those words of the Lord are memorable because they seem to stand directly opposed to his poignant definition of the new covenant we will hear in Jeremiah 31:34. In fact, the Lord went further. He told Jeremiah, "Do not pray for the well-being of this people." At this point we might be surprised that Jeremiah was praying for them at all. After experiencing persecution from his hometown, Jeremiah could have simply written off the very people to whom he was called to prophesy.

How often do you pray for the people who called you? Pastors pray for others on a Sunday morning . . . when they remember. Teachers include students in their prayers when the child suffers from a dangerous illness. Yet these are probably not the daily prayers for your people that Jeremiah exhibits with such love. Jeremiah prays for the very people who would want him dead! We can do a far better job of praying for our members, even the ones who would prefer us not to be their called worker. Those individuals certainly need our prayers!

Jeremiah knew his people needed his prayers. Yet the Lord's response remained ominous. He had stopped listening. He told

Jeremiah that he did not need to intercede this time around. The drought would remain because Judah's sins and backsliding remained. The Lord would be "a stranger in the land" because his own people had chosen not to know him.

We would do well to incorporate some of these detailed verses Jeremiah writes in this chapter into our own confession of sins. We must also admit with Jeremiah and Judah: "For we have often rebelled; we have sinned against you." This word *backsliding* speaks to the apostasy of the people. For generations God's people had been "backsliding" into false gods and pet sins. No sooner had the Lord made spiritual headway up the hill with his people than they slid back into their old spiritual sins, succumbing to temptation all over again!

The Lord's warning of backsliding should resonate with us and our people, too. By the power of the Holy Spirit, there are days when we faithfully climb the hill of sanctification. But there are other days, or other parts of the day, when we slide back into our old sins. For a called worker, these sins can mean the difference between standing strong in the ministry and being forced out of it. Yet backsliding into secret sins, the kind no one ever would know about, is a spiritual danger, too. This is why pastors and teachers need to daily admit these backsliding sins to the Lord in prayer and ask for his forgiveness through Jesus. The strength to stop backsliding will come from the Lord and the encouragement of our fellow believers.

Jeremiah did not seem to have much encouragement. He and his people were surrounded by false prophets who were predicting, "You will not see the sword or suffer famine. Indeed, I will give you lasting peace in this place." It was true. These prophets were certainly speaking lies, yet it was no excuse for the wicked backsliding and false beliefs of the people. "The people they are prophesying to will be thrown out into the streets of Jerusalem" the Lord tells Jeremiah. In the eyes of the Lord there are never any excuses for sin—circumstantial or otherwise.

The people of Judah had only themselves to blame for acting like that miser with God and his word. King Josiah's reformation had given Judah the treasure of the gospel all over again when he had dug it up in the temple. Yet they never made use of it. The word of the Lord might as well have been replaced by a rock. And actually, it was. The "worthless idols" (14:22) the people trusted to bring rain couldn't give them a drop. If anything, Judah had become worse than Aesop's rich miser. They had *willingly* given up the treasure of God's word for the worthless rock of idolatry!

That lack of water led to a sad irony. Judah was experiencing a disastrous drought behind a vail of tears. "Judah mourns, her cities languish; they wail for the land, and a cry goes up from Jerusalem." Jeremiah himself was crying out to the Lord on behalf of his people. Then, at the end of it all, the Lord also cried. "Let my eyes overflow with tears night and day without ceasing." If tears could water the land, the drought would have ended long ago.

Yet even in the midst of Judah's spiritual crisis and physical disaster, Jeremiah does not give up hope. "Do any of the worthless idols of the nations bring rain? Do the skies themselves send down showers? No, it is you, O LORD our God. Therefore our hope is in you, for you are the one who does all this."

Jeremiah's hope remains your hope. When members fall away, when children are taken out of your school, when physical disasters affect the community to which the Lord called you, continue to place your sure and certain hope in him. Let your prayers continue to rise to your Savior on behalf of those who have left, and use his word to avoid the type of backsliding that gives you into your temptations.

The spiritual desert in which you were born compares well to Judah's drought. That is why you were baptized. Judah wanted physical water without God's word. You have been given both together. You are a baptized child of God, washed and cleansed. Such children are not to be misers with the treasures they have received. They are faithful servants, taking God's word to heart. And when you do, you are privileged with the task of showing others how to do the same.

Prayer

"God's own child, I gladly say it: I am baptized into Christ!
He, because I could not pay it, Gave my full redemption price.
Do I need earth's treasures many? I have one worth more than any
That brought me salvation free, Lasting to eternity!" Amen.

—CWS 737:1

"If you repent, I will restore you"

Jeremiah 15

The word *intercede* is one of those terms that floods the mind with an ocean of pictures. A priest sacrifices between a sinner and his almighty God. An ambassador walks out through the massive door from a city under siege to the yelling, swarming enemy beyond. To intercede is to be the priest in the middle. It means walking as the ambassador between rival armies. This role of intercessor remains important. He is the only one preventing all-out destruction and death. And yet, while the position is vitally important, it is rarely appreciated.

If there was any man in scripture who understood the lifesaving role of intercessor, it was Moses. He often stood between his own complaining, hot-tempered, and occasionally idolatrous people and their holy God. After receiving God's Ten Commandments on two tablets of stone, Moses and Joshua walked down the mountain to hear a frightful noise. As they approached the camp, Moses saw the dancing, the carousing, and the golden calf at the center of it all. Worlds once again collided as Moses angrily threw down God's engraved tablets toward the image Aaron had made with his own hands. Punishment ensued. This was followed by Moses' loving intercession. "Oh, what a great sin these people have committed! They have made themselves gods of gold. But now, please forgive their sin—but if not, then blot me out of the book you have written" (Exodus 32:31–32).

Moses understood the seriousness of intercession. He was willing to stand in front of his own sinfully defiant, idol-worshiping people—even if it meant his own removal from God's written history. Moses interceded to ask for Israel's forgiveness. Graciously, the Lord forgave them.

Later, after the spies brought back their report of the Promised Land, God's people again turned against their Lord. The same doubt-filled cries rang out from the people, "If only we had died in Egypt! Or in this desert!" (Numbers 14:2) and finally "We should choose to go back to Egypt" (Numbers 14:4).

When Moses and Aaron tried to convince the people of the Lord's power, even over giants, the Israelites talked about *stoning* them! Then Moses once again had opportunity to intercede for his people. The Lord, in turn, proclaimed, "I will strike them down with a plague and destroy them, but will make you into a nation greater and stronger than they" (Numbers 14:12).

As any good intercessor would, Moses returned to the promises of the Lord: "The LORD is slow to anger, abounding in love and forgiving sin and rebellion. Yet he does not leave the guilty unpunished" (Numbers 14:18). So the Lord gave his verdict to his intercessor, Moses, "I have forgiven them, as you asked" (Numbers 14:20). Yet the Lord did not leave the guilty unpunished. The generation that saw Egypt would not be allowed to see the Promised Land. Once again Israel was saved through intercession.

Moses wasn't the last intercessor. Samuel was also given ample opportunity to go between his people and their Lord. The situation at that time was as dire as it ever had been for Israel. The ark of the covenant was in Philistine hands, and they were looking to wipe out Israel once and for all. It seemed God had given Philistia the perfect opportunity. Samuel assembled all Israel at a place called Mizpah. We don't hear of any Israelite weapons or battle plans . . . just Samuel. In the meantime, the Philistines noisily approached. Their massive army had arrived and was moving in to wipe out their ancient enemy.

Samuel remained unafraid. As their lives hung in the balance, he calmly stated to his people, "I will intercede with the LORD for you" (1 Samuel 7:5). The people soon also confessed with Samuel, "We have sinned against the LORD" (1 Samuel 7:6). Soon the sky thundered so loudly that the attacking Philistines were sent into a panic. In one of the quickest turn-arounds in Israel's battle history, the Israelite army went out and routed the scattering men of Philistia.

By the end of the reign of King Josiah, those accounts of Moses and Samuel seemed distant memories. Now it was the prophet Jeremiah's turn to pick up the mantle of intercession on behalf of his angry, godless nation. Like Moses before him, Jeremiah's own people were ready to kill him for the words he shared from the Lord. Like Samuel, Jeremiah and his people were facing the eventual invasion of a powerful foe.

Up to this point in chapter 15, Jeremiah has faithfully and lovingly interceded for his people. With words that sounded like they came from Moses himself Jeremiah pleaded, "We acknowledge our wickedness, LORD, and the guilt of our ancestors; we have indeed sinned against you. For the sake of your name do not despise us; do not dishonor your glorious throne" (Jeremiah 14:20–21a). Then once again Israel's intercessor held God to his promises, "Remember your covenant with us and do not break it" (Jeremiah 14:21b).

To this the Lord gave a response neither Moses nor Samuel ever heard. "Even if Moses and Samuel were to stand before me, my heart would not go out to this people. Send them away from my presence! Let them go!" Death and the sword and starvation and captivity were coming for God's people. Even Jeremiah's words of intercession could not stop those consequences now.

What an ominous position to be in—standing between a people about to be obliterated and the very God who is about to obliterate them! Such is the role of an intercessor. How easy it would be to simply step to the side. Jeremiah must have given that choice a cursory thought. Why die with a godless people doomed to destruction? Stand to the side and watch them get the punishment they deserve!

Have you let that thought creep into the recesses of your mind? After a particularly feisty meeting, after a member calls you out erroneously, after someone threatens your life, you also may have thought about stepping to the side to watch the fire of God eventually consume this individual. If you have not yet experienced situations like these, you simply have not been in ministry long enough. They will come. The devil will make sure of it. And when they do, how will you act? Will you step aside, or will you stand between?

For all the times we did step out from our God-given go-between role of minister or teacher, we have one who never did. Moses and Samuel and Jeremiah may have been great intercessors, but they still needed someone to intercede for them. Enter your Great High Priest, the one who came to stand between the sinful world and the actual wrath our Lord sent our way. Jesus interceded throughout his ministry: "During the days of Jesus' life on earth, he offered up prayers and petitions with fervent cries and tears to the one who could save him from death, and he was heard because of his reverent submission" (Hebrews 5:7).

Jesus died interceding. Your go-between took all of your hell upon himself so that they only thing to fall upon you would be the shadow of his cross. This is the ultimate fulfillment of the role of intercessor. The forgiveness Moses pleaded for from God, the forgiveness Samuel's people looked to God for, all came to them, and us, through the Great High Priest, Jesus.

While Jesus fulfilled the role of intercessor, he has not abolished it. He gives his called workers opportunity to continue the role of intercessor through his gift of prayer. He gives you the ability to sing with the psalmist: "May my prayer be set before you like incense; may the lifting up of my hands be like the evening sacrifice" (Psalm 141:2). He gives you marvelous Old Testament examples of loving intercessors like Moses and Samuel and Jeremiah to appreciate and imitate. He gives you New Testament encouragements to intercede: "I will continue to rejoice, for I know that through your prayers and God's provision of the Spirit of Jesus Christ what has happened to me will turn out for my deliverance" (Philippians 1:18–19).

And most of all, he gives you the loving strength not to step aside. It can be very tempting for a pastor to move out of the way of his people to watch them die. Don't give in to Satan's appeal to self-preservation at the cost of watching your people incur God's wrath. Pray on their behalf. Stand with them on God's life-giving word. And if need be, stand between them and their God like Moses, Samuel, and Jeremiah once did.

Let God's words of comfort to Jeremiah be your comfort, too. After so many words of law, after refusing Jeremiah's words of entreaty on behalf of his people, the Lord had a special reminder for his prophet . . . and for you.

> Therefore this is what the Lord says: "If you repent, I will restore you that you may serve me; if you utter worthy, not worthless, words,

you will be my spokesman. Let this people turn to you, but you must not turn to them. I will make you a wall to this people, a fortified wall of bronze; they will fight against you but will not overcome you, for I am with you to rescue and save you," declares the Lord. "I will save you from the hands of the wicked and deliver you from the grasp of the cruel."

Prayer

"Jesus, heav'nly hosts adore you, Seated at your Father's side.
Crucified this world once saw you; Now in glory you abide.
There for sinners you are pleading, And our place you now prepare,
Ever for us interceding Till in glory we appear." Amen.

—*CW* 351:3

"I will send for many fishermen"

Jeremiah 16

Ministry often seems to attract difficult situations. The causes can be various. The world around us labels our faith "ignorant." Individuals angry with church practices aim their barbs at the called worker. Those disillusioned by hypocrites in the church speak out against all Christians.

These attacks all took place in Jeremiah's ministry at one time or another, too. Yet in this chapter, Jeremiah's personal ministerial struggles seem to come directly from the Lord. God now commands Jeremiah to do something no other person in scripture was ever asked to do. "You must not marry and have sons or daughters in this place." How can the Lord ask his prophet to avoid the blessing of marriage and children—especially in the midst of a long and difficult ministry? Perhaps you personally know just how much of a blessing a spouse can be during the joys and struggles of faithfully carrying out the Lord's work.

So why not Jeremiah? The command of the Lord was actually given out of love for the prophet. "They will die of deadly diseases. They will not be mourned or buried but will be like dung lying on the ground. They will perish by sword and famine, and their dead bodies will become food for the birds and the wild animals."

God's command of ministerial celibacy no longer applies to called workers today, and we can thank our Lord for it. Yet that is one thanksgiving prayer we do not pray as often as we should. It can be easy to fall into the temptation of thinking ourselves better off with the free time a single ministry would provide. Most likely the opposite would be true. Do not take God's blessings for granted, especially his blessings of a spouse and children. God uses these people in our lives to encourage us and make us stronger. We are able to lean on them when we are weak. In turn, we are given the opportunity to help and encourage them.

Jeremiah, the loner prophet, may have missed those blessings of a wife and children. However, he was about to get lonelier still. The Lord further commanded him, "Do not enter a house where there is a funeral meal; do not go to mourn or show sympathy, because I have withdrawn my blessing, my love and my pity from this people." Just when Jeremiah thought he couldn't be hated any more than he already was, the Lord commanded him not to mourn for the deceased or attend a funeral. No exceptions are made, even for family members.

Once again there was a reason for this command from the Lord. "Both high and low will die in this land. They will not be buried or mourned, and no one will cut themselves or shave their head for the dead." Jeremiah once again was a living parable for Judah's coming death.

Then came the final command: "And do not enter a house where there is feasting and sit down to eat and drink . . . Before your eyes and in your days I will bring an end to the sounds of joy and gladness and to the voices of bride and bridegroom in this place." Jeremiah was not to share in the joy or sadness of his people. Instead, within his own lifetime, death and destruction would come upon everyone.

Weddings and funerals were a very important part of Jewish life. There was no sense in earthly joy at this point in Jeremiah's ministry. The weddings could only offer an empty, temporal happiness. The funerals would only be a precursor to the countless bodies that would be strewn unburied throughout the land.

There have been periods in human history when this has been the case. The days before the flood looked like any other day: people were conducting business, marrying, and giving in marriage. Then the floodwaters washed everything away. The days leading up to the destruction of Jerusalem in AD 70 must have seemed similarly pointless. The temple was about to be destroyed, along with much of the city itself.

Five centuries after Christ, the eastern half of the Roman Empire experienced a similar world-altering disaster. The worst outbreak of bubonic plague struck the empire. The effect was terrifying. Travelers would come upon once-thriving cities only to find eerily quiet ghost towns. Entire Roman provinces looked like a modern post-apocalyptic movie. Bodies were half-buried as the deadly plague had even interrupted funerals. Wedding decorations could be seen without anyone around them; those invited were either dead or dying.

This was how the Lord saw his people in the days of Jeremiah. They were dead, and they didn't even know it yet. Festivities before destruction seem deeply ominous. Funerals *before* death aren't sad enough.

Jesus' ministry epitomized the opposite. His disciples didn't fast because Jesus, the Bridegroom, was in their midst. Jesus mourned with the friends and family of Lazarus at his tomb—even though he was about to raise him back to life. Jesus rejoiced with those at the wedding at Cana. But then at the end, when Jesus was carrying his cross to Calvary, his words sounded eerily similar to the prophecies of Jeremiah. He told the women weeping for him: "For the time will come when you will say, 'Blessed are the childless women, the wombs that never bore and the breasts that never nursed!'" (Luke 23:29).

Spiritually appropriate emotions can only pour forth from a heart in tune with God's grand plan. He doesn't reveal all of his plan to us here on earth, only the details we need to know. This means that as Christians, there will be times when we will mourn while the world rejoices. The time will also come when we rejoice in God's word and work even while the world fights and mourns.

Such deviation from cultural norms will lead to being ostracized. As Jeremiah soon found out, feeling ostracized can sometimes seem like a prerequisite for ministry. Being out of touch may feel like a new norm for pastors and teachers called by Christ. In fact, Christ was always very up front about this. He told his disciples, "If the world hates you, keep in mind that it hated me first. If you belonged to the world, it would love you as its own. As it is, you do not belong to the world, but I have chosen you out of the world. That is why the world hates you" (John 15:18–19).

Jeremiah's unrelenting nightmare of a ministry would eventually end with the conquering of Jerusalem, the destruction of the temple, and the scattering of his people. And it was quite possible that at this moment everything was now sinking in for the prophet. So in his love, the Lord points his prophet to the big picture—the one that matters.

Even after all the coming destruction and sadness, not all would be lost. While the Babylonian captivity would be as great of a national disaster for Judah as enslavement in Egypt had been, God's salvation for his people, after seventy years of captivity, would be just as glorious as their rescue from Pharaoh.

In fact, the Lord promised even more than that. The tribes of Israel had been scattered, some even seemed to be wiped out entirely. But the day would come when the Lord would send out fishermen to catch them and hunters to hunt his remnant down. Ultimately, Christ himself was that fisherman who lovingly caught the remnant. He was the hunter who sought us for himself. Then the words of the prophet Isaiah would finally be fulfilled: "Those the LORD has rescued will return. They will enter Zion with singing; everlasting joy will crown their heads. Gladness and joy will overtake them, and sorrow and sighing will flee away" (Isaiah 51:11).

As the Lord eventually caught his remnant and brought them back from Babylon, so he has also caught you. You are one of the "many fishermen" that the Lord has sent for. What a privilege to stand as Jeremiah did, faithfully proclaiming God's gospel even in the midst of pain and sadness! The apostle Paul speaks specifically to this when he writes to the Philippians, "I consider everything a loss compared to the surpassing greatness of knowing Christ Jesus my Lord, for whose sake I have lost all things. I consider them garbage, that I may gain Christ and be found in him" (Philippians 3:8–9).

Even in the face of being shunned and persecuted, Jeremiah ends the chapter with the beautiful response of a called worker. The Lord *is* our strength and fortress, our refuge in time of distress. Those around us still need to be taught, as the Lord continues to teach us through his word. And so once again the words of Jeremiah are placed in our mouths. His care for his people fills our hearts. We join with the prophet and continue to recount the timeless word of the Lord with bold confidence:

Therefore I will teach them—
this time I will teach them
my power and might.
Then they will know
that my name is the LORD.

Prayer

"In the cross of Christ I glory, Tow'ring o'er the wrecks of time.
All the light of sacred story Gathers round its head sublime.

Bane and blessing, pain and pleasure By the cross are sanctified;
Peace is there that knows no measure, Joys that through all time abide."
    Amen.

—*CW* 345:1, 4

"Engraved with an iron tool"

Jeremiah 17:1–18

Around 400 BC, a man named Mausolus was contemplating his future. As a powerful Greek king, he had achieved success on every front. He had conquered the surrounding territories. He successfully revolted alongside Artaxerxes. Then he successfully revolted against Artaxerxes. Most memorably, Mausolus moved his capital to the city of Halicarnassus.

Then, as old men tend to do toward the end of their lives, Mausolus began considering his legacy. What would he be remembered for? His love of Greek culture? His conquests? Even Mausolus had to admit these accomplishments would probably not stand the test of time. But what could?

After much contemplation, Mausolus decided that a giant stone structure would do the trick. Not only would this structure stand for all time, he thought; it would also serve as a fitting legacy for his great name. The completed structure came to be known as "The Mausoleum of Halicarnassus." The ancients called it one of the seven wonders of the world.

Ironically, the structure's name is the only surviving piece of Mausolus' legacy. "Mausoleums" continue to stand as stone structures of remembrance for the deceased. For most, these stone buildings stand as the only marks of those who have gone before, their inscriptions the last will and testament of the decaying bodies inside.

Unless the Lord returns soon, this will also be the case for you someday. After a few generations, all that will bear your memory on earth will be an inscribed tombstone or mausoleum. Your name might be remembered in the family genealogies of your descendants, but your personality, your characteristics, and your loves will all be lost to the ages.

For all of our technological accomplishments, inscribed rock still remains the best way to leave a lasting mark. Houses crumble. Hard drives fail. But rock lasts almost forever.

Such permanent qualities of rock could not have been a comfort to Judah when she heard what the Lord planned to engrave on it. "Judah's sin is engraved with an iron tool, inscribed with a flint point." Imagine your tombstone listing your most heinous sins below your name. That would certainly be the opposite of the type of legacy you would wish to leave.

Yet Judah had engraved her own sins. The marks of her godless defiance could still be seen etched on the altars of false gods. Under the giant spreading trees and on the tops of mountains the rocky remains of Asherah poles still stood. "Even their children remember." Children pay attention to the symbolism carved upon rocks even more than adults.

Worse than sin engraved on stone is guilt written on the heart. The Lord often speaks in these terms. He longed to use his law to turn the hearts of his people away from their false gods. He yearned for his gospel to turn his people's hearts back to him.

They had only themselves to blame for their rejection of the true God. "Through your own fault you will lose the inheritance I gave you." Enslavement in a foreign country would be Judah's deserved future.

Inscriptions in rock last a long time. The stones themselves last even longer. Yet in the end, the Lord outlasts them all. That is what makes the Lord's next words so frightening: "For you have kindled my anger, and it will burn forever."

Spiritual trust issues sat at the center of Judah's defiance. Their issues with trusting God meant they looked to their own strength and the power of armies and rulers. The Lord had a strong warning for all those who put faith in the small, infinitesimally weak flesh. "Cursed is the one who trusts in man, who draws strength from mere flesh and whose heart turns away from the LORD."

Instead of trusting the Lord to guide their decisions, most of Judah's kings had ruled their own way. The priests of Jeremiah's day aided the people in their false worship, telling them to trust in these broken sacrifices to their mute gods. And the false prophets were the worst of the bunch. They spoke lies that directly opposed what the Lord had spoken through Jeremiah. When Jeremiah spoke a warning, these men cried out, "Peace!" They all trusted in their own abilities rather than in the Lord's perfect wisdom and strength.

Does that sound familiar? Do you have spiritual trust issues? Jeremiah's world illustrates just how easy it is for called workers and church leaders to shift the object of their trust. Like a slow-moving pendulum, trust swings back and forth from the Lord to the individual. And it is precisely when that pendulum rests above us, and our trust is self-focused, that everything begins to fall apart.

What is your church struggling with right now? Are there financial issues? Is a negative, vocal minority steering meetings and functions in the wrong direction? Are you expected to "get numbers up" this next year? No doubt you feel every one of those pressures. No doubt you feel the temptations that come next. To trust in your own strength is selfishly something we all think ourselves capable of.

What problems is your school wrestling with? Are there financial issues? Is a negative, vocal minority of families steering school meetings and functions in the wrong direction? Are you expected to "get school numbers up" this next year? Once again, you must feel those pressures and struggles. Then come the temptations. You begin to think that the school, and the faith of your children, rest on your capable shoulders. What pressure! To think that such a ministry hangs in the balance because your spiritual strength holds it in place!

The danger with trusting in yourself to hold your ministry together is that it looks like such a noble cause. We feel like the mighty Atlas struggling to hold the entire world of our ministry atop our heads. What if I fail? What if I drop one part of ministry and the entire thing comes crashing down?

Trusting in yourself is not just dangerous. It is also arrogant. No wonder why Jeremiah writes, "The heart is deceitful above all things and beyond cure." The Lord completely sees you for who you are. He knows how your pendulum of trust often swings from trusting in him to trusting in yourself. "I the LORD search the heart and examine the mind, to reward each person according their conduct, according to what their deeds deserve." That inscribed stone forever lists what our deeds deserve.

Thanks be to God that he does not treat us as our sins deserve. Instead, he treated his Son, Jesus, the way we deserved to be treated. Jesus didn't just perfectly trust his heavenly Father. Jesus trusted him enough to willingly drink every last drop of punishment on the cross. As Jesus' enemies allowed his body to be placed in a new tomb, they thought that the sealed stone rolled in front would stand as Jesus' legacy. *Such is the end of all who dare stand against the Jewish leaders,* they thought.

On Easter Sunday, that stone in front of Jesus' tomb became a different sort of marker, establishing a far different legacy. It was not the tombstone of the deceased. Not anymore. Now the stone rolled away stands as Jesus' legacy of eternal *life* for all who believe.

Job looked forward to that. Perhaps standing in his family's cemetery, he looked to the writing that mattered. He saw the inscriptions that would last even longer than the rocks they were written upon.

> Oh, that my words were recorded, that they were written on a scroll, that they were inscribed with an iron tool on lead, or engraved in rock forever! I know that my redeemer lives, and that in the end he will stand on the earth. And after my skin has been destroyed, yet in my flesh I will see God; I myself will see him with my own eyes—I, and not another. How my heart yearns within me! (Job 19:23–27)

You can trust your resurrected Lord. You can trust that your Savior has completely taken your sins away. You can trust in him even when your ministry seems to be crashing down around you. You can trust that he holds your every minute intact and preserves even the hairs on your head. And you can trust that your Lord knows what he is doing in your life, in your family, and in your ministry.

By the grace of God that kind of a trust remained Jeremiah's legacy. May his trusting words forever be yours: "Heal me, LORD, and I will be healed; save me and I will be saved, for you are the one I praise."

Prayer

"Grant that we your Word may cherish And its purity retain.
Lord, unless you are the builder, All our labor is in vain.
Keep us from all pride and boasting, Vanity and foolish trust,
Knowing that our work without you Soon will crumble into dust.

"God of grace and love and blessing, Yours alone shall be the praise.
Give us hearts to trust you truly, Hands to serve you all our days.
Lord, bestow your future blessing Till we join the heav'nly host,
There to praise and serve you ever, Father, Son, and Holy Ghost." Amen.

—*CW* 623:3–4

"Keep the Sabbath day holy"

Jeremiah 17:19–27

"So I declared on oath in my anger, They shall never enter my rest" (Psalm 95:11). Those remain some of the strongest words God ever spoke. With them he actually denied rest to his people. Centuries later, the writer of the book of Hebrews quoted that psalm verse as a warning to New Testament believers. The message was simple: "Don't do what Israel did."

So what had Israel done that was so bad? The writer of Hebrews answers that, too. "Do not harden your hearts as you did in the rebellion, during the time of testing in the wilderness" (Hebrews 3:8). Rebellion led to God's withdrawal of rest. The generation that had witnessed God's ten plagues on Egypt, who had walked across the Red Sea, who had eaten manna for forty years, who stood at the foot of the thundering Mount Sinai, continued to rebel at every turn. For their defiant grumbling and audacious anger, the Lord took away from them a most precious gift: rest.

"They shall never enter my rest." Eventually, that is what God does with rebellious hearts. Day after day, when they want to find their own rest apart from God, he finally gives them their desire. This means taking away from them what he wanted to give them. C. S. Lewis put it this way: "There are only two kinds of people in the end: those who say to God, 'Thy will be done,' and those to whom God says, in the end, 'Thy will be done.'"[1] Moses' entire generation of Israelites stood in the latter camp.

---

[1] C. S. Lewis, *The Great Divorce* (New York: HarperOne, 2009), 90.

So what about Jeremiah's generation? Had God's people finally realized that his rest is the only rest that matters? Had they finally learned from the rebellious actions of their ancestors? Jeremiah was about to find out.

The Lord sent his prophet to Jerusalem, saying, "Go and stand at the Gate of the People, through which the kings of Judah go in and out." The "Gate of the People" literally translates as "the gate of the sons of the people" and probably refers to the common people. Everyone went through this gate, from commoners to kings. There was no better place for Jeremiah to preach this sermon on true rest than this east gate of the temple.

As the people were walking to worship, the Lord warns them, "Be careful not to carry a load on the Sabbath day or bring it through the gates of Jerusalem." Apparently, God's people had been working on the Sabbath. After hearing about Jerusalem's worship of false gods and careless attitude toward their impending doom, this warning may not come as a shock to us. But it would have meant a great deal to the people.

They must have thought that they were keeping that ancient command of the Lord: "For six days, work is to be done, but the seventh day is a Sabbath of rest, holy to the LORD" (Exodus 31:15). They could not have been more wrong. It is quite possible that as Jeremiah spoke these words, people were carrying animals and supplies through the gate in direct conflict with God's law. This warning was clearly aimed at these defiant souls. They were rebelling as their ancestors had rebelled.

Work on the Sabbath may seem like a foreign idea to us New Testament believers. No such rule of rest exists for us anymore. We are free to worship when we want and how we want. Yet, sinful nature instantly latches on to that freedom to twist it for selfish gain. Our sinful nature finishes this misguided logical thought process: "If I am free to worship whenever I want, then I must be free not to worship at all. If I can worship however I want, I must be free to insert selfish motives into the service."

We see how far the guise of "Christian freedom" has taken the Christians of our culture. Overall worship attendance among Christians in America continues to drop down to record lows every year. The amount of offerings given by American Christians has slipped to the same levels of giving that believers offered during the Great Depression.

You have probably seen evidence of this low view of God's rest in your ministry as well. At some point every called worker ends up asking, "Where is everybody?" By now you probably know the responses your people will give you when you ask where they have been. Members were at work. Children needed to attend the weekend tournament. They needed to get away to the lake place for the weekend. They slept in. The impending meeting was happening that Sunday, so they made sure to be absent. The list goes on.

Jeremiah's words were aimed at those people. They were too busy for the Sabbath. They remained too lazy to partake in God's rest. They had forgotten God's Sabbath rest was meant to be one of God's greatest weekly gifts.

However, Jeremiah's words were not just aimed at the lay members of Jerusalem. He warned kings and priests and prophets about keeping the Sabbath as well. I wonder if our people arrived at a low view of worship because we have inadvertently given them that impression. As a pastor, have you embodied the "gladness of heart" God wants his people to have before worship, or have you made it look more like a job? Have your church functions had to schedule around football games? Have your worship services themselves been poorly constructed and hurriedly put together? Was the sermon a last-second retread?

This is a temptation for teachers as well. What has your attitude been when your children sing in church? Does it look like a chore? Are you just happy to get it over with?

Sometimes we get tired of God's rest. As in Jeremiah's day, the devil is hard at work among called workers. He knows that if he can get us to avoid resting with God's word then he can also pull away those entrusted to our care, too.

I can still picture the Bible passage painted above the entrance of the church in which I grew up: "I rejoiced with those who said to me, 'Let us go to the house of the LORD'" (Psalm 122:1). Even as a child I knew what those words meant. I *should* be happy to go to God's house. I can *rejoice* with my fellow brothers and sisters in the faith. Now as an adult, I must admit I weekly struggle with that simple invitation from the Lord. I have not always been glad to hear

God's word. There have been times I wanted to be somewhere else, even while I was leading God's people in worship.

Sins against the third commandment can seem especially selfish. The more we look at them, the more we see those sins for what they are. We have taken for granted one of God's most precious gifts.

Yet God's response to the repentant sinner comes to us at the beginning of that very day of rest. After we confess, "Lord, have mercy on me, a sinner," the Lord himself through his called worker emphatically states, "I forgive you all your sins."

Then that reminder of true rest floods our hearts. Then we are ready to hear God's word gladly. Then we can praise his name with beautiful hymns and responses and offerings. Then, by the grace of God, we can live as faithful called workers. Pastors can feel privileged that they are able to lead worship at all. They can spend appropriate time preparing edifying sermons that grow out of the personal study of God's word. They can carefully select hymns that tie the service together.

God's forgiveness enables teachers to joyfully show their children what worship really means. They can explain to the next generation the importance of confessing sins and the beautiful reminder of forgiveness in Christ. Teachers can prepare their children for worship by practicing the hymns we sing in worship and explaining their rich meaning and history.

Above all, we get to point our members and their children to the boy who refused to leave the temple. Shockingly, his parents were not able to find him. They looked all over. Frantic, they ran to the temple. There they saw a scene no one could have imagined. Their boy was sitting in the middle of the room surrounded by Jerusalem's greatest teachers.

Joseph and Mary were indignant with their son. Why had he put them through all of this? If you are a parent, you can understand their frustration. But as a servant of the Lord, you can understand the boy Jesus' frustration even more. "Why were you searching for me? . . . Didn't you know I had to be in my Father's house?" (Luke 2:49).

That gospel-filled attitude toward God's rest could have led Jeremiah's Jerusalem to the beautiful reality suggested by the Lord: "People will come from the towns of Judah and the villages around

Jerusalem, from the territory of Benjamin and the western foothills, from the hill country and the Negev, bringing burnt offerings and sacrifices, grain offerings and incense, and bringing thank offerings to the house of the LORD."

That was Jeremiah's dream. It became Christ's reality. May it continue to be our great heritage.

Prayer

"God's Word is our great heritage And shall be ours forever;
To spread its light from age to age Shall be our chief endeavor.
Through life it guides our way; In death it is our stay.
Lord, grant, while worlds endure, We keep its teachings pure
Throughout all generations." Amen.

—*CW* 293

"Like clay in the hand of the potter"

Jeremiah 18–19

Ostraca is one of those Greek words that sounds more important than it actually is. Archaeologists use the term to describe broken pieces of pottery. Ostraca were everywhere in the ancient world. Often discarded, they filled refuse piles. Even today, archaeologists find more ostraca than any other artifacts.

With so much ostraca laying around, the leaders of ancient Athens decided to implement a recycling plan. They encouraged the re-use of these broken pieces of pottery. These leaders even led by example. When a citizen of Athens was found guilty of a crime, the decision to exile that person was put to a vote. These men wrote their vote on the pieces of ostraca. If they voted in favor of exile, then the person would be banished for a period of ten years. Today, we would say that person had become "ostracized."

The prophet Jeremiah had his moments of feeling ostracized. It seemed no one wanted to hear the words of the Lord anymore. So the Lord sent his much-maligned prophet to a potter's house to witness a living illustration. The prophet would not soon forget the scene.

"I went down to the potter's house, and I saw him working at the wheel." If you have worked with clay, then you know the skillful touch it takes to successfully form a pot on the wheel. The recipe for a well-made pot sounds simple, but it takes quite a bit of practice to make the "simple" successful. Take one part strength, two parts finesse, and then finish with a graceful stir.

Don't feel bad if your pot doesn't turn out the first time. Even potters fail to make *every* pot perfectly. "The pot he was shaping from the clay was marred in his hands." Jeremiah saw the potter's initial failure firsthand. But the potter remained undeterred. "The potter formed it into another pot, shaping it as seemed best to him."

What was going through Jeremiah's mind at this point? Perhaps he was marveling at the potter's ability to fix his mistake by reforming the pot. Perhaps he was simply waiting for the Lord's explanation. But maybe, just maybe, the scene brought Jeremiah back to that very first day the Lord called him to be his prophet. "Before I formed you in the womb I knew you." Jeremiah's Potter had formed him carefully, expertly, and lovingly. The Potter formed his pottery prophet for the tasks expected of him.

Now it was time for the Potter to speak about the people he had formed. "Then the word of the LORD came to me. He said, 'Can I not do with you, Israel, as this potter does?' declares the LORD. 'Like clay in the hand of the potter, so are you in my hand, Israel.'"

But there was a problem. The created had forgotten their Creator. "If at any time I announce that a nation or kingdom is to be uprooted, torn down and destroyed, and if that nation I warned repents of its evil, then I will relent and not inflict on it the disaster I had planned." What mercy! The very uprooting and tearing down and destroying for which the Lord prepared Jeremiah could actually be prevented. The pots simply needed to repent, acknowledging their Potter who formed them.

This had happened before. King Jehoshaphat and his army faced obliteration when they allied with the wicked King Ahab. But in the heat of battle, Jehoshaphat cried out to the Lord for mercy, and he was spared. The prophet Jonah eventually arrived at Nineveh and preached the Lord's message of repentance. The entire city repented, and the Lord withdrew his impending destruction.

Then there were the occasions when cities refused to repent. To this day archeologists have not found a single piece of pottery from Sodom and Gomorrah. The Lord's fire and brimstone wiped them off the map because of their wicked actions. Ten plagues brought the ancient and powerful kingdom of Egypt to its knees when Pharaoh stubbornly defied the Lord.

Now it was Jerusalem's turn to choose. "This is what the LORD says: Look! I am preparing a disaster for you and devising a plan against you. So turn from your evil ways, each of you, and reform your ways and your actions." Would the pottery listen to the warnings of the Potter who formed them? The Lord doesn't keep his prophet in suspense for long.

"But they will reply, 'It's no use. We will continue with our own plans; we will all follow the stubbornness of our evil hearts.'" The Lord knew the answer before he ever asked the question. These defiant vessels would stand against their maker.

Then the situation escalates. Linguistically, the Lord switches from prose to poetry, lamenting, "My people have forgotten me." At that very same moment, the people began to make a conscious effort to ostracize the prophet Jeremiah. "Come, let's make plans against Jeremiah; for the teaching of the law by the priest will not be lost, nor will counsel from the wise, nor the word from the prophets. So come, let's attack him with our tongues and pay no attention to anything he says."

In reply, Jeremiah makes a linguistic shift himself, switching from prose to poetry with his cry for help to the Lord. "Listen to me, O LORD; hear what my accusers are saying!" Jeremiah's enemies had dug his pit, and now he called for the Lord's punishment on the people. It all happened exactly as the Lord predicted.

Now the Lord needed to present the second half of his object lesson. "Go and buy a clay jar from a potter. Take along some of the elders of the people and of the priests and go out to the Valley of Ben Hinnom." This was the valley where the godless of Jerusalem had sacrificed their children in the fires. It was the scene of some of the worst crimes in Judah's history. Now it became the location for God's most poignant lesson yet in Jeremiah's ministry.

After speaking against every atrocity Judah had committed in that valley, the Lord finally commands Jeremiah to "break the jar." Then God says why: "I will smash this nation and this city just as this potter's jar is smashed and cannot be repaired." The same message was then spoken in the court of the temple of the Lord.

It all made perfect sense. God had carefully and lovingly formed his people with the purpose of praising his holy name. Instead, they refused to acknowledge their Maker. So the Lord could not go back on his word. Destruction had to come. The Lord's pottery would be smashed into ostraca. The Lord's useful vessels would be made into what they had wanted all along: useless artifacts.

Like Jeremiah, you have been personally formed by the hands of your perfect Potter. Like Judah, you have been hand-crafted to joyfully worship your Creator. Like countless men and women formed before you, you have been called to be a faithful servant, a clay jar carrying a priceless message.

The apostle Paul once appraised the contents residing inside your clay exterior. "We have this treasure in jars of clay to show that this all-surpassing power is from God and not from us" (2 Corinthians 4:7). Paul has to give you that reminder because it doesn't come naturally. By nature we look at ourselves the way the people of Jerusalem did. We think that as jars we are more important than the treasure we carry inside. Nothing could be further from the truth! We exist as fragile clay pots. We do not last a long time. And most humbling of all, we are never going to be as important as that treasure of the gospel residing inside of us.

We are often tempted to think otherwise. And for all of those arrogant thoughts, we also deserve the fires of the valley of Ben-Hinnom. We should be broken to pieces. And as ostraca, we deserve to be ostracized from our Lord forever.

Remember that first pot the potter worked with? It didn't turn out too well, but he didn't give up on it. The patient potter reshaped it. He made it useful again before it hardened. Your patient Potter has done the same with you. Through the waters of baptism, he has "re-formed" you before you could harden.

The Lord has made you useful in the most humbling way. He made you able to carry out his work. By his power you can accomplish that work as a clay jar without taking away from the treasure you are blessed to carry. The Lord formed you in the exact way you needed to be formed. He placed the treasure of the gospel inside you so you can carry it to everyone you come into contact with.

Then watch as that treasure of the gospel re-forms other pots. Witness how the Holy Spirit saves other souls once doomed to the fires of the trash heap of hell. And thank him like the clay jar you are, daily remembering the Lord's words to you: "Before I formed you in the womb I knew you."

Prayer

"Take my love, my Lord, I pour At thy feet its treasure store.
Take myself, and I will be Ever, only, all for thee." Amen.

—*CW* 469:6

"You deceived me, LORD"

Jeremiah 20

The scene is still vividly seared on my memory. My family and I had just returned from Sunday morning church. Worship had gone as it always did. After lunch, my children and I began playing on the floor of our parsonage living room. Then, all of a sudden, my wife gasped. When I looked up, I saw her holding her phone to her ear. Her eyes were wide open. Her face looked shocked.

"You had better listen to this message," she finally said to me as tears filled her eyes. I listened. It was a death threat. I was confused. A person had called and left the message on my wife's phone during church that morning. I tried to check the number where the call came from, but it was restricted.

I didn't handle the situation as well as I should have. I was in shock. So I just sat there in the living room with my children still playing around me. I felt ready to lash out, and I felt defeated all at the same time. Then, finally, after too much time had passed, I got up and found my wife in the bedroom. She was shaking.

As I held her in my arms, questions flooded my mind. Why would anyone threaten to end someone else's life like this? Why did the person call during church? Why was the number restricted? Why did he call my wife's phone instead of mine? That angered me the most. If someone wanted to come at me, why would he attack my wife with his words? Why couldn't he just attack me?

There was a much larger question that all of those little questions eventually led to: Why did God allow this to happen? The following days led me to realize that I wasn't just angry with the anonymous coward who threatened our lives. I was angry with God for putting us in this position. As I soon realized, anger toward God is a dangerous emotion.

There stood Jeremiah in the temple of the Lord, prophesying the law-filled messages from the previous two chapters. "In this place I will ruin the plans of Judah and Jerusalem. I will make them fall by the sword before their enemies, at the hands of those who want to kill them" (19:7).

A priest named Pashhur did not like what he heard from this prophet of the Lord. He was determined to do something about it. "He had Jeremiah the prophet beaten and put in the stocks at the Upper Gate of Benjamin at the LORD's temple." Pashhur's logic was simple, even if it was not sound. He was punishing Jeremiah for preaching such a strong law message. He was getting back at Jeremiah for what seemed to be a personal slight.

So Pashhur made an example of the prophet. For three long days, the stocks bound Jeremiah's hands and feet. At that public place, everyone saw the example that Jeremiah was made out to be. Perhaps Pashhur thought that he could seal Jeremiah's fate with the temple itself: "So, Jeremiah, you think temple and everyone in it will be destroyed? Now you are stuck here, too. If the temple is destroyed, then you will be too."

At the end of three days, Jeremiah was released. He was probably ready to die. But before he could think about what came next, the word of the Lord came to him again. This message was meant specifically for the priest, Pashhur. "The Lord's name for you is not Pashhur, but Terror on Every Side. . . . I will make you a terror to yourself and to all your friends; with your own eyes you will see them fall by the sword of their enemies."

It may have felt liberating for Jeremiah to be released from the stocks. It may have felt personally gratifying to finally speak those brutal parting words of law to Pashhur. I know that I wanted to shout similar words at the person who threatened my wife's life. But there was something more important to Jeremiah's message than the outcry of personal vengeance. It was the reminder that all of his suffering was according to God's will.

That was what sent Jeremiah sinking down into the deep, dark water of questions we all have. Why, Lord? Why do you allow these awful things to happen to your called servants? As he so often does, Jeremiah speaks on behalf of all called workers. Listen for your own gripes with God in Jeremiah's emotion-filled complaint. "You deceived me, LORD, and I was deceived; you overpowered me and prevailed." Jeremiah listed the different crosses he was forced to bear because of the words he spoke from the Lord. To his credit, he had the wherewithal to understand that all of these crosses came from the Lord. And he was right!

But had the Lord really *deceived* Jeremiah? No, of course not. At the very beginning, the Lord told Jeremiah exactly what his ministry would entail: "Today I have made you a fortified city, an iron pillar and a bronze wall to stand against the whole land—against the kings of Judah, its officials, its priests and the people of the land" (1:18). There was no deception in those words, only loving honesty.

Admittedly, it is easy for us to understand Jeremiah's complaint. These are the words of a man who has seen his fair share of persecution. There would be many more persecutions to come. There are far more hardships coming in your ministry as well.

Perhaps you have had your life threatened because of the message you share. Maybe you have faced physical enemies and attackers. Perhaps the poisonous words of members and nonmembers have led you to the dark environs of depression. These are the crosses all called workers bear at one time or another.

The devil loves to jump on these dark times in our lives with temptations of doubt and loneliness. "What's the point?" he gets us to ask. "Why am I even doing this?" In the face of such sadness, Satan throws two extreme temptations our way. He either pulls us into an uncontrollable vengeance that can end a ministry, or he pulls us to extremely dark depression where the mind wonders if this life is even worth living. Both temptations are equally dangerous for you and your ministry. Doubt crouches in the shadows of both of these extremes, questioning the very love of the Lord himself.

The walls of doubt had once again imprisoned Jeremiah. Dire straits had led the prophet of the Lord to the most shocking place he ever found himself in his ministry. Jeremiah had actually attempted to stop speaking the Lord's message!

Can you see how Jeremiah reached that conclusion? He figured that if he stopped speaking the word, he would avoid all the pain and misery it had brought him. He was trying to remove the crosses he carried for Christ.

Can you see the times when you have attempted to remove your crosses you carry on behalf of Christ? His word brings so much hardship that in our darker moments, we attempt to silence ourselves. We only speak portions of the word to select people at certain times rather than speaking all of God's word to everyone at any time.

Jeremiah's vow of silence did not work out the way he expected. "But if I say, 'I will not mention him or speak any more in his name,' his word is in my heart like a fire, a fire shut up in my bones. I am weary of holding it in; indeed, I cannot." The Lord opened Jeremiah's mouth, even on the days Jeremiah tried to keep it shut. We sometimes find ourselves in these "Jonah-like" situations, too. The Lord will use you to speak the word, even if that means using you in spite of your apprehensions.

Sinful arrogance has led every called worker at one point or another to think he or she is undergoing the worst of persecution. Pride leads us to believe we are in the midst of the heaviest fighting on the front lines of this spiritual battle. The Lord reminds you, as he had to remind Jeremiah, that you are not alone. He stands with you. And your brothers and sisters in the ministry stand beside you, too. The apostle Peter, who suffered as much as anyone, often reminded his hearers of this. "Dear friends, do not be surprised at the fiery ordeal that has come on to test you, as though something strange were happening to you. But rejoice inasmuch as you participate in the sufferings of Christ, so that you may be overjoyed when his glory is revealed."

Can you believe he said that? *Rejoice* in the sufferings of Christ! No other walk of life, no other religion, no other context ever tells people to *rejoice* in sufferings. Following Christ will forever remain different from every other aspect of life. And why? Once again, it is because of Christ. He carried your cross. He suffered your hell. He endured your punishment and won heaven for you. That is why you can rejoice.

And wouldn't you know it, rejoicing is exactly what Jeremiah begins to do. "But the LORD is with me like a mighty warrior; so my persecutors will stumble and not prevail." This shift in tone from Jeremiah is quite jarring. But is it any different from our daily shift from self-anguish to selflessness? "Sing to the LORD! Give praise to the LORD! He rescues the life of the needy from the hands of the wicked."

Then comes the next jarring shift. Jeremiah was still struggling with the cross. Immediately after his words of praise, we hear the lament of a saddened heart. "Cursed be the day I was born!" This back and forth within the confines of Jeremiah's heart might sound strange to us. Yet there is honesty in his words—brutal honesty. These are some of Jeremiah's most personal confessions in his entire book. Jeremiah's struggle with persecution, with his crosses, with his ministry, and with his very life exemplifies our struggles.

My wife and I were not ready for that awful phone message on that Sunday afternoon. How could we be? I'll be honest—the questions still sometimes arise even now: Why would God allow such a thing? Why are we here facing such vitriol?

And yet, the Lord knows the weight of the crosses he can give us. And it is love that places those crosses on our backs. In the days and months and years that have followed, my wife and I are closer to one another and closer to our Lord than ever before. That is not a testament to us as people. We remain poor, miserable sinners. It is, as always, a testament to our Lord. His ability to use poor, frail, emotionally compromised people remains a show of his ultimate power and strength. Most of all, it embodies his love.

The call might come your way someday, if it hasn't already. The threats might grow. The anger among our people will continue. And sadly, you will face much of the fallout. Ministers have always made good targets for the hurting and the lost. But at those dark moments, when the Lord walks you through this valley of the shadow of death, be strengthened by his words through Jeremiah. The Lord will always stand as your mighty warrior. Your persecutors will not attack you forever. The Lord will rescue your life. "They will fight against you but will not overcome you, for I am with you and will rescue you" (1:19).

Above all, your Savior has *already* rescued you eternally. Of course he will fulfill his personal promise to you: "Surely I am with you always, to the very end of the age." Sear that image onto your heart forever.

Prayer

"I pass through trials all the way, With sin and ills contending;
In patience I must bear each day The cross of God's own sending.
Oft in adversity I know not where to flee
When storms of woe my soul dismay; I pass through trials all the way.

"Grim death pursues me all the way; Nowhere I rest securely.
He comes by night, he comes by day, And takes his prey most surely.
A failing breath, and I In death's strong grasp may lie
To face eternity today. Grim death pursues me all the way.

"I walk with Jesus all the way; His guidance never fails me.
He takes my ev'ry fear away When Satan's pow'r assails me,
And, by his footsteps led, My path I safely tread.
In spite of ills that threaten may, I walk with Jesus all the way." Amen.

—*CW* 431:2–4

"The way of life and the way of death"

Jeremiah 21

The Israelites stood on the precipice of the Promised Land. An unknown territory loomed in front of them. To understand what they were up against, Moses sent out spies to secretly travel throughout the land. After returning to Moses, they shared their twofold report: "We went into the land to which you sent us, and it does flow with milk and honey! Here is its fruit" (Numbers 13:27). At this point they must have shown the whole Israelite community the giant cluster of grapes that was so large it took two men to carry on a pole.

Then came the second half of the report. "But the people who live there are powerful, and the cities are fortified and very large" (Numbers 13:28). Not only were the people large and powerful, but they also lived everywhere. The Israelites sighed and scoffed at this news, just as we would expect. But Caleb silenced the people. Not all the spies were in agreement. He and Joshua remained far more optimistic. "We should go up and take possession of the land, for we can certainly do it" (Numbers 13:30).

Nobody believed them. "We can't attack those people; they are stronger than we are" (Numbers 13:31). The fire of pessimism spread throughout the whole community. Their words burned against the Lord and his command to march against the giants and their fortresses. The next day the people were ready to stone Moses for suggesting such a march!

The Lord came down hard on his people that day. "Not one of them will ever see the land I promised on oath to their forefathers" (Numbers 14:23). The ensuing Israelite response may have surprised even Moses. They admitted, "We have sinned" (Numbers 14:40). But then they took it too far to the other extreme. "We will go up to the place the LORD promised" (Numbers 14:4).

The problem was that it was too late. A perturbed Moses exclaimed, "Why are you disobeying the LORD's command? This will not succeed!" (Numbers 14:41). They marched into the Promised Land anyway. Scripture does not hold back on how it details this rebellious raid. "In their presumption they went up" (Numbers 14:44). Denial of sin, denial of its consequences, and denial of the Lord's punishment all led to Israel's presumptuously disastrous plan. "The Amalekites and Canaanites who lived in that hill country came down and attacked them and beat them down" (Numbers 14:45).

Sinful arrogance had led Israel to refuse to walk into the Promised Land. Then, after the Lord reprimanded them by keeping them out of the Promised Land, sinful pride led Israel to try and attack the Promised Land anyway. This is the definition of rebellion! Sin always works toward the opposite of what God commands.

Forty years after the Israelites tried to fight their way into the Promised Land against God's will, their children stood upon the same precipice. They were about to do what their parents refused to do. They were about to enter the Promised Land to conquer it. Moses gave a final warning to this next generation of Israelites.

> If you then become corrupt and make any kind of idol, doing evil in the eyes of the LORD your God and arousing his anger . . . You will not live there long but will certainly be destroyed. The LORD will scatter you among the peoples, and only a few of you will survive among the nations to which the LORD will drive you. (Deuteronomy 4:25–27)

Almost one thousand years later, God's people once again found themselves on the precipice of disaster. For hundreds of years, kings, prophets, and priests had faithfully carried the word of the Lord. Throughout Israel's entire history, the ancient warning of Moses continued to sound in the background.

In Jeremiah 21, that background warning is brought into the foreground. The year was 588 BC, two years before the destruction of Jerusalem. Judah's last king, Zedekiah, now sat on the throne.

Scripture tells us he had become corrupt. Secular historical records also show he had rebelled against Nebuchadnezzar. The rebellion was a mistake of the highest degree. Now the Babylonian king was making his way down to Judah to stamp out Zedekiah's pathetic flicker of pride.

Judah's king had gotten them into quite a mess. There was nothing he could do as destruction slowly marched down toward them. The bowl was tipping toward Jerusalem from the north.

Now, after all of this, Zedekiah is finally ready to hear what the Lord has to say. This was not an admonition of guilt or an attempt to repent. It was a simple desire to know how all of this will end up. It was Zedekiah's audacious request for a miracle from the God he never acknowledged. "Perhaps the Lord will perform wonders for us as in times past so that he will withdraw from us." It was the epitome of "too little, too late."

There is nothing new under the sun. Have you had delinquent members who come calling only when they need some cash? Many come to the Lord only when it is convenient for them or when they have nowhere else to turn. On other occasions these members ask you to pray for them because they will be undergoing surgery. Then they tell you that they also asked the other pastors, priests, and rabbis in the area to pray for them, too.

Students enjoy walking down this road, too. After not listening to a single lesson, after wasting most of his day, your student finally asks for help with one minute left in school. Or perhaps even worse, the child asks for help with the hope that the teacher can do most of the work. Parents can be just as bad. After a semester of informing a parent of the difficulties his child is having, the parent finally decides to get involved. Usually that comes only when the difficulty has affected something at home.

To say these incidents in ministry are merely frustrating is to understate them. There are times when we let these frustrations boil over. We get angry with those we are called to serve. Worst of all, we are tempted to refuse to help those in need because of the *way* they asked or the timing of *when* they asked. Patience is more than just a virtue in ministry. It is a necessity.

If we are being honest with our own prayer life, we have to admit that we are guilty of similarly audacious requests. We must concede we have been less than faithful in going to the Lord in prayer. And when we do pray, it is often to simply ask the Lord for something we want in the moment.

To put it another way, if you were to categorize the types of things you pray about, how many would fall under the headings of "praise" or "confession" or "thanksgiving"? How many could you categorize as "requests for others"? If you were to add up all of those categories, would they even come close to the number of self-focused prayer requests?

Jeremiah had been guilty of selfish requests as well. The difference between the called worker and the wicked king Zedekiah is where we land after sin. Zedekiah had no time for repentance. By the grace of God, Jeremiah did. By that same grace, so do you.

When King Zedekiah had the gall to ask the Lord for a miracle to save Jerusalem, Jeremiah had to hold his own opinions to himself. Only the Lord could tell the king what was going to happen. "I am about to turn against you the weapons of war that are in your hands, which you are using to fight the king of Babylon and the Babylonians who are outside the wall besieging you."

This disaster sounded an awful lot like what the Lord originally promised through Moses when his people first entered the Promised Land. Now they would hear it again, right before being taken out of the Promised Land. Zedekiah would be handed over to Nebuchadnezzar. The officials would be killed. The wicked priests would be taken captive. And all the false prophets who lied about peace would experience the wrath of God.

It all came down to one simple truth. "This is what the LORD says: See, I am setting before you the way of life and the way of death." This warning was both physical and spiritual. Those who walked out to the Babylonians, who physically walked away from Jerusalem's wickedness, would be saved. Those who stayed would suffer with the rest of the city.

Spiritually, those who listened to their Lord would be saved. Those who defiantly refused the Lord faced a much worse reality than any Babylonian king could give them. The Lord declares, "I will punish you as your deeds deserve."

It all goes back to what an ancestor of Zedekiah's once said. As he wrote Psalm 103, King David simultaneously looked backward and forward: "[The Lord] made known his ways to Moses, his deeds to the people of Israel" (Psalm 103:7). While that law of Moses convicts us, David trusted in the fulfillment of that law. "He does not treat us as our sins deserve or repay us according to our iniquities" (103:10).

Now, as we approach our Lord in prayer by faith, we can remember what is worth asking for. We can remember that our Father in heaven always hears and always answers. "As a father has compassion on his children, so the LORD has compassion on those who fear him" (103:13). And we can look forward our heavenly Promised Land, without audacity and arrogance, but with a sure, certain, and humble hope, saying with David and Jeremiah and faithful believers throughout the centuries, "Praise the LORD, my soul" (103:22).

Prayer

"Lord, teach us how to pray aright, With reverence and with fear.
Though dust and ashes in your sight, We may, we must draw near.

"We suffer if we cease from prayer; Oh, grant us pow'r to pray.
And when to meet you we prepare, Lord, meet us on the way.

"Give deep humility; the sense Of godly sorrow give;
A strong desire, with confidence, To hear your voice and live." Amen.

—*CW* 412:1–3

"Why has the Lord done such a thing?"

Jeremiah 22

She was a city like none other. In the west, her massive land walls had kept armies at bay for a thousand years. In the east by the sea, her impressive bulwarks towered over the golden waves of the Bosporus as they flowed into the Mediterranean. Safely behind these ramparts lived almost a million people busily conducting business, worshiping, or arguing with one another about doctrine and politics.

This was Constantinople, the emerald of Late Antiquity and the beacon of orthodoxy in an ever-darkening world. From her grand chariot-racing stadium to her enterprising forum to the majestic Hagia Sophia, this city ruled all others. She sat enthroned as the queen of civilization.

Then, on May 29, 1453, that thousand-year-old light was ingloriously snuffed out. After a seven-week siege, the Ottoman armies were finally able to blast their way through the city's mighty walls. The cries of Christians in Constantinople that day echoed throughout Europe. The few men who remained were tortured. The women were raped and murdered. Even the children were killed.

Now those who passed by the ancient city marveled for new reasons. Christians lamented as they gazed upon the rubble. They watched as the grandest churches in Christendom were methodically converted to mosques. Many put ink to paper in those early days of desolation as they struggled to internally appraise this unthinkable horror. This is one of the oldest:

O most merciful fount of all hope,
Father of the son whose weeping mother I am:
I come to complain before your sovereign court,
about your power and about human nature,
which have allowed such grievous harm
to be done to my son, who has honored me so much.[1]

Those who were alive when this great Roman city fell would forever remember what they were doing the moment they heard the disastrous news. Lamentations for the lost ruin of a city resounded throughout Christendom:

To you, the only God, I submit my complaints,
about the grievous torment and sorrowful outrage,
which I see the most beautiful of men suffer
without any comfort for the whole human race.[2]

Destruction like this has a way of stopping time in its tracks. Falling steeples and silenced bells suspend a person's everyday rush. They ominously grab our attention, pulling us in for a closer look.

Jeremiah brings us in for that closer look. He takes us within the great walls of Jerusalem, walking from the glorious temple at the summit of the city down to the beautiful and ornate palace of the king. Although it has not happened yet, he shows us the city's coming destruction. It wouldn't be long now.

This destruction had been a long time in coming. After centuries of warning, Jerusalem's kings, priests, prophets, and people still refused to listen. On this day, Jeremiah gave one of the last warnings they would ever hear. "This is what the LORD says: Do what is just and right. Rescue from the hand of the oppressor the one who has been robbed. Do no wrong or violence to the foreigner, the fatherless or the widow, and do not shed innocent blood in this place."

---

[1] Rima Devereaux, "Reconstructing Byzantine Constantinople: Intercession and Illumination at the Court of Philippe le Bon," *French Studies* 59.3 (2005): 297–310.

[2] Ibid.

Judah's leaders were supposed to be carrying out what was right and just. Instead, they epitomized selfishness. Justice was long gone. Violence ran rampant. Innocent blood filled the streets.

If only God's people had listened to his warnings . . . *any* of his warnings. "Then kings who sit on David's throne will come through the gates of this palace, riding in chariots and on horses, accompanied by their officials and their people." Isn't that what Judah's leaders wanted? If so, then why did they continue to defiantly stand against the Lord?

You know the answer by now. The king and his officials wanted to rule God's people on their own terms. They had refused to acquiesce. Now the Lord was going to remind them of what was coming. He started with the very palace Jeremiah was standing in. "I will surely make you like a wasteland, like towns not inhabited."

In many ways Jerusalem's annihilation would be a precursor to the destruction Constantinople endured two thousand years later. Walls would be breached. Palaces would be battered into ruins. Even their majestic place of worship would be turned to rubble.

The reactions of onlookers would be similar, too. "People from many nations will pass by this city and will ask one another, 'Why has the Lord done such a thing to this great city?'" And this will be the answer: "Because they have forsaken the covenant of the LORD their God and have worshiped and served other gods."

The lamentations for Constantinople refused to place blame on the victims who endured her last days.

> Do not accuse the king, masters,
> nor his lords, nor his soldiers.

The Lord refused to show Jerusalem's rulers that kind of leniency. "Do not weep for the dead king or mourn his loss; rather, weep bitterly for him who is exiled, because he will never return nor see his native land again." Some had already been exiled into Egypt. Many more were about to be thrown all the way into Babylon, doomed to live out their days agonizing over everything they lost.

What does a minister do in these awful situations? Sometimes, like Jeremiah, we feel stuck behind the same walls as the rabble who defy God. We find ourselves caught under the power of unjust leaders. Violence continues to spread. Innocents suffer.

Once again, the ruins of Jerusalem pull us in for a closer look. Yet this inspection need not lead us to eternal lamentation. The rubble of the city is a silent reminder. Dark days arrive because we live in a sin-darkened world. Like Jeremiah, you may feel caught between unjust rulers and violent citizens. Someday, you may even find yourself on the walls looking out at the enemy standing at the gates.

Dark days like these can shake us. No doubt Jeremiah had his moments of worry, wondering what Jerusalem's disaster would mean for his own ministry . . . or his own life. Would there be anyone left to whom he could preach the word?

Have you thought that recently in your ministry? As membership declines and pews look emptier, have you wondered whether there would be anyone left? Perhaps that is the source of your lamentations. Or maybe you secretly enjoy the losses because you think they somehow equate your ministry to that of Jeremiah's. It is understandable, human even, to mourn the loss of believers. But don't send them out in an effort to force yourself into a difficult ministry. The Lord finds all sorts of ways to give you crosses. You do not need to seek them out to make yourself a better servant.

Whether the number of souls in your ministry is increasing or decreasing, you can faithfully hold on to the same confidence that sustained Jeremiah. Wicked rulers, enemy armies, and dwindling numbers of Christians will continue to be crosses placed on your back. Such matters are not in our hands, and we can thank the Lord for that. What graciously remains in our hands is the word of the Lord. Share it with a just and upright heart. Look after those forgotten by society: the alien, the fatherless, and the widow. You are to be a minister in the original sense of the word: a servant.

You are also to be faithful, even to the point of death. Then walls won't matter. Earthly palaces and temples will fade away. Then you will finally see your home city with gates wide open. Then you will see the Light that will never be snuffed out. Then you will behold the Lamb at the center, shining more gloriously than the sun itself. Then, at the beginning of eternity, you will see your crown of life.

Prayer

"Built on the Rock the Church shall stand Even when steeples are falling.
Crumbled have spires in every land; Bells still are chiming and calling,
Calling the young and old to rest, But above all the soul distressed,
Longing for rest everlasting.

"Grant then, O God, your will be done, That, when the church bells are
    ringing,
Many in saving faith may come Where Christ his message is bringing:
'I know my own; my own know me. You, not the world, my face shall see.
My peace I leave with you always.'" Amen.

—*CW* 529:1, 5

"I myself will gather the remnant"

Jeremiah 23:1–24

On March 13, 1964, a woman by the name of Kitty Genovese was walking through the streets of Queens, New York. She was heading home after work when the unthinkable happened. A man came out of the shadows. He attacked her, stabbed her, and then killed her. The entire assault took thirty minutes. At the end of it, the murderer fled the scene.

The murder case turned the city upside down. As the murderer was hunted down, detectives started to put the pieces together. When they reconstructed everything, they discovered a heart-wrenching detail. After talking with the neighbors in the area, they realized that thirty-eight people had witnessed the murder. Now think about that. Thirty-eight people had *witnessed* an assault and murder that lasted for half an hour, and not one of them helped Kitty. Not one of them called the police until after the killer had left.

How could that happen? Were these people just coldhearted New Yorkers who were used to looking the other way when a murder happened? That just didn't seem to be the case. On other occasions individuals had heroically helped one another. There were times when individuals had even prevented murders. So why not this time? Why didn't any one of those thirty-eight people help Kitty?

Sociologists seem to have found the answer. It is called the "bystander effect." Here's what it means: the more people who are present when someone is attacked, the less likely any one of them is to help. But again, why is that? Are we just wired that way as people?

Well, sociologists seem to have come up with an answer to that as well. People are less likely to help in a group setting because of what sociologists call a "diffusion of responsibility."

So here is the bottom line. The more people there are when something bad happens, the less likely any one of them is to help *because* no one wants to take responsibility. And that isn't just a modern American problem. Groups of people have been doing nothing for thousands of years now.

Just look at how many spiritual bystanders sat around in Jeremiah's Jerusalem! The very shepherds God had called to lead his people to the green pastures of his word were watching their own sheep spiritually die. They refused to help. And while there were a lot of them, the Lord does not allow for any sociological excuses. Neither the bystander effect nor the diffusion of responsibility could get them out of their punishment. "Woe to the shepherds who are destroying and scattering the sheep of my pasture!"

The Lord sets the bar of faithfulness very high for those called to preach and teach. Because Judah's teachers scattered the Lord's flock entrusted to them, strong punishment was headed their way. "Because you have scattered my flock and driven them away and have not bestowed care on them, I will bestow punishment on you for the evil you have done." The Lord reserves the harshest discipline for those who should know better.

Failure to carry out the task the Lord has given you is dangerous enough. What awaited the false prophets who openly spoke lies about the Lord? The Lord now assesses just how dark Jerusalem's spiritual situation had become: "The prophets follow an evil course and use their power unjustly. Both prophet and priest are godless; even in my temple I find their wickedness."

The Lord is not unemotional about this. He cries, "My heart is broken within me." These are not the cold, calculating responses of a distant God. These are the spiritual pleas that pour forth from a heart in love. It is out of that love that the Lord disciplines his people. When it comes to his word, the Lord cannot let spiritual passivity and prophetic lies stand. "Therefore their path will become slippery; they will be banished to darkness and there they will fall." To these people who "commit adultery" with false gods and "live a lie" the Lord states, "I will make them eat bitter food and drink poisoned water."

This was not what the Lord originally established these Old Testament offices for. Priests were supposed to sacrifice to the true God, not to false gods. Prophets were supposed to speak the truth of God's word to the people, not trumpet their own lies. And the king was supposed to keep these offices in check with God's word. Instead, he was playing politics with other rulers and persecuting God's true prophets.

So far in the book of Jeremiah, you have heard the Lord's strongest warnings aimed at Judah's called workers. This chapter is no different. But in the midst of such harsh warnings, temptations creep into our hearts. We are tempted to think of ourselves as living above the temptations that Jerusalem's priests and prophets had succumb to. After all, aren't we better shepherds than those guys?

But let's be honest—we have had our struggles too. As servants called by the Lord, we have also been spiritual bystanders. We have fallen for the diffusion of responsibility. We have looked at those spiritually suffering and thought, *Someone else can help*. Instead of lovingly showing our flock their sins, we sometimes look the other way. Rather than helping a brother or sister in the ministry, we leave that difficult and taxing work to someone else.

The prophet Ezekiel, a contemporary of Jeremiah, once heard the Lord's strongest warning against spiritual bystanders. "When I say to the wicked, 'You wicked person, you will surely die,' and you do not speak out to dissuade them from their ways, that person man will die for their sin, and I will hold you accountable for their blood" (Ezekiel 33:8).

We need that reminder. When we see someone living in sin, it becomes far too easy to look the other way. We are even nice enough to come up with excuses for that person. "Well, I'm sure he has everything under control" or "It's none of my business how she lives her life." And then there is the biggest bystander effect of them all: "Someone else can show him his sin; I'm not going to do it."

We've all been spiritual bystanders. We've all sat on the sidelines when it would have been so easy to help. And the Lord is clear about how seriously he takes our inaction. As he stated through the prophet Ezekiel, acting out sins isn't the only offense. Not helping someone else spiritually is just as bad of a sin.

A couple of years ago, a high school in Pakistan faced a situation no school would ever want to face. A suicide bomber approached the school, strapped with thirteen pounds of explosives. Everybody watched as he got closer and closer. Fifteen hundred student lives hung in the balance. Then, one of the teenagers in the school *stood up*. His name was Aitzaz Hasan. He actually *walked out* to the bomber. The two struggled. The bomber tried to rush to the school. Hasan kept stopping him. Finally, when he realized Hasan was not going to let him get to the school, the bomber set off his explosives, killing both him and Hasan. When an entire school was in peril, a teenage boy gave his life to save fifteen hundred other lives.

Jesus was no bystander. He said what needed to be said. He told adulterers and adulteresses to leave their lives of sin. He warned the Pharisees about their hypocrisy and their made-up rules. He gave the hard truths of sin to the crowds. And for all of this brutal honesty, Jesus was put on trial and beaten and crucified.

There were a lot of bystanders in Jerusalem when Jesus was suffering. No one went to help him. And it had to be that way. We had to be a world of bystanders as Jesus died on the cross for our sins. He is our perfect Shepherd, our righteous Branch, who laid down his life for us, his sheep. Or to put it another way, he took our sins as his responsibility.

And now he reminds you of your responsibility to those who called you. "I will place shepherds over them who will tend them, and they will no longer be afraid or terrified, nor will any be missing." The Shepherd has placed you as a shepherd over his flock. The King who reigns in your heart has made you a leader in his church. The Prophet enables you to speak God's word to his people.

Sometimes we think that saying nothing is the loving thing to do. It isn't. Love speaks to others. Love shows sin. Love shows your Savior's forgiveness.

Prayer

"Let none hear you idly saying, 'There is nothing I can do,'
While the multitudes are dying, And the Master calls for you.
Take the task he gives you gladly; Let his work your pleasure be.
Answer quickly when he calleth, 'Here am I—send me, send me!'" Amen.

—CW 573:4

"I had a dream!"

Jeremiah 23:25–40

You can't escape God's prophecy. If God foretells something about you, it is going to happen. As a culture, the Greeks may have understood that aspect of prophecy better than most. It is said that an oracle once prophesied to the Greek playwright Aeschylus that he would one day die when something fell on his head.

Aeschylus was no dummy. To try and escape the fulfillment of this morbid prophecy Aeschylus slept outside every night for the rest of his life. This seemed to be a logical response. If something is destined to fall on your head, stay away from falling objects.

One night a vulture snatched up a tortoise into the sky. It sounds strange, but it isn't out of the ordinary. The vulture was going to fly the tortoise up and drop it on the ground to crack it open like a nut. In true Greek fashion, this tortoise landed on Aeschylus, who just so happened to be sleeping outside to avoid falling objects. It landed on his head and killed him. It was a real-life fable. The lesson? You can't escape prophecy.

But what happens when the prophecy isn't true? It seems that the ancient Greeks understood that some prophecies would come true and others wouldn't. This led them to take an ominous view of prophecy. They could either live fatalistically or hope that their gods were wrong.

Of course, you know better. The oracle at Delphi doesn't really know what will happen to us. The horoscopes in the paper can't accurately predict your future either. Even historically successful sooth-sayers like Nostradamus needed to keep their predictions vague enough to make them appear believable.

Phony prognosticators were just as numerous in the Old Testament as they are today. Jeremiah struggled with their false prophecies throughout his ministry. That is why the Lord told Jeremiah, "I have heard what the prophets say who prophesy lies in my name. They say, 'I had a dream! I had a dream!' How long will this continue in the hearts of these lying prophets, who prophesy the delusions of their own minds?"

Delusional. That's what God calls these false prophets. They had become so effective at tricking other people that they had actually succeeded in fooling themselves. These were not the omniscient words of the Lord. They were the impotent ramblings of imitators. If the word of the Lord burned like a fire, then the words of false prophets flickered like flashlights. If the Lord's word flew down like a sledgehammer, the false prophets' words floated as ineffectively as an imitation Styrofoam prop.

Everything hinged on the meaning of that word: *oracle*. The original Hebrew word actually carries two different meanings that happen to be opposite in their definitions. The Hebrew word for "oracle" can either mean "a future prophecy" or "a burden." Only context can dictate the meaning. So when the Lord commands in verse 33: "Say to them, 'What message? I will forsake you, declares the LORD,'" which *oracle* is he talking about?

The false prophets may have thought they were genuine oracles. They had taken God's word and changed it into a message the people wanted to hear. Ironically, that is precisely what made their "oracles" burdens.

The Israelites didn't seem to mind. As long as the predictions were good news, everyone was happy. Those false prophets always obliged with crowd-pleasing predictions of peace and victory.

God's prophecies, however, were far more grim. He told his people that the temple would be destroyed like Shiloh (7:12–26). He prophesied to the king that his palace would become a ruin (22:5). He warned "disaster from the north" and "terrible destruction" (4:6). The Lord even used the false prophet's words against them: "We hoped for peace but no good has come" (8:15).

Hearing a sermon from God's prophets usually meant bad news. It is no wonder, then, why the false prophets garnered such a following. Their news always sounded nice. They predicted victories. They prophesied happiness.

There are many churches today that have gone that route. They overlook the Lord's "bad news" and share only the nice-sounding things. Theologically speaking, they withhold the law and give only the gospel. Of course, this is a theological problem that becomes readily apparent. Without the law, the gospel fades into a social teaching of civil righteousness. Without the law, the gospel ceases to matter. And without the law, the gospel ceases to be the gospel!

These are the "reckless lies" of today's false prophets. And they can be quite tempting. Mainstream Christian vocabulary permeates religious books and TV shows. Some of our people tell us to talk about what other Christian denominations (or nondenominational churches) are discussing. After enough nagging, we are tempted to give in.

One of the most dangerous of these teachings focuses on our personal feelings and emotions. It tells believers to trust their feelings as "proof" of faith and "evidence" of a connection with God. The temptation for the called worker is to focus on these mainstream feelings to appease our people, or to win over our visitors.

Of course, the problem with feelings and emotions is that they are so volatile. Even the most steady of individuals can find herself on a rollercoaster of emotion based on the situations in her life. Faith, on the other hand, is not volatile. Faith is created by the Holy Spirit and sustained by the gospel in word and sacrament. Certainly faith overflows into all sorts of godly emotions, but these emotions are *products* of faith, not the *source* or *proof* of saving faith.

Perhaps mainstream Christian vocabulary is not a temptation for you. But there are others. The false prophets of Jeremiah's day were taking God's words and changing them. One addition here or one key subtraction there and God's word became a false oracle. These subtle changes can be a very real enticement for pastors and teachers, too. When it seems fewer people want to come to hear God's word, we are tempted to add things to the message. Why not add gimmicks to the service to "rope people in"? When visitors enter the sanctuary on a communion Sunday, it can be tempting for the pastor to wish the Lord's Supper would rather be offered the *next* Sunday to avoid offending the visitor.

Not causing offense to others is important, but not as important as remaining steadfast in the word of the Lord. To be honest, that word of God *will* cause offense at times. There will be occasions when individuals do leave the church because a portion of the message offended their sinful nature. You have probably seen that in your church.

Words did not differentiate false prophets from Jeremiah. To the uniformed, the words sounded similar. The illustrations appeared interchangeable. So what *was* the difference? It was actually quite simple: God's prophecies came true. The false oracles didn't.

How blessed you are to hold God's entire, true word! Don't let the false inclinations of your heart try to convince you that God's word needs your changes. It doesn't. God's word has been creating faith in countless hearts long before you were ever born. Don't let the sweet-sounding words of the Christian-sounding social gospel pull you in. That "gospel" is not God's gospel.

Like Jeremiah, you are a minister of the Lord surrounded by a lot of false words and actions. It can feel overwhelming. But like Jeremiah, you are armed with God's pure word. And like Jeremiah, you get to lovingly share the message of the Prophet, Jesus, who came to fulfill every Messianic prophecy. You get to boldly confess Christ crucified, an oracle that is a stumbling block for many. But not for you. For you, Christ is the prophecy you would never want to escape.

Prayer

"We have a sure prophetic Word
By inspiration of the Lord,
And, though assailed on ev'ry hand,
Jehovah's Word shall ever stand." Amen.

—CW 291:1

"A heart to know me"

Jeremiah 24

I'm not sure if Americans still call it "brain drain." It used to go by that name. The official designation is "human capital flight," and it refers to the migration of the best and the brightest from one community, or country, to another. This has been happening ever since the Tower of Babel. When the city of Constantinople stood on the edge of destruction, many of her scholars and artists and clergy fled to Italy. When Louis XIV expelled the Protestants with his Edict of Fontainebleau, the Huguenots escaped to places like England, Switzerland, Norway, Prussia, and even South Africa. In 1933, when the Nazi regime began promoting antisemitic rhetoric, many of Germany's academic elite, including a man named Albert Einstein, fled to America.

Each of these examples of human capital flight took place in a period of tragic political shifting. In each instance, the repercussions were profoundly and historically important. Constantinople's philosophers and scholars and artists brought the beacon of their learning to a darkened Europe. Many of their works led to the achievements of the Renaissance, while the biblical texts they imported helped men like Erasmus and Martin Luther to translate the Bible from the original languages.

The Huguenots benefited every country they escaped to. They became winemakers in South Africa and potato farmers in Ireland. Some, like Henri Basnage de Beauval in the Netherlands and Abel Boyer in London, became well-respected writers and historians. While the Huguenot flight benefited many countries, it nearly broke the French academically. Decades would pass before France would recover from their self-inflicted brain drain.

Germany faced a similar problem in the 1930s. While the Nazi propaganda machine was revving up, many of Germany's best and brightest decided to flee. From Albert Einstein to the family of Niels Bohr, Germany gave away their most intelligent individuals. America was happy to have them.

Brain drain is not a new phenomenon. Long before Constantinople's foundations were set and well before anyone knew what a Huguenot or a Nazi was, Jerusalem experienced a form of human capital flight. The secular historian would attribute this to another regime change. The Lord attributes it to himself. And naturally, he uses a couple of baskets of figs tell the story.

Let's let Jeremiah describe the scene: "The good ones are very good, but the poor ones are so bad they cannot be eaten." Like every other inspired message from the Lord, there is no middle ground. There is only good and bad.

The Lord gives the good news first. "Like these good figs, I regard as good the exiles from Judah, whom I sent away from this place to the land of the Babylonians." They will one day be brought back. "I will build them up and not tear them down; I will plant them and not uproot them. I will give them a heart to know me, that I am the LORD." Then the Lord goes on to share some of his most beautifully comforting words: "They will be my people, and I will be their God."

Then comes the bad news. "But like the bad figs, which are so bad they cannot be eaten . . . so will I deal with Zedekiah king of Judah, his officials and the survivors from Jerusalem." The Lord knew some of these survivors were thinking about escaping to Egypt. He quickly declared that he will deal with them "whether they remain in this land or live in Egypt."

It gets worse. "I will make them abhorrent and an offense to all the kingdoms of the earth, a reproach and a byword, a curse and an object of ridicule, wherever I banish them." Then comes the final warning. "I will send the sword, famine and plague against them until they are destroyed from the land I gave to them and their ancestors."

The difference could not have been more pronounced. The Lord promised to bless and preserve those taken into captivity in Babylon.

But he promised only suffering and ridicule, and eventually destruction, to those left behind.

So what was the difference? Was the Lord putting an emphasis on the intelligent and the skilled above the weak and uneducated? Does the Lord love painters more than farmers or professors more than shepherds? Not hardly. The difference is so simple that even those left behind in Jerusalem could understand it. The Lord states that those carried into captivity "will return to me with all their heart." That's the difference. Faith differentiated the one group from the other.

Have your community and church been experiencing brain drain? Are your best and brightest leaving your town for better jobs and better pay elsewhere? A look at American demographics in general and Christian synodical statistics specifically illustrates the effects that human capital flight continues to have on our congregations.

The situation can be maddening. No sooner does a young family start regularly attending worship and becoming involved than they leave for a better job in a bigger city. Pretty soon, the only time you see these young families is when they visit their parents, or grandparents, at your church around the holidays. This type of Jeremiah chapter 24 ministry quickly fosters feelings of defeat.

Just imagine how defeated Jeremiah must have felt while he saw the Lord's figs! He watched as Nebuchadnezzar carried off "the officials, the craftsmen and the artisans of Judah." These were his friends. More than that, as the Lord describes them, these were faithful individuals. And Jerusalem needed faithful, skilled people now more than ever!

I bet Jeremiah felt like he needed them, too. Along with the educated crowd that migrated to Babylon were young men like Daniel and Shadrach, Meshach, and Abednego. So who was even left for Jeremiah? It seemed all that remained were the unbelievers, the weak, and the uneducated.

Losses like those cut deep in ministry. Have you watched brothers and sisters in the faith move on to pastures that look greener? Have you felt like you are "left behind" with the weak like Jeremiah was? You probably have. When it happens, the devil strikes with all sorts of haughty temptations. He makes you think you are the last educated person in your community. He convinces you to feel sorry for yourself when your happy, well-educated families leave. He reminds you just how weak and dumb you must be to have been left behind in such a ministry.

Such temptations may have been thrown at Jeremiah, too. In the nadir of his loneliness, Jeremiah may have even murmured Elijah's sad ministerial description: "I'm the only one left." If anything, that statement may have described Jeremiah's ministry more accurately than Elijah's.

But Jeremiah was never alone. He may have felt as though he was left behind. He may have felt defeated. But he wasn't. Jeremiah had his Lord, and that was enough. The skilled men and women may have been long gone in Babylon, but that was only because they needed to be there. Your members who have left also need to be in their new locations, helping those ministries and ministers. You need to be where you are now. The Lord planted you there to preach and teach the people he has entrusted to you. They might be weak. They may not be the most academically educated. These things don't matter. See your people the way their Lord sees them. Your people are loved. Your people are baptized. Your people, from the smallest child to the oldest grandparent, have *real* knowledge.

When the temptation of envy for the best and the brightest rears its ugly head, cast it aside with the word of the Lord. You do not serve Jeremiah's Jerusalem. You are called to serve God's children right here, right now. And you, more than your people, exemplify just how powerful the Lord is at using the weak and secularly uneducated for his good purpose.

Your loving Lord might as well have been talking about you and your people when he said to Jeremiah so long ago: "They will be my people, and I will be their God, for they will return to me with all their heart."

Prayer

"I pray you, dear Lord Jesus,
My heart to keep and train
That I your holy temple
From youth to age remain.

Oh, turn my thoughts forever
From worldly wisdom's lore;
If I but learn to know you,
I shall not want for more." Amen.

—*CW* 510

"I have spoken to you again and again"

Jeremiah 25:1–14

"Well, it's Groundhog Day . . . again."

A perturbed Bill Murray spoke those memorably sarcastic words into the camera in the movie *Groundhog Day*. He had good reason to be nervous. He had woken up that morning to a day he had already lived. The next day would be the same. So would the one after that. On and on the days would continue, every day exactly as it was before. Trying to come to grips with this new repetitive reality, Murray remarks, "Well, what if there is no tomorrow? There wasn't one today!"

Bill Murray's character was caught reliving the same day over and over again. And if that wasn't bad enough, the strange situation was made even worse by his location. He hated the town he was waking up in. He despised the people. And he especially loathed the event he was reliving: Groundhog Day.

Believe it or not, the movie is actually a comedy. And although the premise sounds ridiculous, the film reveals interesting insights into the human character. A man is caught in a place he detests, surrounded by people he loathes. Yet he remains stuck reliving that same day, among those same people.

After getting his bearings in this strange situation, Murray decides to make the most of it. He gradually gets to know the town and its people. But his initial motives are devious. He only understands the people enough to take advantage of them. He steals money. He punches old classmates. He tricks women into sleeping with him.

Again, believe it or not, this is a comedy.

But abusing people with his growing knowledge of the town doesn't foster lasting happiness. Quite the opposite. Murray falls into a deep despair. At his nadir, the character summarizes his hopelessness in one of the most memorable quotations of the movie. Talking about the groundhog's winter prognosis, Murray decides to give one of his own: "It's gonna be cold, it's gonna be gray, and it's gonna last you for the rest of your life."

At that point, Murray spirals into the kind of deep despair that leads to suicide. He tries every way imaginable to rid himself of his situation. Nothing works. The cycle continues. He feels destined to relive the same day forever.

It was Groundhog Day in Jeremiah's Jerusalem. The cycle of sin that began during the time of the Judges was now culminating with the open idolatry of Judah. Every circling cycle spun God's people further away from their Lord and his word. Every step over the Lord's line stretched out further beyond the last one.

The prophet Jeremiah must have had his moments when he felt stuck. He stood in a town that despised him, among people who hated him. Every day seemed to be the same. He watched as people shrugged off their Lord. He heard the poisonous words of the false prophets work their way into the hearts of his people. He saw Jerusalem's kings make deals with the neighboring rulers rather than approach the King of kings.

It was Groundhog Day in Jerusalem. Even the responses of the Lord sounded familiar. "You did not listen to me . . . and you have aroused my anger with what your hands have made, and you have brought harm to yourselves." They had heard it all before. The kings, the priests, the false prophets, the people, and even Jeremiah knew how this sermon ended.

"Though the Lord has sent all his servants the prophets to you again and again, you have not listened or paid any attention." I wonder what emotions flooded Jeremiah's senses when he said these words to the people. Frustration? Anger? No doubt those emotions could easily have become Jeremiah's common companions. But there must have been another emotion, one harder to grasp. Jeremiah was probably sinking into deep depression.

Prophet after prophet had spoken God's words to God's people. Day after day the people refused to listen and withheld their repentance. This infamous cycle seemed to continue into infinity. This must have worn on Jeremiah.

Has it been wearing on you? Are there moments when your ministry feels caught in a sort of Groundhog Day situation? Every day feels the same. The same people commit the same sins. The town you live in continues as it always has. Some scriptural warnings are heeded, while others seem to be ignored. And there you are, caught in the repetition.

The human character exhibited in that movie *Groundhog Day* remains frighteningly accurate. Pastors and teachers placed in a role of power among trusting people are daily tempted to abuse their power for selfish purposes. Sinful defiance comes up with a solution to the repetitive ministry: "If I'm stuck here, then I might as well get what I want."

There are times when we have fallen for those temptations. Like Murray's character, we are tempted to abuse the trust of others to get power we want, or the possessions we desire, or even the people we want. Short-term sins often lead to long-term problems. Like Murray, we eventually see that tricking people into providing us with our selfish desires leads to disaster. These actions of ours cannot break the cycle of sin. In fact, our sins only spin it faster!

This is when depression slips in to the mind and emotions of a called worker. Nothing seems to matter. Your hard work is undone by budget cuts. Your painstaking efforts at building relationships with others are immediately severed in a moment of anger or disagreement. Nobody listens anymore . . . and that is assuming they ever listened before. So you arrive at a ministerial Groundhog Day, secretly affirming Murray's mantra: "It's gonna be cold, it's gonna be gray, and it's gonna last you for the rest of your life."

And you would be right. Ministry often feels cold. Living as a pastor or teacher brings gray days. And for most of us, it will in fact last the rest of our lives. So what is the difference? Are we doomed to a sad ministerial cycle that sends us into a depressing tailspin until death mercifully ends it all? The Lord's answer is a resounding no!

The glaring difference between Murray's character in *Groundhog Day* and the ministry the Lord has blessed you with is spiritual perspective. Murray had no hope because he had no faith. The happy ending the movie provides is founded on Murray's change of heart, which leads to his change of circumstances. The more he learned about the people he formerly hated and the town he despised, the more he grew to like them.

Hollywood's portrayal of a change of heart doesn't come close to what your Lord has done for you. When the Lord converted you, he turned you around. In so doing, he changed your worldview. Equipped with this new spiritual perspective, you are able to view your ministerial situation the way the Lord wants you to view it. Instead of a dead-end town, you see opportunity. In place of bitter, angry, unfocused people, you see souls bought by Christ's blood. Instead of an unbreakable Groundhog Day cycle, you are privileged to lead your people in the daily rhythm of confession, absolution, and sanctification.

Jeremiah's Jerusalem would soon see the Lord break their cycle of sin. Nebuchadnezzar was coming. Destruction would be his hallmark. Captivity would be the fallout. Mercifully, this captivity would last *only* seventy years. Lovingly, the Lord would preserve a remnant. A man named Daniel would lead those faithful few as they waited for the Lord, as they watched his working through leaders, and as they listened to his word.

As harsh as this chapter of Jeremiah sounds, these words would actually become a source of comfort for Daniel and the rest of the exiles. "I, Daniel, understood from the Scriptures, according to the word of the LORD given to Jeremiah the prophet, that the desolation of Jerusalem would last seventy years" (Daniel 9:2).

Jeremiah may not have seen anyone in Jerusalem repent from these words, but a thousand miles away in captivity, Daniel did.

> We have sinned and done wrong. We have been wicked and have rebelled; we have turned away from your commands and laws. We have not listened to your servants the prophets, who spoke in your name to our kings, our princes and our ancestors, and to all the people of the land. (Daniel 9:5–6)

Jeremiah wasn't stuck in his ministry, and neither was Daniel. They repented. They believed the Lord's pronouncement of forgiveness. And while every day may have looked similar, they viewed it through the lens of faith. Opportunistic souls perceive the possibilities of sanctification. The Holy Spirit gives us that spiritual sight. He enables our movements.

You are not stuck in your ministry. The Lord has not doomed you to a cold, gray eternity of misery. Quite the contrary! Like Jeremiah in Jerusalem, and like Daniel in Babylon, the Lord has placed you exactly where and when he wants you to be. He has armed you with his powerful word. He promises to you support you through the words and works of the members who called you to serve them. And most of all, your Lord will continue to be with you always, to the very end of the age.

How can we possibly respond to the Lord for all of this? Perhaps Daniel said it best when he prayed to the Lord: "We do not make requests of you because we are righteous, but because of your great mercy. Lord, listen! Lord, forgive! Lord, hear and act! For your sake, my God, do not delay" (Daniel 9:18–19).

Prayer

"When all their labor seems in vain, Revive their sinking hopes again;
And when success crowns what they do, Oh, keep them humble, Lord, and
     true
Until before your judgment seat They lay their trophies at your feet." Amen.

—CW 542:3

"You must drink it"

Jeremiah 25:15–38

The Israelites had just gotten settled at Mount Sinai. Rest became a welcome sight after their three-month trip from Egypt. The cries of Pharaoh and the screams of Egypt now faintly gurgled under distant waters. How Israel must have looked forward to the quiet provided by those secluded mountains of Sinai! To drink in the sights and sounds of peace and security after the frightening shouts of slavery would be nothing short of a blessing from the Lord.

But this camping trip would be no vacation. Thunder and lightning filled the sky above Mount Sinai. A thick cloud enveloped the mountain. A loud trumpet blast echoed off the rock walls. The whole mountain trembled violently. The Lord commanded the Israelites to leave the mountain untouched. The frightened responses of the people seemed to render that command superfluous.

Most frightening of all was the Lord's command to Moses. He ordered Moses to ascend the mountain to stand in the very presence of the Lord. Can you imagine? As a million people shuddered, the Lord ordered Moses to climb the shaking, trumpeting, thunderous mountain.

It was a good thing he did. On Mount Sinai the Lord gave Moses the Ten Commandments, along with his civic and ceremonial laws. The entire situation was frightening . . . but it remained necessary. The Lord hid just enough of his glory to dictate his commands to Moses without killing him with holiness. What an experience it must have been for Moses!

Then, all at once, it was over. The Lord told Moses to descend the mountain. Armed with the two stone tablets, Moses and Joshua approached the Israelite camp. But something didn't sound right. People were shouting. Joshua's ears perked up. "There is the sound of war in the camp" (Exodus 32:17).

But these were not the sounds of war—at least, not a physical war. A spiritual battle had been waged, and God's people had lost. And Moses knew it instantly. In one of the most ominous poems in all of scripture, Moses tells Joshua:

> It is not the sound of victory,
> it is not the sound of defeat;
> it is the sound of singing that I hear. (Exodus 32:18)

It was bedlam. Moses saw his people dancing and worshiping the false god. Many were drinking heavily. And at the center of this idolatrous storm stood the idol itself, the golden calf handcrafted by Moses' very own brother, Aaron.

It was all too much. Filled with anger, Moses threw down the stone tablets, breaking them in to pieces. He marched straight to Aaron and yelled, "What did these people do to you, that you led them into such great sin?" (Exodus 32:21). Aaron's answers remained unconvincing.

Short of destruction, what punishment would appropriately illustrate how rebellious these actions were? Moses came up with perhaps the most memorable punishment of all. "He took the calf the people had made and burned it in the fire; then he ground it to powder, scattered it on the water and made the Israelites drink it" (Exodus 32:20).

The very people blessed enough to drink in God's show of power at Mount Sinai now had to drink down an idol of their own making. It was time for God's people to literally swallow the consequences of their sin. There is no more sobering brew than that.

Hundreds of years later, God's people continued to drink to gods of their own making. This new generation of Jeremiah's day had become drunk on the same idolatry as their ancestors. In turn, their same holy Lord became perfectly angry. Fittingly, the same punishment given at the foot of Mount Sinai would be prescribed again in Jerusalem. The Lord dusted off that cup for his people to drink anew. "Take from my hand this cup filled with the wine of my wrath and make all the nations to whom I send you drink it." They would be forced to gulp it down to the bitter dregs.

Ultimately, the Lord was giving his people and their neighbors what they had been begging him for. Each nation, from Egypt to Philistia to Arabia to Judah, was fixed to the fate they originally desired. These self-hardened hearts were now sealed in stone by the Lord himself.

All of this from a drink! "Drink, get drunk and vomit, and fall to rise no more because of the sword I will send among you." The Lord would hand that sword to Nebuchadnezzar. "Look! Disaster is spreading from nation to nation; a mighty storm is rising from the ends of the earth."

Perhaps some noticed the effects this drinking brought on and refused. But it was too late. "If they refuse to take the cup from your hand and drink, tell them, 'This is what the LORD Almighty says: You must drink it!'"

Jesus heard those same words in the garden of Gethsemane. He was looking up at the tumultuous, stormy, hellish Mount Calvary with a wrenched heart. Like those Israelites at the foot of Mount Sinai, Jesus' disciples must have been unnerved by what their Lord had to say: "My soul is overwhelmed with sorrow to the point of death" (Matthew 26:38).

Those are feelings that we can only know in part. While we sip from the cup of suffering in this world, Jesus was about to drink it all down. Yet this cup would prove to be so unbearably and eternally painful that Jesus actually asks if it is possible that he not drink from it. "My Father, if it is possible, may this cup be taken from me. Yet not as I will, but as you will."

Jesus knew the answer to his prayer from eternity. The very cup of wrath prescribed as Israel's punishment at Mount Sinai in Moses' day, the very cup of punishment filled up in Jeremiah's day, the very cup of suffering that should have been yours and mine was now grabbed by Jesus. He drank down your eternal suffering so you would never know what it would feel like.

When it was all finished, the Son of God had suffered the hell of every person who ever lived. Yet even in that moment he still had the perfect wherewithal to understand that scripture still needed to be fulfilled. And so he said from the cross, "I am thirsty" (John 19:28). He who had the spiritual thirst for our cup of suffering now cried out in physical thirst from the physical torment of crucifixion. It marked the end of it all. At the very moment that sponge touched Jesus' lips and he received the drink, Jesus declared our justification with these words: "It is finished" (John 19:30).

Now Christ has a drink for you. He hands you the living water of his word and tells you to drink deeply. These are the waters that refresh your soul. Christ also hands you his drink from the cup of the new covenant in his blood. In the Supper Christ instituted, he pours out his forgiveness for all of your wrongs. Take and drink from this fountain of forgiveness as often as you can.

But your Lord also holds another cup from which you are to drink. He hands it to you daily, and it is a bitter brew. It is your daily cup of suffering. Downing this drink means tasting the bitter persecutions of the world around you. It means consuming the devil's ire. It means death to self with all its evil wants and desires.

This cup brings hardship. Your Lord was very forward about this. In his prayers before his capture in Gethsemane, Jesus prayed to his Father, "I have given them your word and the world has hated them." Surprisingly, he requested, "My prayer is not that you take them out of the world but that you protect them from the evil one."

Jesus prayed to keep you where you are. He prayed that you be handed a cup of suffering. It is not the straight suffering he drank. Lovingly, Jesus dilutes your drink of suffering to preserve you. And while it is not always easy to digest, your Lord promises to enable you to drink it to the dregs.

All of this is temporary. Soon the spiritual drink of our physical sufferings will end. The cup will be empty. And the foretaste of heaven we consumed every time we drank in the Lord's Supper will give way to God's glory itself. The quaking, thunderously sinful world will give way to a trumpet blast. Then we will stand with the Lord on holy Mount Zion. Suffering will cease. Death will be done.

"Whoever is thirsty, let him come; and whoever wishes, let him take the free gift of the water of life" (Revelation 22:17).

And for eternity you will get to drink it all in.

Prayer

"I heard the voice of Jesus say, 'Behold, I freely give
The living water, thirsty one; Stoop down and drink and live.'
I came to Jesus, and I drank Of that life-giving stream;
My thirst was quenched, my soul revived, And now I live in him." Amen.

—*CW* 338:2

"Do not omit a word"

Jeremiah 26

Jerusalem, Jerusalem, you who kill the prophets and stone those sent to you, how often I have longed to gather your children together, as a hen gathers her chicks under her wings, and you were not willing. Look, your house is left to you desolate. For I tell you, you will not see me again until you say, "Blessed is he who comes in the name of the Lord." (Matthew 23:37–39)

Those were the last words Jesus publicly preached. The remainder of his teachings would be directed at his disciples, his enemies, and those standing at the foot of the cross. This lament of Jesus might possibly be the saddest in scripture. The Savior who yearns with every fiber of his being to save his people cannot bear the fact that they have rejected him. He makes it clear that this is not the first time he has cried over this ancient city. Every stone thrown at a prophet sent a tear to the very eye of God. Each sword that pierced a faithful servant also pierced the heart of God.

Right before his lament over Jerusalem, Jesus shared one of his final parables with the crowds. It would be one of the most vividly tragic teachings of his entire ministry. "There was a landowner who planted a vineyard. He put a wall around it, dug a winepress in it and built a watchtower" (Matthew 21:33a). This landowner created his vineyard perfectly. Towers and walls protected every side. The winepress enabled the vineyard to be efficient and successful. All he needed were workers.

"Then he rented the vineyard to some farmers and moved to another place" (Matthew 21:33b). Everything went according to plan. The workers worked. The grapes grew. Then the harvest came. That was when everything fell apart. "When the harvest time approached, he sent his servants to the tenants to collect his fruit" (Matthew 21:34).

The unthinkable happened. "The tenants seized his servants; they beat one, killed another, and stoned a third" (Matthew 21:35). We are left with the same questions the original hearers had: Why would the tenants do this?

Simply put, the tenants wanted the vineyard for themselves. They had come to think that they owned the vineyard. Delusion led to defiance as the tenants fought off the landowner and his servants.

In this parable the vineyard is Jerusalem. The Lord gave her everything she would ever need. He protected her. He enabled her to succeed both physically and spiritually. The tenants were God's people. And somewhere along the line, they began to believe that this vineyard God had given them was actually theirs. Defiantly they guarded the walls of Jerusalem against the very God who gave it all to them.

Jeremiah 26 provides the historical background for Jesus' parable. Once again the Lord sent his servant, Jeremiah, into the harsh confines of the vineyard of Jerusalem. "Tell them everything I command you; do not omit a word." We are not made privy to Jeremiah's emotions at this point, but the patient love of the Lord shines throughout the account. He tells Jeremiah, "Perhaps they will listen and each will turn from their evil ways." Through wars and plagues, in the midst of siege and defeat, God's goal for his people always focused on repentance.

But to bring about true repentance God's law must first show sin. So the Lord commands Jeremiah to speak these words: "If you do not listen to me and follow my law, which I have set before you, and if you do not listen to the words of my servants the prophets, whom I have sent to you again and again (though you have not listened), then I will make this house like Shiloh and this city a curse among all the nations of the earth." This was not the dark, distorted lens the false prophets had been holding up to the people. These were the harsh truths that only a mirror can show. Every imperfection became exposed. The result of continued defiance remained clear.

Shiloh. The Hebrew word that means "peace" had become the definition of destruction. To even bring up such a tragic memory around Jerusalem's leaders, on the temple grounds no less, was to bring a death sentence upon oneself. "As soon as Jeremiah finished telling all the people everything the LORD had commanded him to say, the priests, the prophets and all the people seized him and said, 'You must die!'"

Poison filled their words. "You *must* die!" There was no other recourse in their minds. Jeremiah would be the next servant in a long line of persecuted prophets. He even tells us about one of them. Uriah had also prophesied these words and was chased all the way to Egypt, where he was hunted down and murdered.

Quickly, officials from the king's palace rushed up to the temple to calm the mob. The level-headed elders reminded the people that the prophet Micah pronounced the same warnings from the Lord to King Hezekiah. Then a man named Ahikam arrived. He had been an official of Josiah and realized the importance of Jeremiah's message. And so, because of these few remaining faithful tenants, Jeremiah, the servant sent into the dangerous vineyard, was spared.

Fast forward again to Holy Week. The time had come for the landowner to send his final envoy. This man would be greater than any of the servants the vineyard had seen. "Last of all, he sent his son to them" (Matthew 21:37). Do you see what is happening here? The very Son of the landowner is speaking this parable to those wicked tenants! If they don't understand their rebellion now, can there ever be any hope for them?

"When the tenants saw the son, they said to each other, 'This is the heir. Come, let's kill him and take his inheritance'" (Matthew 21:38). Rebellion and sin may seem rational in the moment, but time and perspective always show just how illogical it really is. Did they really think they could avoid punishment by killing the landowner's son? How could they really believe their actions would be free of consequence?

Time and perspective greatly benefit our view of this parable. But we are not so removed from it. Who are *we* in this parable? Often, by the grace of God, we have the privilege of working as the servants of the landowner. He sends us to show the rebellious their sins. We are equipped with the mirror of the law to show sin for the defiance it really is.

These are not easy tasks! Showing the law will inevitably incur angry recourse. So in reaction we are tempted to dilute the message. Instead of showcasing the seriousness of sin, we cast it as annoying or inconvenient. These same temptations threatened Jeremiah, too. That is why the Lord actually had to tell him, "Tell them *everything* I command you; *do not omit a word*."

But another, far scarier threat looms. We are not always numbered with the perfect servants sent to the vineyard. There are times when we have acted as defiantly as the tenants. Whenever we refuse to listen to the Lord's law, or when the Pharisee inside of us makes us feel above the consequences of sin, we have shed our servant moniker to be numbered with the rebellious tenants.

How can we respond when rebellion threatens to change us from faithful servants to defiant tenants? Listen again to Jesus' loving lament.

> O Jerusalem, Jerusalem, you who kill the prophets and stone those sent to you, how often I have longed to gather your children together, as a hen gathers her chicks under her wings, and you were not willing. Look, your house is left to you desolate. For I tell you, you will not see me again until you say, "Blessed is he who comes in the name of the Lord." (Matthew 23:37–39)

By our God-given faith, we are those who cry out in repentance, "Blessed is he who comes in the name of the Lord." We sing, "Hosanna," understanding that we need every bit of what that word asks for: "Lord, save us!"

Remember that amazing fact: the landowner *willingly* sent his Son to die in that vineyard. All of your sinful rebellions, defiant thoughts, and poisonous words have been taken away. And while the Lord still laments the loss of his people, the promise still stands for you. The Lord's kingdom is now "given to a people who will produce its fruit" (Matthew 21:43). By God's grace, by Jesus' death and resurrection and by the Holy Spirit working in your heart, you are able to produce that fruit of repentance.

Such fruit will inevitably bring about suffering in this world. Enemies may threaten you as they once did Jeremiah. Rufinus of Aquileia, a church father living in the fourth century, was not oblivious to the importance of suffering and death. He once insightfully stated, "Understand that God is a physician, and that suffering is a medicine for salvation, not a punishment for damnation."[1]

Like Jeremiah, consider your suffering pure joy. Like Jeremiah, boldly proclaim *all* of God's Word. And like Jeremiah, remember God's personal promises that he made to you when he first called you:

> "Get yourself ready! Stand up and say to them whatever I command you. Do not be terrified by them, or I will terrify you before them. Today I have made you a fortified city, an iron pillar and a bronze wall to stand against the whole land—against the kings of Judah, its officials, its priests and the people of the land. They will fight against you but will not overcome you, for I am with you and will rescue you," declares the LORD. (Jeremiah 1:17–19)

Prayer

"The servants you have called And to your Church are giving
Preserve in doctrine pure And holiness of living.
Your Spirit fill their hearts And charge their words with pow'r;
What they should boldly speak, Oh, give them in that hour!" Amen.

—CW 546:4

---

[1] "Intelligat homo medicum esse Deum, et tribulationem medicamentum esse ad salutem, non poenam ad damnationem." Rufinus of Aquileia, *In LXXV Davidis Psalmos Commentarius*, vol. 21, *Patrologia Latina*, ed. J.-P. Migne (Paris, 1849), 720. Translation by the author.

"The yoke of the king of Babylon"

Jeremiah 27

Sometimes respecting the authority God has placed over us in this world comes at a cultural cost. Can you imagine how difficult it must have been to be a Christian in the years leading up to the American Revolution? Scripture tells us to submit to the governing authorities. That submission should come even when taxation takes place without representation. How should the believer act in such circumstances? Should he honor his king or side with his rebellious neighbors? The choice was not so easy. Cultural implications threatened those who chose to stay loyal. Patriots viewed those loyal to the crown as enemies. "Loyalists" were called "persons inimical to the liberties of America."[1] That was a loyalist's cultural cost. To say the price was high would be an understatement.

"These are the times that try men's souls."[2] Thomas Paine's words had become even more true than he realized. He went so far as to compare the fight for these revolutionary ideals to the battle between heaven and hell, "Tyranny, like hell, is not easily conquered; yet we have this consolation with us, that the harder the conflict, the more glorious the triumph."[3]

---

[1] Barbara Smith *The Freedoms We Lost: Consent and Resistance in Revolutionary America*. (New York: New Press, 2013), 142.

[2] Thomas Paine, *The American Crisis* (CreateSpace Independent Publishing Platform, 2017), 5.

[3] Ibid.

Revolution had thrust a difficult choice upon believers: choose rebellion or be hated by your people, your culture, and even your family. These were trying times indeed for the searching soul!

Yet the American cause was hardly the first battle between culture and faith. The distinguished scholar Avishai Margalit noted that Josephus struggled between these two choices, too. Living at the time of Jesus, Josephus had witnessed just how oppressive the Roman government could be. But he also saw the ruinous errors of the Jewish rebellions against that authority. Josephus was a Jew caught between his government and his culture. In the end, he refused to back rebellion. When he fled, he was labeled a traitor.

Margalit took his study of Josephus one step further. He stated that Josephus' difficult choices had made him strikingly similar to the prophet Jeremiah. They both held a God-given respect for the foreign government God established. Neither rebelled. Both were ostracized.

Jeremiah's choice between his culture, his people, and the foreign Babylonian government of Nebuchadnezzar started to take a toll on his ministry. The words the Lord had him say during the reign of Judah's final king, Zedekiah, sounded more like treason than scripture. "Make a yoke out of straps and crossbars and put it on your neck." This physical illustration of people being yoked like animals would get the message across loud and clear. "Now I will hand all your countries over to my servant Nebuchadnezzar king of Babylon."

Just think of the cultural implications of preaching that message in Jerusalem! Nebuchadnezzar had already sacked the city and taken away her king, along with the city's best and brightest individuals. How do you think people would feel when they heard Jeremiah promoting Babylonian propaganda?

Of course, this wasn't propaganda at all. This was a prophecy of the Lord. Jeremiah was simply the mouthpiece through which this message came. If anything, the Lord was the one who sounded like a traitor. And while the people would consider Jeremiah a conspirator, deep in their souls they probably thought Jeremiah's God was one too. Why else would he turn against their sacred city of Jerusalem? Why else would the Lord prophesy against their temple and their king?

The world of Jerusalem had turned upside down. The cries of rebellion had led God's people to declare his prophet a traitor. They called God's message a lie. And while many still wouldn't say it out loud, deep down Judah's rebellion looked to remove God from his throne so that they themselves could reign upon it. And in the end, isn't that the goal of every rebellion?

Jerusalem's false prophets only stoked these rebellious flames. Diviners, dream-interpreters, mediums, and sorcerers all perpetuated the lie of rebellion by blatantly proclaiming, "You will not serve the king of Babylon." Such a message must have sounded pleasantly patriotic. Who could argue with such a message of freedom? Anyone who *did* argue would be labeled an unpatriotic traitor and a threat to the crown. Jeremiah's message made him look the part of a traitor, even though he remained one of the last faithful followers of God.

What was the last difficult choice you had to make between your culture and your faith? Perhaps a recent conversation brought you at odds with an old friend over God's blessing of marriage. So many Christians have begun the gradual slide toward culture's mistaken acceptance of homosexuality, same-sex marriage, and even abortion. Most aren't afraid to call you "unloving" for standing against such cultural ideals.

The false prophets of our age make this battle even more difficult. They dress in sheep's clothing by combining scriptural-sounding messages with the cultural mores around us. The poison of their teaching slowly kills their people's faith. The drink tastes sweet, but it will be bitter in the end.

Even our language distances us from our culture. We speak respectfully of our leaders because of the offices they hold. Most in our culture refuse to use those respectful words. They even become offended when we use them. We speak of this world as being created by God. Most of the world uses evolutionary language and becomes indignant when we refuse to acknowledge their stance.

Every year we find ourselves more divergent with our country, our people, our neighbors, and even our own family members. Have we really become traitors? Does God's message *have* to mark us as cultural turncoats?

Look no further than the prophet Jeremiah for the answer. God's word will never truly align with our world's culture. God's law will never sound as sweet as the misguided sayings of sociologists. God's gospel will never make the rational sense our enemies so desire to hear. And really, God never set out to manipulate our culture. God doesn't care about having the best-looking band poster in the subway. His word *changes* hearts. The faith he gives us *transforms* our worldview. It *reforms* our language.

As we will see in the coming chapters, Jeremiah and his ministry will pay for these transformative aspects. False prophets will smash his yoke in an attempt to break his message. He will be thrown into the cistern. He will be forced to flee with rebels. For all of Jeremiah's faithful service to the Lord, he will be labeled a traitor and a criminal. The people Jeremiah loves so deeply will hate him so completely.

Ministry has a way of inviting those persecutions into your world. Family members speak against your traditional, old-sounding beliefs. Your neighbors keep you at arm's length because you work at the "strict church" in town. Your school makes the local news for all the wrong reasons as reporters tag your ministry with harsh, unloving labels. Parents pull their children out of your school because you refuse to give in to the cultural view of transgender opinions. No doubt more cultural battlegrounds will appear in the coming years. It can all become so overwhelming!

In our darker moments, our sinful nature advises us to take off this anticultural yoke. Or if we must wear it, we carry it in hidden places and take it off when the crowds are looking. The people in our lives tempt us with acceptance all the time. The cost for such acceptance will always be God's very word. And there are times when we have considered the trade.

While men like Josephus and Jeremiah took a costly stance against their cultures, it is Christ who paid the highest price. He respectfully followed the cultural mores of his day when they aligned with scripture. But he wasn't afraid to eat with tax collectors and prostitutes and people that his culture had labeled as "sinners." He healed lepers. He talked with women and Samaritans (and at least one person who was both). He chose fishermen and a tax collector and a zealot to be his disciples.

Most of all, Jesus stood against his culture when his culture stood against his word. He accomplished this perfectly, not with rebellion but with sacrifice. That symbol of sacrifice, the cross, may be fading from favor these days. In Jesus' day, the very thought of the cross was horrific. Who would ever take such an abomination upon himself?

Jesus would. He set himself apart from his culture and his very own people. In the end, he had to hang opposite his very Father. On that dreadful cross, Jesus thought nothing of earthly perception. He thought about you.

Thomas Paine once wrote: "Heaven knows how to put a proper price upon its goods; and it would be strange indeed if so celestial an article as freedom should not be highly rated."[4] He's right, but for all the wrong reasons. Although your sins made you worthless in God's sight, Jesus treated you as priceless. His death won your eternal freedom. This is a freedom from your slavery to sin, from your slavery to the devil, and even from your slavery to the expectations of your culture.

Go tell your people just how eternally peaceful that freedom is.

Prayer

"Take the world, but give me Jesus! In his cross my trust shall be
Till with clearer, brighter vision Face to face my Lord I see.
Oh, the height and depth of mercy; Oh, the length and breadth of love!
Oh, the fullness of redemption, Pledge of endless life above!" Amen.

—*CW* 355:3

---

[4] Ibid.

"Only if his prediction comes true"

Jeremiah 28

There Jeremiah stood, a man alone in the midst of a sea of people. He looked ridiculous. He had just preached a stirring sermon, but hardly anyone listened. They were all busy looking. It was quite a sight to behold. There in the house of the Lord, Jeremiah, the prophet of the Lord, carried a yoke around his neck. It was the type of physical sermon a servant of the Lord was unable to shrink away from. Every priest, every official, and all the citizens of Jerusalem fixed their eyes on the burdened prophet.

No doubt Jeremiah was feeling the weight of that burden. Yokes are heavy; after all, they are built for oxen, not humans. But this yoke carried a spiritual burden that pushed down on him harder than the harness. Jeremiah was once again proclaiming a law message to a people who were quickly tiring of it. "If, however, any nation or kingdom will not serve Nebuchadnezzar king of Babylon or bow its neck under his yoke, I will punish that nation with the sword, famine and plague, declares the LORD" (Jeremiah 27:8).

A yoke is not the type of device that garners supporters. That is probably why few churches use it as a symbol. Few pastors talk about their "yoke ministry," and I have yet to see a "Yoke Christian School" in any directory. Yet if there was one symbol that best captured Jeremiah's ministry, it might be that yoke. A much-maligned prophet, surrounded by his own disbelieving people, physically preaching a law message by wearing a heavy yoke—that epitomizes Jeremiah's ministry.

But the picture wouldn't be complete without an approaching Hananiah. Once Jeremiah finished his sermon, Hananiah walked straight up to him with resolute purpose. He had a message of his own to share with that gathered crowd. "This is what the LORD Almighty, the God of Israel, says . . ." His words *sounded* so official. Their religious tone seemed to mimic Jeremiah's address.

This was not the first time a liar attempted to imitate God's message. The devil accomplished the same feat in front of a perfect crowd in the garden of Eden. By mixing his lies with half-truths, he convinced Adam and Eve that his words stood on the same level as the Lord's. Nothing could have been further from the truth.

Hananiah revealed himself to be as capable an imitator as the devil himself. The attribute remains a hallmark among false prophets to this day. The message also persists. "I will break the yoke of the king of Babylon." Talk about a crowd-pleasing proclamation! This was the good news Jerusalem so desperately yearned to hear. It was refreshingly different from the foreboding proclamations Jeremiah continued to promote.

Now that Hananiah perked up the crowd's ears, he continued by giving the types of details people often want to hear. "'Within two years I will bring back to this place all the articles of the LORD's house that Nebuchadnezzar king of Babylon removed from here and took to Babylon. I will also bring back to this place Jehoiachin son of Jehoiakim king of Judah and all the other exiles from Judah who went to Babylon,' declares the LORD, 'for I will break the yoke of the king of Babylon.'"

Do you understand Satan's play here? Not only is he proclaiming a lie through Hananiah in the name of the Lord, he is also flooding the prophetic market. Jerusalem's inhabitants now felt they were choosing between equally valid messages. The devil was trying to throw enough conflicting reports at the people that they would be content to continue as they had been, on the path away from the Lord.

The song remains the same today. So many scriptural-sounding messages have flooded the religious market that individuals excuse themselves from having to think through any one of them. False doctrines contain truthful-sounding words. Conflicting messages provide the illusion of biblical contradictions. With so many spiritual voices crying out, how is the man of God supposed to rise above the fray?

Jeremiah and his message from the Lord had just been publicly rejected. Now Jeremiah *had* to publicly object. He needed to remove all doubt from the confused crowd. And the approach he takes might surprise you. "He said, 'Amen! May the LORD do so! May the LORD fulfill the words you have prophesied.'"

Relish the days when you are blessed to use ministerial sarcasm appropriately. This was one of those days for Jeremiah. He wanted to see the fulfillment of this sweet-sounding message as much as anyone at the temple! Alas, this was not the Lord's message. Nor *had* this been the message of the Lord. "From early times the prophets who preceded you and me have prophesied war, disaster and plague against many countries and great kingdoms."

Jeremiah had not been the first law preacher in Judah's history. Nor would he be the last. So how could the people decipher which message was true? How can we today? Let's let Jeremiah give the final word on the matter: "The prophet who prophesies peace will be recognized as one truly sent by the LORD only if his prediction comes true." Prophecy simultaneously remains that simple and that profound.

Hananiah was not about to let Jeremiah have the last word on the matter, so he increased the stakes. "Then the prophet Hananiah took the yoke off the neck of the prophet Jeremiah and broke it." The message was clear. Hananiah physically backed his own message of freedom by breaking Jeremiah's yoke.

"At this, the prophet Jeremiah went on his way." What thoughts drove Jeremiah's actions at this point? Which emotions rushed through his mind now that he seemed to have lost this prophetic battle at the temple? Perhaps he was so angry with Hananiah's blasphemous actions that he had to remove himself before he did something rash. Or maybe Jeremiah felt defeated, once again embarrassed in front of Jerusalem's crowd.

Those would certainly be human responses we have all experienced. In a public debate about a scriptural truth, did your adversary mock you and win the day in the eyes of those gathered? Did that nonmember attempt to come up to communion and then make a boisterous show after the service in front of you and your members?

Did that angry family in your school publicly pull their children out and air your dirty laundry in the streets of your community—or even worse, on social media? If that has happened to you, and it probably has in one form or another, then you have stood with Jeremiah. The crowd agrees with your accuser, and you are left to walk away with fists clenched in anger while tears stream down your cheeks.

But Jeremiah may have walked away for another reason altogether. There are times when God has his prophets leave the crowds to make a point. The point Jeremiah may have been making was to preach a silent message. Beware when the prophet of the Lord closes his mouth! It usually means God has ceased to put up with his people's stubborn rejections.

Jesus did this in his ministry. After his hometown of Nazareth rejected him and tried to throw him off the local cliff, Jesus stopped preaching to them. That silence must have been deafening. The gospel of Mark records the one thought that accompanies this silence: "He was amazed at their lack of faith."

But the Lord wasn't done speaking to Jeremiah's Jerusalem. Not yet anyway. Once again the prophet who may have preferred to walk away was thrust back into the fray. The Lord told Jeremiah to return to Hananiah with this message: "This is what the Lord says: You have broken a wooden yoke, but in its place you will get a yoke of iron." Hananiah could break all the yokes he wanted. The Lord's prophecy would still be fulfilled.

A broken yoke sure is tempting. The significance becomes even greater when we remember the history behind our own yokes. When a pastor places a stole around his neck for worship, he is clothing himself in a powerful symbol. The fabric hanging around his neck reminds both him and his congregation that the yoke of the Lord's ministry has been placed on him. It might look fancy and prestigious, but the stole is actually a reminder of selfless service. Beasts of burden wear yokes. Servants put on cloths to wash feet. In this way your stole illustrates the definition of your title "minister." You are a servant of the Lord.

Hananiah was not a servant of the Lord. He took the first chance he got to break his yoke. False prophets never allow themselves to be burdened like true prophets. In fact, false prophets have something far more burdensome on the horizon. Ironically, or perhaps tragically, they never see it coming.

"Listen, Hananiah! The LORD has not sent you, yet you have persuaded this nation to trust in lies. Therefore, this is what the LORD says: 'I am about to remove you from the face of the earth. This very year you are going to die, because you have preached rebellion against the LORD.'"

Two months later, Hananiah died. We see no tears on the cheeks of the crowds in Jerusalem. We hear no crying in the streets. No holiday marked his passing for future generations. When the devil is done using false prophets, he usually spits them out into the gutter. Hananiah stood with the devil against the Lord. In the end, the Lord defeated both.

What about Jeremiah? He may have "won" the temple dispute, but the reward did not include the hearts of his people. If anything, more of his fellow citizens would stand against him in the coming days. As his ministry continued, Jeremiah's yoke would weigh even heavier.

How heavy has your yoke felt lately? Have the demands of your people weighed you down? Are your ministerial knees buckling under the pressure of producing? Remember that you do not bear the weight of your ministry alone! Your Lord and Savior lifts your burden with you. And he knows all about weighty burdens. After all, he took the burden of your sins, your punishment, and your death. Of course he will carry today's struggles with you! Of course he will be with you always!

He promises.

> Come to me, all you who are weary and burdened, and I will give you rest. Take my yoke upon you and learn from me, for I am gentle and humble in heart, and you will find rest for your souls. For my yoke is easy and my burden is light. (Matthew 11:28–30)

Prayer

"'Come unto me, ye weary, And I will give you rest.'
O blessed voice of Jesus, Which comes to hearts oppressed!
It tells of benediction, Of pardon, grace, and peace,
Of joy that has no ending, Of love that cannot cease." Amen.

—CW 336:1

"I know the plans I have for you"

Jeremiah 29:1–23

"By the rivers of Babylon we sat and wept when we remembered Zion" (Psalm 137:1). How difficult it must have been for those first-generation Judean exiles. They had lost everything. Their ancestral homes had been destroyed. Their family land, passed down from every father to every son since Joshua's conquest, was stolen away forever. So was their culture. They now lived in a foreign land as prisoners of war coping with the prospect of living as Babylonian subjects.

The spiritual implications of exile would prove to be the most difficult. "How can we sing the songs of the Lord while in a foreign land?" (Psalm 137:4). This first exiled generation vowed to never forget their homeland. "If I forget you, Jerusalem, may my right hand forget its skill" (Psalm 137:5). How *could* they forget? They yearned for Jerusalem as long as they lived.

It is precisely in days of longing when the devil tempts us to ask, "Why?" Certainly these exiles were asking the question. *Why* did God exile us? Did we do something particularly sinful? *Why* must we long for Jerusalem when those still living in the city continue to possess everything?

Someone needed to answer these questions of longing. So the Lord had the prophet Jeremiah write a letter to these exiles. Jeremiah may not have known it at the time, but this letter would become one of the most comforting chapters the prophet ever penned. To those longing to return to Jerusalem, Jeremiah wrote: "Build houses and settle down; plant gardens and eat what they produce. Marry and have sons and daughters; find wives for your sons and give your daughters in marriage, so that they too may have sons and daughters. Increase in number there; do not decrease."

Quite a shocking command for these Judean exiles to follow! "Settle down" the Lord tells them, "because you are going to be there a long time." These were not the encouraging words the exiles were hoping for. Escape must have been considered. Perhaps the exiles even contemplated revolution. The Lord gave a surprising response to each of these rebellious ideas: "Also, seek the peace and prosperity of the city to which I have carried you into exile. Pray to the LORD for it, because if it prospers, you too will prosper."

Pray that Babylon *prospers*? Jeremiah must have sounded out of his mind! This may have been the point where the reader of the letter had to double-check to make sure this was really signed by the prophet Jeremiah. It was, of course. And this barrel of exiles needed these commands because a few bad apples had been exiled with the bunch. "Do not let the prophets and diviners among you deceive you. Do not listen to the dreams you encourage them to have. They are prophesying lies to you in my name. I have not sent them." Even in Babylon these false prophets were convincing people that this exile was not so bad. "This will only be a short stay—a vacation!" the dreamers proclaimed. They couldn't have been more wrong.

"This is what the LORD says: 'When seventy years are completed for Babylon, I will come to you and fulfill my good promise to bring you back to this place.'" Seventy years—the number must have hit their hearts with a thud. They knew what that number meant. It meant their generation would never see Jerusalem again. Such a realization can shatter people's confidence and make them question whether the Lord knows what he is doing.

Does the Lord know what he is doing? So much in our lives feels random. Or worse, hardship seems to seek and destroy us while others in this world run free of sin's consequences. Ministry especially feels this way. Pastors deal with not only their own difficulties but the difficulties of their members, too. Teachers must lovingly teach children who have been cast off by their parents. Even worse, teachers must effectively educate children even when their parents constantly get in the way.

The effects of people's sins on your ministry can threaten to lead you to the dark thought of retribution. Why should I keep putting up with people's stupid choices? Why do I continue to feel punished for someone else's mistakes? It doesn't seem fair!

No doubt the exiles had come to the same realization. The party in Jerusalem continued while they suffered the humiliating sadness of exile. What was left for these exiles now? What was the plan? *Was* there a plan?

To every worry and fear, in the face of every question and doubt, the Lord gives a most comforting reminder: "'For I know the plans I have for you,' declares the LORD, 'plans to prosper you and not to harm you, plans to give you hope and a future.'" The Lord knew his plans for his people. He even told them what those plans were: prosperity and safety, hope and a future during seventy years in Babylon.

The Lord shared his plans for Jerusalem. Their idolatrous party was about to end. "I will send the sword, famine and plague against them and I will make them like figs that are so bad they cannot be eaten." Everything would switch. God would destroy Jerusalem and the exiles would be safe. The Lord told these exiles that their captivity would actually mean safety!

Only the Lord can work through awful, sinful situations for the good of his people. Only the Lord could use this Babylonian exile as a means of safety. Only the Lord can work all things for the good of those who love him. That includes you.

Have you felt exiled? Has the ministry removed you from family and friends that you have been forced to leave behind? Are you living in a foreign world among strange people with strange customs? The Lord has a way of using the ministry to plant us in uncomfortable ground. He moves you to use you effectively. Like those exiles, the Lord puts you in those sometimes difficult situations to keep you safe.

In this way, we are all exiles. You may not always live where you prefer to be. But your home and the place to which you were called is even better. It is the place that the Lord wants you to be. Like he told those exiles, the Lord also tells you to "settle down" and to "seek the peace and prosperity" of your community and your local leaders. Pray for them.

We have been comparing ourselves to exiles, but can you imagine what it was like to be born into exile? Every day you would hear about the "good ol' days." The old-timers would describe the grandeur of Jerusalem to you. They paint pictures of how the sun glimmered off the beautiful walls of the temple. The old women would recall the sounds and smells of their old houses passed down from one generation to the next. "But you never saw it. You have no idea," they would say longingly.

The early years must have been the most difficult for those second- and third-generation exiles. All they could do was listen to what used to be. They were longing for something they had never seen. They would hear about a homeland they had never lived in.

You are that kind of exile. You have been hearing your entire life about a fatherland that you have never seen. Like those Babylonian exiles, you read the words from the prophets about what your homeland is like. But like those second- and third-generation exiles, you start to wonder if the wait is even worth it. You ask, as they did, "How long, O Lord?"

Then comes the encouragement for exiles, the Lord's perfect plans for you: "'For I know the plans I have for you,' declares the Lord, 'plans to prosper you and not to harm you, plans to give you hope and a future.'" Is there a more comforting promise for servants called away from their earthly homelands? You have been called to your location precisely because the Lord wants you there. He knows his plans for you, and those plans are described with words like *prosper* and *hope* and *a future*.

And someday, dear exile, the seventy years will be up. The Lord will return and take you to the home you have been waiting your entire life to behold. No more longing. No more wandering. The rivers of Babylon will give way to the river of the water of life flowing down the middle of your new city. Worldly thrones will crumble in the presence of the throne of God. And your Savior will open his doors and you will be home.

Forever.

Prayer

"I'm but a stranger here; Heav'n is my home.
Earth is a desert drear; Heav'n is my home.
Danger and sorrow stand Round me on ev'ry hand.
Heav'n is my fatherland; Heav'n is my home.

"Therefore I murmur not; Heav'n is my home.
Whate'er my earthly lot, Heav'n is my home.
And I shall surely stand There at my Lord's right hand.
Heav'n is my Fatherland; Heav'n is my home." Amen.

—*CW* 417:1, 4

"He has preached rebellion"

Jeremiah 29:24–32

John Mark must have felt awkward. There he stood, silently listening as the church's two greatest missionaries argued. They were arguing about him. Barnabas wanted to bring him along on their second great missionary journey. Paul had his doubts.

John Mark probably agreed with Paul. After all, he *had* abandoned Paul and Barnabas on their last missionary journey. But Barnabas, ever the encourager, saw more in the young man. He knew John Mark could be faithful if he was just given another chance.

Paul didn't want to take that chance. And so the two great stalwarts of mission work in the church had a sharp disagreement. What emotions passed through John Mark's mind as he heard their disagreement over his character, his failures, his sins? What guilt he must have felt as he watched Paul walk one way and Barnabas another!

Blessed with the benefit of hindsight, we can see how the Lord used this disagreement for the good of his church. One missionary journey turned into two. Twice the amount of ground was covered. Perhaps even more importantly, the Lord graciously gave John Mark a second chance. He went on to become both a faithful missionary and according to tradition, an evangelist.

Disagreements happen in the church. If Paul and Barnabas could fall into such a sharp argument, so can we. While the subjects of our disagreements are usually much smaller than what Paul and Barnabas disagreed about, they often begin in the same way. Disagreements are born from differences in character and opinion.

Soon the subject of disagreement is forgotten, and the people themselves become the issue.

That can be a real problem for called workers. Are there people in your ministry who you struggle to work with? Do their characteristics, their words, or their way of operating paralyze you? Chances are good that a person or a group of people have been making your ministry difficult. Why is that? What is it about that person that makes ministry so challenging? Perhaps a more introspective question is in order. Are you the only one who struggles to work with this individual, or has everybody had run-ins with this person?

The criminal psychologist Robert Hare gave a shocking description to people who poison a work environment. He called them "psychopaths in the workplace."[1] Such people, Hare asserted, use bullying and stress to manipulate others into submission. They turn a healthy, positive setting into a stressful, destructive environment.

One of the most effective forms of confrontation these people use is called "character assassination." Rather than patiently participate in a conversation about your opposing views (like Paul and Barnabas did), these individuals attack your character. They attempt to destroy your credibility and reputation so others listen to their opinion rather than yours.

If that has happened in your ministry, you are not alone. Jeremiah knew better than anyone how it felt to have his character assassinated. In verse 24 the Lord tells us that an exile named Shemaiah exerted astonishing force. He had been playing the role of puppet master as he used his letters to pull the strings of Jerusalem's leaders. His letters must have been convincing. Through them Shemaiah incited a priest named Zephaniah to depose the high priest, Jehoiada! Zephaniah in turn took the open position of high priest.

Shemaiah's thousand-mile-long puppet strings didn't stop manipulating. Acting as the de facto king in absentia, he called for Jerusalem's last true prophet, Jeremiah, to be reprimanded and thrown into the stocks and neck irons. With one letter, this false prophet nearly

---

[1] Robert Hare, *Snakes in Suits: When Psychopaths Go to the Workplace* (New York: HarperCollins, 2007), x.

succeeded in upending Jerusalem's three most important offices: prophet, priest, and king.

Perhaps worst of all, Shemaiah attempted to destroy Jeremiah's ministry. Acting as one of Robert Hare's psychopaths, he made an assassination attempt on Jeremiah's character. To do this, he referred to Jeremiah as a "madman." Destroy a minister's character in the eyes of the people and you effectively destroy his ministry. Even this false prophet knew that "A good name is more desirable than great riches" (Proverbs 22:1).

The assassination of a minister's character can still take a pastor or teacher down today. In fact, a called worker is always one accusation away from the end of his ministry. The accusation need not even be true! It simply must ignite a spark of doubt in the minds of people. When the flames of doubt arise, then trust is burned up. So is that person's ministry.

No wonder the apostle Paul spends so many verses reminding called workers of how to carry themselves. In 1 Timothy 3 he reminds you to be above reproach, faithful spouses, temperate, self-controlled, respectable, hospitable, and able teachers. He warns you not to be violent or quarrelsome or drunkards but rather gentle. Not one of us has perfectly followed this list. And when we fall short, the devil is quick to remind both us and our enemies of that fact.

So what is stopping him? Why doesn't the devil reveal our deepest, darkest-sounding sins to our members? Shining a light on those sins would surely provide more than enough doubt in the minds of our parishioners. Once they found out, your ministry would be over.

The answer rests in the love of your Lord. Instead of allowing Satan to parade all of our secret sins before our people, he placed them on his Son, Jesus. Jesus made our sinful humiliation his own. When we deserved the ridicule of this world it was Jesus who "was despised and rejected by mankind" (Isaiah 53:3a). Our ministry-threatening sins should have shamed us. Instead, Jesus became "like one from whom men hide their faces" (Isaiah 53:3b). And when our secret sins could have revealed us to be the worst of called workers, Jesus took our painful, humiliating suffering as he "took up our infirmities and bore our suffering" (Isaiah 53:4). Even in death, Jesus was mired in our disgrace. "He was assigned a grave with the wicked" (Isaiah 53:9).

So what is stopping Satan from revealing the sins that could undermine your ministry? Christ. Satan has been rebelling from the beginning, from Absalom's rebellion against his father, David, to Korah's rebellion in the wilderness to the first rebellion of humankind in the garden of Eden and all the way back to Satan's own rebellion against the Lord. Shemaiah became another rebel in Satan's army against the Lord. The Lord never holds back on punishing rebellion. Shemaiah would be no different. "He will have no one left among his people, nor will he see the good things I will do for my people, declares the LORD." Then comes the ominous reason for this punishment: "Because he has preached rebellion against me."

When false accusations target God's servants, he always treats those attacks as rebellion. By his grace God preserved Jeremiah's ministry in Jerusalem. The flaming arrows of the evil one continued to fly, yet the Lord extinguished them all. He preserved the ministry of his prophet, sinful as that prophet was.

He promises to preserve you, too. The arrows of accusation will continue to fly. Satan will continue to incite rebellion against the ministry the Lord has blessed you with. When that battle rises again, flee to your Savior. He is ever your refuge and strength. He remains your source for living a faithful ministry—one embodied by faithfulness and self-control.

When the apostle Paul encouraged Timothy and his congregation to exhibit these faithful characteristics, he maintained how such a lifestyle could be possible in the daily struggle of a sinner. He stated that he gave these encouragements so that "you will know how people ought to conduct themselves in God's household, which is the church of the living God, the pillar and foundation of the truth" (1 Timothy 3:15).

Then he told Timothy how Christ would one day embody your ministry. "He appeared in a body, was vindicated by the Spirit, was seen by angels, was preached among the nations, was believed on in the world, was taken up in glory" (1 Timothy 3:16).

Prayer

"O highest Comfort in ev'ry need,
Grant that neither shame nor death we heed
That e'en then our courage may never fail us
When the foe shall accuse and assail us. Lord, have mercy!" Amen.

—*CW* 190:4

"I will restore you to health"

Jeremiah 30

Half a millennium ago, in 1565, Malta was a small Mediterranean island with a big problem. This little, Christian island saw an entire fleet of Muslim Turks sailing directly toward them. Conquest was on their minds. No one gave the Maltese much of a chance at survival. They could only amass an army of a couple thousand men while the mighty Turkish military threw their entire force at the little island.

To make matters worse, this Turkish military was experienced. They had been slowly conquering the entire world, from Iran and Iraq, to Egypt, Jerusalem, Constantinople, Greece, and North Africa. They were at the gates of Europe, and poor little Malta stood in their way.

Everything happened like you might expect. When the Turks arrived, they overran cities. They burned fields. They destroyed the forts. Thousands of Maltese men, women, and children died. The few remaining Maltese people fled to their last standing fortress, a place named St. Michael.

In the midst of this final stand, the Maltese leaders sent word to the rest of Europe, pleading for help. Those hot July days passed on to August. The fort remained, but no help came.

In the meantime, that Maltese fort was strong, but the Arab army seemed stronger. It was only a matter of time before the Turkish cannons blew through the walls of the fort. Soon the people would be taken off into slavery and the island would be conquered. Already a third of the population of the island was dead. And no help had come.

Can you imagine standing in that Maltese fort, clutching your family and slowly coming to the realization that you are about to witness the extinction of your culture? To describe the emotion as simple sadness is to downplay the grief of the Maltese. To label them afraid would be to undercut just how terrified they felt.

Perhaps most of all, the Maltese felt frustrated. Where was the rest of Christendom? Their little island of Malta faced the full force of the Muslim army, and the rest of Christian Europe was simply watching! It is hard to imagine ourselves in that type of sad situation, but it is not impossible. Believers have faced those kind of long odds and pitiful moments before.

Jeremiah stood as the quintessential example of a man caught in a hopeless situation. For twenty-nine chapters you have been reading a book whose words bleed for its author. You stood and listened along with him when the Lord first bestowed his warning-filled ordination upon his prophet. You watched Jeremiah's family shun him. You heard Jeremiah's fellow citizens shouting out against him. You felt the wooden stocks that bound him to the temple courtyard. And most of all, you have heard those law-filled prophecies. Sadness and sword, doom and destruction continue to spill forth from Jeremiah's bitter pages.

Where is the hope in all of this? Jeremiah must have wondered. How could he not? He felt betrayed. He appeared to be alone. All that was left for this weeping prophet was to witness the destruction of his city, the obliteration of his temple, and the murder of his people. Jeremiah might as well have been crouching behind the fortress walls with the rest of the Maltese, waiting for the arrival of death.

At first, chapter 30 appears to be no different. "This is what the LORD says: 'Cries of fear are heard—terror, not peace.'" Here we go again. To make matters worse, the Lord now tells Jeremiah to write everything down. Not only would Jeremiah preach these words to his people; he would also record them forever.

In the midst of men grasping their stomachs and the people of Jerusalem turning a white shade of death, the Lord adds something else to his message. This beautiful *something* has been in short supply throughout Jeremiah's book. Jeremiah has begged for it, and now, finally, he hears it. The Lord now gives his prophet *hope*.

"How awful that day will be! No other will be like it. It will be a time of trouble for Jacob . . ." Now comes the Lord's wonderful adversative, his turn in the message, the *but* that makes all the difference. ". . . but he will be saved out of it."

The yokes Jeremiah prophesied would eventually be broken! Their slavery would eventually end! False prophets like Hananiah or Shemaiah would not be the cause behind this great reversal. Judah's salvation will come from the only one who could win it for them: the Lord. "'I am with you and will save you,' declares the Lord. 'Though I completely destroy all the nations among which I scatter you, I will not completely destroy you.'"

The Lord's salvation became the medicine Judah needed, and no one needed it more than the prophet who preached it. No wonder the Lord had Jeremiah write the words down! He could read and reread these gracious promises the rest of his life, even when the Babylonians surrounded Jerusalem and tore down her walls. Jeremiah could hold these words close even when he was whisked away toward Egypt. The prophet could clutch God's glorious gospel during his personal depression. If we still had Jeremiah's original copy, chapters 30–33 might be the most worn pages.

Which pages of scripture are most worn in your Bible? When ministerial depression comes, when your life begins to fall apart, or when all hope seems lost, where do you turn? *Have* you been turning to God's word? Jeremiah was reminded that true, lasting hope can only be found on the pages of scripture.

The reverse is also true. Hope always seems lost without God's word. A look back on your ministry might just reveal a pattern emerging. Problems arise in the ministry precisely when God's word has left the called worker's schedule. With the crises comes depression. With depression comes the sickness of hopelessness.

Listen again to the Lord's hopeful words that pour forth from Jeremiah's pages: "'But I will restore you to health and heal your wounds,' declares the LORD." And all that after Jeremiah had been called "an outcast." He wasn't an outcast, of course. In fact, listen to what the Lord calls Jeremiah and his fellow believers: "So you will be my people, and I will be your God."

My people. *Your* God. "Personal" barely begins to describe your Father. "Perfectly loving" gets closer. But the best description might still be what Jeremiah needed most. Your Lord is a Lord of *hope*.

I wonder if any of the Maltese Christians read these verses of Jeremiah while they awaited their death at the Turkish hands. To be surrounded on all sides, to face the end of your family and people, to be rid of all hope is to understand Jeremiah's plight. All those who have been devoid of hope can relate.

On September 7, hope finally arrived. Don Garcia, the Spanish general, landed on the island with thousands of men. They lured the Turks away from the fort just before it could be destroyed. The knights in the fort then swept out and chased the large Muslim force off the island. The long Maltese siege had finally ended. Against all odds, in the midst of hopelessness and despair, the little island of Malta stood up to the greatest army in the world . . . and survived.

How did things change so swiftly? You see, that Turkish army might have looked invincible, but they were starting to tire during their long siege. The Muslim soldiers began to bicker with one another. By the time those reinforcements landed on the island with Don Garcia, the enemy was ready to run.

To show their gratitude toward Garcia and his men, the people of the island labeled them *Gran Soccorso*, which fittingly means "the great relief." Your enemy looks similarly strong but is just as vulnerable. In fact, your enemies already stand defeated by your Savior, Jesus. He is your "great relief." No siege of ministry can break through your Savior's walls. No enemy can snatch you out of his almighty hands. He has won your victory, your eternal crown, your heaven forever. And when you arrive within those heavenly walls, you will finally see with your eyes what you have always believed by faith: your God. He will hold you tightly and whisper, "You will be my people, and I will be your God."

Prayer

"Guide me, O thou great Jehovah,
Pilgrim through this barren land.
I am weak, but thou art mighty;
Hold me with thy pow'rful hand.
Bread of heaven, Feed me till I want no more.

"Open now the crystal fountain
Whence the healing stream doth flow;
Let the fiery, cloudy pillar
Lead me all my journey through.
Strong Deliv'rer, Be thou still my strength and shield.

"When I tread the verge of Jordan,
Bid my anxious fears subside;
Death of death and hell's Destruction,
Land me safe on Canaan's side.
Songs of praises I will ever give to thee." Amen.

—*CW* 331:1–3

"After I strayed, I repented"

Jeremiah 31:1–30

Had it all been a dream? Perhaps. Then again, maybe it was more like a nightmare. Jeremiah watched the horror pass through his mind. An entire nation had been forced out of their homes. The massive force from the north arrived. Darkness enveloped Jerusalem, murdering men, abusing women, kidnapping children. Those fortunate enough to escape fled into the hopeless expanse of the wilderness. They had survived the sword only to suffer starvation.

Jerusalem itself looked like a desert. Only charred vineyards remained in the enemy's wake. Nothing grew. Dust and ashes covered the once-beautiful city. Those cursed with blindness were considered blessed. They couldn't see the destruction. Those paralyzed remained as weak as ever. Perhaps every survivor felt that weak.

Then came the crying. Weeping louder than Jerusalem had ever heard burst forth into the void of the heavens. No one appeared to be listening. Such was the weeping of Rachel, Jacob's wife who died giving birth to Benjamin. Scripture always compares the most heart-wrenching tears to hers. This comparison was not hyperbole. Jerusalem, and her weeping prophet Jeremiah, mourned louder than ever before.

Jeremiah's dream continued with a view of a few faithful priests. In their wickedness, the people had not supported them. Starvation would find these religious leaders of Jerusalem just as it found the rest of the people suffering under the Babylonian siege.

Then, everyone was gone. The streets, once crowded with happy Israelite children playing and wealthy merchants conducting business, now lay deathly silent. The families had been ripped apart. The people were filed away into a captivity they would never see the end of.

Only a poem remained. It was the type of poem that made sense only to the sleeping mind. "The parents have eaten sour grapes, and the children's teeth are set on edge." The sins of the fathers hovered above the human wreckage of the city.

Precisely at this point the dream twisted, as dreams often do. Its themes and tones turned in on themselves. As the dreaming Jeremiah soon realized, the Lord was the one doing the twisting, and this nightmare of a dream would soon become one of the most beautiful and comforting prophecies in all of scripture.

The wandering survivors walked into view first. And the voice from heaven narrated their new future: "The people who survive the sword will find favor in the wilderness; I will come to give rest to Israel." The view was no mirage. The Lord instantly formed the barren wilderness into lush environs. The weary received the rest they so desperately yearned for.

The dust heap of the fields followed. Like a phoenix from the ashes, new growth arose from the charred remains. Again, the voice explained, "Again you will plant vineyards on the hills of Samaria; the farmers will plant them and enjoy their fruit." Like a new creation, the Lord brought everything from nothing. "They will rejoice in the bounty of the LORD—the grain, the new wine and the olive oil, the young of the flocks and herds. They will be like a well-watered garden."

The blind witnessed this great transformation. The lame miraculously walked through it. It was the Voice who enabled them: "Set up road signs; put up guideposts. Take note of the highway, the road that you take."

No tear of sadness could be seen. No somber sounds could be heard. "They will come and shout for joy on the heights of Zion." Then came the dancing. "Then young women will dance and be glad, young men and old as well. I will turn their mourning into gladness; I will give them comfort and joy instead of sorrow." All of this Rachel-like weeping, all of this mourning over what was lost ceased. Once again the voice controlling the dream boomed, "Restrain your voice from weeping and your eyes from tears."

Even the faithful priests changed. No longer did they look starved. The faithful crowds returned to the Lord, bringing with them their numerous offerings. No one could remember a time when such abundance filled Jerusalem. "I will satisfy the priests with abundance, and my people will be filled with my bounty."

The end of the dream zoomed in on a single shepherd. Smiling, his joy overflowed into love for the countless sheep standing around him. They had all been lost, hurt, crying, scared, and alone. But he found them. He found each and every one of them. "He who scattered Israel will gather them and will watch over his flock like a shepherd."

These sheep, at one time defiantly wandering in every direction, had turned back to their shepherd who rescued them. "After I strayed, I repented; after I came to understand, I beat my breast. I was ashamed and humiliated because I bore the disgrace of my youth." The dream that began in such a nightmarish way ended with a joyous apogee.

Then everything faded away. The prophet woke up, and all at once the dream gave way to reality. Jeremiah looked around, trying to sense his surroundings. He had been thrust from the future back into the present. Initially confused, Jeremiah finally admits, "My sleep had been pleasant to me." The message of the dream had everything to do with that.

The dream had been a familiar prophecy. The scenes illustrated how the Lord would fulfill the very first prophecy he ever gave to Jeremiah. Just in case he missed the connection, or just in case we had forgotten the Lord's words of ordination to Jeremiah, he repeats them here: "'The days are coming,' declares the Lord, 'when I will plant the kingdoms of Israel and Judah with the offspring of people and of animals. Just as I watched over them to uproot and tear down, and to overthrow, destroy and bring disaster, so I will watch over them to build and to plant.'"

Your ministry exists in this twilight between dream and reality. The Lord's prophecies miraculously find their way from his word into your heart. What a privilege it is for pastors and teachers to encourage today's sheep in their sojourn through this barren land. You are blessed to give comfort to those mourning the loss of loved ones. You are given the opportunity to share the strength of God's word with the suffering. You get to behold the work of the Holy Spirit as he uses the means of grace to give the sight of faith to spiritually blind sinners. You watch as he exhibits his strength through physically weak workers like you.

And you get to live the joy of the redeemed in full view of the next generation. It isn't a joy based on circumstance and situation, nor is it founded in the stuff of this world. Your joy looks beyond this life. Your joy is founded on what comes *after* the dream of this life.

After all, that is what this world is. Your crying, your frustrations, your long, lonely walk through the desolate reaches of your world all seem so very real. But as the dream collapses, everything that seemed so real fades away. Your sadness leaves you. Your worries cease. Death is forgotten. Had it all been a dream?

At the end of it all, at the beginning of eternity, your Shepherd comes in to view. His flock sits around him. And there he will love you with an everlasting love, for he had drawn you with unfailing kindness.

Prayer

"Jerusalem the golden,
With milk and honey blest
The sight of it refreshes
The weary and oppressed.
I know not, oh, I know not
What joys await us there,
What radiancy of glory,
What bliss beyond compare." Amen.

—*CWS* 728:1

"A new covenant"

Jeremiah 31:31–40

The most infamous treaty in Western civilization was signed in a French train car. The "War to End All Wars" had, in fact, just ended. The nations of Europe could not have been more relieved. Over 40 million people had died during the conflict. Countries were devastated. Decades would pass before nations recovered. Some never would.

So on November 8, 1918, everyone felt it was time to officially end this bloody war of attrition. The French summoned the German leaders, their vanquished aggressors, to a railroad station in the French forest of Compiègne. There, in a special railcar, the Allies spelled out the terms of this armistice. Germany needed to relinquish the territory they conquered during the war. They had to significantly reduce the size of their military. And Germany had to pay an unfathomable $33 billion. Most humiliating of all, Germany was forced to admit they were responsible for starting the entire war.

Begrudgingly, the Germans agreed, and the Treaty of Versailles was signed by all parties. Most memorably, the treaty would take effect on the eleventh hour of the eleventh day of the eleventh month. As Americans, we still celebrate that agreement today.

They did not celebrate the agreement in Germany. In fact, the humiliating treaty fueled the German people to vote for extreme nationalist leaders from the Nazi party. Adolph Hitler, the preeminent Nazi extremist, used that sentiment to shout his way to the top of his German government. Already in 1939, Hitler was sending his

German forces through Poland to reconquer the lands the Treaty of Versailles had taken from his people.

The Allies realized too late that the treaty had not brought a lasting peace. In fact, that most infamous treaty had actually fueled the fire behind a second World War. Germany continued sweeping over Europe. Hitler attacked Norway, then Denmark. Finally, in May 1940, Germany conquered France. To mark the occasion, Hitler designed a treaty of his own for the French. In a moment of premeditated historical irony, Hitler ordered that old French train car found, the one on which the Treaty of Versailles was signed, and placed it at its exact World War I location. Bringing the French leaders into the train car, he had them sign an armistice.

Such are the agreements between sinful men and wicked nations. Vengeance and retribution inflame self-serving treaties. Individuals break promises. Trust shatters like glass. Could a kinder French treaty have prevented World War II? Perhaps not. But the harsh, vindictive, unreachable provisions of the Treaty of Versailles certainly stirred the German storm of reckoning.

Treaties are not always so extreme. Many do, in fact, bring about lasting peace. Our world is filled with them. Agreements between individuals can also be beneficial. Companies sign contracts that hold them to the promise of completing good work on time.

Then there is this story from Japan. A gentleman once brought a few of his friends out to eat at a fine Japanese restaurant. He planned out the money he would need, but at the outset of the meal, he realized that had forgotten his credit card. The establishment did not share the cost of each portion until the very end of the meal. As each course came out, the man became more and more worried. He began to wonder if he had brought enough money to pay the bill. Then the server brought out Kobe beef. At that point, the man knew he was in trouble.

Sure enough, when the bill came at the end of the night, he did not have enough cash to pay it. Surprisingly, the restaurant manager calmly asked the man to write down his address so the bill could be sent to his house. It was a simple solution that both parties agreed to and probably one that could only happen in Japan.

Agreements are wonderful when they work, but they can be deadly when one person cannot live up to what was agreed upon.

If only every exchange went as smoothly as buying Kobe beef at a Japanese restaurant! Usually agreements end tumultuously. Vindictive hearts delight in signing treaties in French railcars.

Parties are forced to nullify contracts every day. Builders do not always show up when they are supposed to. Workers do not always do the quality of work they said they would. And yes, even the marriage bond is broken when husband or wife fails to live up to their marriage agreement.

Jeremiah's Judah was no better at keeping agreements than the people of our modern-day world. Although the law of the Lord was to be a covenant for them, they never lived up to their end of the bargain. Was there a problem with the covenant itself? Did the Lord make things too difficult for his people? Does the Lord make things too difficult for *all* of us?

There was nothing wrong with the law. And there is nothing wrong with the Lord. The broken side of this covenant comes from sinful humankind. And so, when we look at God's law, we can only come to one of two conclusions: either complete despair or complete denial.

A new covenant needed to be formulated. But it could not be like God's original covenant. Something had to change, because nothing about us had changed. The prophet blessed with the task of writing down this new covenant was Jeremiah. The words carried such importance that they would go on to summarize both Jeremiah's book and his ministry.

"'The days are coming,' declares the Lord, 'when I will make a new covenant with the people of Israel and with the people of Judah.'" And just before we say, "I'm not so sure, Lord, I'm all covenanted out," he continues. "It will not be like the covenant I made with their ancestors."

What a relief. That covenant was a bust, and again, it wasn't God who messed it up. "They broke my covenant, though I was a husband to them." God, as our faithful husband, continues to love us even when we have failed to love him perfectly.

"'This is the covenant I will make with the house of Israel after that time,' declares the Lord. 'I will put my law in their minds and write it on their hearts.'" God promises to cleanse us not just on the outside, but on the inside as well. His word won't be a hard, cold, and distant pair of stone tablets but rather his word that governs our lives from within.

"I will be their God, and they will be my people." This isn't a two-way covenant. How could it be? God's two-way covenant failed because of sinful humankind. This is a one-way covenant all the way. God promises to do all the work for your salvation.

In worship you are blessed by that covenant in a very personal way when you celebrate the Lord's Supper. When Jesus instituted that sacrament for you, he "took bread, and when he had given thanks, he broke it and said, 'This is my body, which is for you; do this in remembrance of me.' In the same way, after supper he took the cup, saying, 'This cup is the new covenant in my blood; do this, whenever you drink it, in remembrance of me'" (1 Corinthians 11:24–25).

This remains God's everlasting covenant with you. It is a one-sided covenant, pouring streams of grace down upon you from the endless aqueducts of Jesus' love. Every sin that the law pointed out, every internal trespass only you are aware of, and even those that are hidden from you, are declared "paid in full" by your God.

This is not just a covenant kept. It remains a promise fulfilled. Now, as a servant of the Lord, you are blessed to look back on all the covenants and agreements you have made through the lens of faith. You can live as a faithful child of the Lord through the working of the Holy Spirit in your heart. You can faithfully serve as a son or daughter. You can exhibit selfless love in your commitment of marriage. You can continue to dedicate yourself to God's word, just as you promised at your confirmation.

Against all earthly odds, you can also faithfully carry out your calling as the Lord's called worker. Remember those words you heard at your installation as you stood in front of the believers who called you.

> As an ambassador of Christ, you are to teach the pure doctrine of God's word, to instruct the young in the way of salvation, and always to have in your heart the spiritual welfare of every soul under your care. You are to devote yourself to the meditation and study of the scriptures. You are to be an example to others in godliness and Christian living, putting no stumbling block in anyone's path, so that the ministry will not be discredited. You are to speak the truth in love,

as the apostle Peter reminds us: "Love each other deeply, because love covers over a multitude of sins. If anyone speaks, he should do it as one speaking the very words of God. If anyone serves, he should do it with the strength God provides, so that in all things God may be praised through Jesus Christ. To him be the glory and the power for ever and ever."[1]

These are not the vindictive agreements of the world that hide the fine print or attach unseen strings. These are the tasks assigned to you by the very Lord who promises to help you accomplish them every day. And when you do fail, because you will, you can graciously return to the Lord in repentance and receive forgiveness. After all, that is what his new covenant is all about: "For I will forgive their wickedness and will remember their sins no more."

Prayer

"Come in sorrow and contrition, Wounded, paralyzed, and blind;
Here the guilty, free remission, Here the troubled, peace may find.
Health this fountain will restore; He that drinks shall thirst no more.

"He that drinks shall live forever; 'Tis a soul-renewing flood.
God is faithful; God will never Break his covenant of blood,
Signed when our Redeemer died, Sealed when he was glorified."

—*CW* 106:3–4

---

[1] Commission on Worship of the Wisconsin Evangelical Lutheran Synod, *Christian Worship: Occasional Services* (Milwaukee: Northwestern Publishing House, 2004) 247–248.

"Face to face"

Jeremiah 32:1–5

Soon after Adam and Eve ate from the Tree of the Knowledge of Good and Evil, the Lord blessed them with a son. Having been expelled from the garden of Eden, having lost their perfection, these first-time parents couldn't help but notice something different about their newborn. He was not born in the image in which God originally created *them*. He was born in his *father's* image.

As the boy grew up, that inherited sinful condition reared its ugly head in jealousy. The Lord looked favorably on his brother, Abel, and Abel's offerings, but not on Cain. Scripture's description of Cain's reaction reveals his dangerous disposition. "Cain was very angry, and his face was downcast" (Genesis 4:5). In love, the Lord held a mirror to Cain's anger in a perfect attempt to show him his sin. Cain would have none of it. Instead, he doubled down on his anger by acting on it. After asking Abel to come out to the field with him, Cain murdered his own brother.

Once again the Lord lovingly confronted Cain, now the world's first murderer. Cain dismissed the questions outright. When his parents had sinned for the first time, they at least had the good sense to admit to the Lord that they had sinned. Cain refused to talk about his brother. So the Lord explained that the consequences of Cain's actions garnered an even stricter reprisal than his parents' original sin. "Now you are under a curse and driven from the ground, which opened its mouth to receive your brother's blood from your hand. When you work the ground, it will no longer yield its crops for you. You will be a restless wanderer on the earth" (Genesis 4:11–12).

Cain was aghast. "My punishment is more than I can bear" (Genesis 4:13). Perhaps he knew just how harsh this sinful world could be. Maybe he realized that being hidden from God's presence was worse than death. Whatever was going through his mind, Cain finally revealed his one great worry that outweighed everything else. "Whoever finds me will kill me" (Genesis 4:14b).

Psychologists call that projecting. Cain, a murderer, was worried that someone else might murder him. He was projecting his sinful actions on his own brothers and sisters. When he looked at his family, Cain thought he saw people who looked and acted just like him.

Projecting is an attempt to place our shortcomings on others. When we act out in this way, whether consciously or subconsciously, we inadvertently shine a light on our own thoughts. Cain's actions weren't the only act that showed us he thought like a murderer. His projecting words to the Lord verified the thoughts of his heart.

Projection affects other feelings and emotions, too. If you are often angry, you perceive others in your life to be angry also. If you are afraid, you see others as having that same fear. Sadness is an emotion that finds itself everywhere.

Think back to the different times you projected your own feelings onto others in your ministry. You were worried Sunday school would flop, so you subconsciously thought your members held those same worries. Your anger flared up at a certain family while your thoughts led you to assume their anger was just as fierce. Your personal fears of inadequacy convinced you that everyone else thought you were a pretty shabby servant.

Projection dangerously deceives us in to thinking we are doing just fine while everyone else around us is falling apart. But the opposite often remains true! Our projections are just that—extensions of our own worries, fears, anger, and shortcomings.

Based on this chapter of Jeremiah, it seemed everybody was projecting in Jerusalem. Nebuchadnezzar and his strong, victorious army had finally arrived to place Jerusalem under siege. A large city like Jerusalem could withstand a siege for quite a while, but ominous signs filled her streets. Nebuchadnezzar had never lost a battle, or even a city. Jerusalem, strong though it was, looked to eventually be the next accolade in Babylon's long list of achievements.

Sieges make people do strange things, and Jerusalem had been under siege for about a year and a half at this point. Deception reigns within the walls of surrounded cities. Officials capture and kill anyone they perceive to be a spy. Starvation causes families to eat their dead loved ones. In the midst of these unthinkable circumstances, emotions slowly rise like an ocean at high tide. Waves of people start to crash against one another with their projected emotions.

Of all the people living in the besieged capital, Jeremiah made the best object of others' projections. After all, he was the prophet who predicted Nebuchadnezzar would arrive with his army. He was the man who warned his fellow countrymen that this siege would make them wish they were captives. In the eyes of many, Jeremiah and his treasonous-sounding prophecies seemed positively Babylonian!

So in an act of pure projection, King Zedekiah had Jeremiah arrested and confined to the courtyard of his royal palace. The move didn't make any sense. Why capture a prophet while your entire city is under siege? The move seems akin to rearranging chairs on the deck of the sinking *Titanic*!

Illogical as his actions were, Zedekiah wanted to act on his anger. His pathetic force in Jerusalem could not hope to dislodge Nebuchadnezzar's world-class army, so he decided to turn the prophet Jeremiah into a kind of whipping boy. All of Zedekiah's shortcomings, his people starving to death, his impotent military, and his eventual loss of Jerusalem were projected onto Jeremiah.

What could Jeremiah do? Although he faithfully preached God's warning to his people, his fate seemed sealed with the rest of Jerusalem. Once again, God's words had gotten Jeremiah imprisoned . . . perhaps for the last time.

To be the object of someone's sinful projections might be one of the most taxing aspects of ministry. Your angry family thinks you to be as hot-tempered as they are. Your financially struggling member sees you and the church as the reason for their need—and does not understand why you cannot help him more than you do. Everywhere you look, the intensive care unit that is the Christian church is filled with patients blaming their doctors for their self-inflicted illnesses.

We have been that type of patient who blames the doctor, too. And that type of projection, the one where we throw our shortcomings on our great Physician, is the most dangerous of all. When we are angry, we see God as angry. When we are distant, we perceive God to be distant. When we find ourselves in a ministerial bind, we blame the Lord for placing us there. In the end, these inaccurate accusations only reveal our own sins. All along our projection has really been our own reflection.

Prisoners to projections though we are, Jesus came to loose the chains. Your selfless Savior broke your selfish, sinful bonds by taking them upon himself. He slipped out the nails that held your shackles together so they could be hammered through his hands, binding himself to the cross that set you free. And while he suffered, Jesus had every right to project your sins back on to you. But he didn't. Instead, he exchanged those sins for his own righteousness.

That robe, dear Christian, is what you are privileged to project. Like the moon reflecting the light of the sun, you are blessed to reflect your Savior's love and goodness in your own life. Your problems and sufferings are not his fault. They are his opportunity. They stand as your reminder of just how loving and powerful your Savior really is. Project that truth in the pulpit, in the classroom, in the world around you, in chains, and even in death. Then you will receive the *real* crown of life, which is far greater than any projection.

Prayer

"Fast bound in Satan's chains I lay;
Death brooded darkly o'er me.
Sin was my torment night and day;
In sin my mother bore me.
Yet deep and deeper still I fell;
Life had become a living hell,
So firmly sin possessed me.

"My own good works availed me naught,
No merit they attaining;
My will against God's judgment fought,
No hope for me remaining.
My fears increased till sheer despair
Left naught but death to be my share
And hell to be my sentence.

"But God beheld my wretched state
Before the world's foundation,
And, mindful of his mercies great,
He planned my soul's salvation.
A Father's heart he turned to me,
Sought my redemption fervently;
He gave his dearest treasure." Amen.

—CW 377:2–4

"Once more fields will be bought"

Jeremiah 32:6–44

By the end of his life, Abraham's footprints covered the Middle East. After hearing God's initial command to move to Canaan, Abraham walked his family up north through Babylon to Haran, then down south through Damascus. Step after step, the crowd slowly, methodically made their way to their new home.

Upon arrival, most sojourners would have dug a foundation, built their dream home out of long-lasting bricks, and settled down for good. Not Abraham. He continued to roam throughout the land, finding green pastures for his flocks and friendly confines for his family. He preferred to live in tents. He never built a house, either for himself or for his servants. In fact, the only building projects Abraham ever completed were stone altars. To Abraham, these altars were the most important structures he could ever build.

Holding to that mind-set, Abraham never attempted to establish a permanent residence anywhere. And of all the lands his feet tread upon, Abraham never attempted to own any of it . . . except one, small field. The situation surrounding this purchase must have grieved his heart. Abraham's wife, Sarah, had just died. Not owning any land meant Abraham had no burial plot. Where would his wife's final resting place be?

After mourning over the loss of his wife, Abraham took care of business. Going to the Hittites, the regional landowners, Abraham purchased a field in Machpelah near Mamre. In that field stood a cave. There Abraham said a momentary goodbye to his wife.

Surprisingly, Genesis 23 focuses more on how Abraham obtained the land for Sarah's burial. Instead of summarizing Sarah's life, the chapter's final verse summarizes Abraham's purchase. "So the field and the cave in it were deeded to Abraham by the Hittites as a burial site" (Genesis 23:20).

The purchase of that field took trust. The man who once was ready to sacrifice his own son because he believed in God's power over death now once again looked to the Lord of the living at the death of his wife. This cave, the only land Abraham ever owned, showed that he trusted the Lord to keep his promises. And there were a lot of those promises. God had promised Abraham a son, through whom would come a nation, from which would come a Savior who would bless the entire world. And all of that would take place in the very land in which Abraham roamed. The bold footprints he left while walking into that cave looked ahead to the day in which his wife, Sarah, would one day walk out. That land purchase pointed ahead to the eternal Promised Land won for Abraham by his coming descendant.

Land acquisitions rarely seem that important. Yet while Abraham's land purchase was meaningful, Jeremiah's purchase was essential. Just seventeen miles from the cave Abraham bought from the Hittites stood the area of Anathoth. The Lord had told Jeremiah what was going to happen regarding that field: "Hanamel son of Shallum your uncle is going to come to you and say, 'Buy my field at Anathoth.'"

Two important stipulations left Jeremiah little choice in the matter. His uncle explains the first, which had to do with Judah's law code. "As nearest relative it is your right and duty to buy it." Like Boaz purchasing Naomi's land in the book of Ruth, so Jeremiah was duty-bound to keep this land in the family.

The second stipulation was a command from the Lord himself. After God's prophecy was fulfilled and Jeremiah's uncle asked him to buy the land, Jeremiah realized that the Lord indeed wanted him to purchase it. "I knew that this was the word of the LORD."

At any other point in Judah's history, the purchase of a field might be considered a blessing. But not in these dark days. Nebuchadnezzar had placed Jerusalem under siege, surrounding the city for months. But surprisingly, by this point in chapter 32, he and his army had left.

Jerusalem was granted a momentary reprieve, and Jeremiah's uncle was going to make the most of it. Finding Jeremiah under arrest in the courtyard of the guard, the uncle sold his land to his nephew and left with the money while he still could.

What a blunder on Jeremiah's part! Who would buy land in Judah right before her demise? The purchase was akin to buying a timeshare on an iceberg! And yet the Lord specifically orchestrated this land acquisition for Jeremiah. As always, the lesson remained vitally important, not just for Jeremiah, but also for the returning remnant.

Jeremiah instantly realized this land lesson. To purchase land in a country about to be conquered illustrates the strongest kind of trust. It is using what you own to say, "We *will* return." Understanding this gospel message from the Lord, Jeremiah loudly prays about the Lord's goodness and blessing to his people in every generation. The Lord had indeed shown love to thousands. The Lord most certainly saved his people from Egypt. And even now, as Babylonian siege ramps would soon ascended to the tops of Jerusalem's walls, Jeremiah declares, "You, Sovereign LORD, say to me, 'Buy the field with silver and have the transaction witnessed.'"

According to legend, someone once asked Martin Luther what he would do if he knew the Lord would return tomorrow. His answer sounded positively Jeremiah-like. "Even if I knew that tomorrow the world would go to pieces, I would still plant my apple tree."[1] Complete trust in the Lord shows itself in many ways. Jeremiah stood at the door of destruction . . . and bought a field. Luther looked at Armageddon . . . and stood ready to plant his apple tree. Both men understood the Lord's rhetorical question: "I am the LORD, the God of all mankind. Is anything too hard for me?"

Jerusalem's coming punishment was well deserved. Her future redemption was not. And yet in divine love, the Lord promised both. And both were coming quickly. "As I have brought all this great calamity on this people, so I will give them all the prosperity I have

---

[1] Richard Allen Landes, *Heaven on Earth: The Varieties of the Millennial Experience* (USA: Oxford University Press, 2011) 48.

promised them." That is why Jeremiah's field purchase remained so important. "Once more fields will be bought in this land."

Sometimes the Lord reserves his greatest gospel for the times when we are surrounded by the greatest evidence of his law. During these most difficult days of Jeremiah's ministry, the gospel poured forth from heaven on him like a deluge. Surrounded by Jerusalem's punishing fire, Jeremiah soaked in God's goodness.

Distress and disaster continually threaten your church and your ministry, too. Buildings may not be toppling in your community, but Christian morals and faithful perspectives certainly are falling. Waves of anger and skepticism roar and foam as they wash against your church and your people. Your people might struggle with those worldly attitudes even more. After all, they are the ones working in the world, surrounded by that anger and skepticism every day.

How can twenty-first-century believers possibly show the kind of stalwart faith that Jeremiah so boldly demonstrated in a besieged Jerusalem? How can we possess the confident stillness that led Luther to casually proclaim he would plant a tree on the eve of Judgment Day? Remember your Lord's promises. By the grace of God, that is what those men did. Jeremiah trusted that the Lord would return his remnant to the land he purchased. Luther believed that the Lord would surely bring him home to heaven.

By the working of the Holy Spirit among you and your people, you are granted similar opportunities to live your bold faith as well. In the midst of tumultuous times, believers can still establish new churches. While Christianity's numbers dwindle, we can confidently purchase land on which to build, believing in the fulfillment of Christ's promise, "Where two or three gather in my name, there am I with them" (Matthew 18:20).

Then there are the beautiful words the Lord reiterated to his imprisoned prophet—words that reveal the true picture of an almighty Shepherd holding his flock of believers gently in his hands. "They will be my people, and I will be their God." This is the third time in as many chapters that the Lord has spoken this phrase to Jeremiah. It sits at the core of God's gospel in this portion of the book. It is why the Lord gave Jeremiah the promises that he did. It is why Luther could hold on to his sure and certain hope of eternal life. And this remains your confidence to establish, build, and plant in Christ's name until he returns.

You belong to God's people, and he ever remains your God.

Prayer

"Lord, you I love with all my heart;
I pray you ne'er from me depart;
With tender mercies cheer me.
Earth has no pleasure I would share;
Heaven itself were void and bare
If you, Lord, were not near me.
And should my heart for sorrow break,
My trust in you no one could shake.
You are the treasure I have sought;
Your precious blood my soul has bought.
Lord Jesus Christ, My God and Lord, my God and Lord,
Forsake me not! I trust your Word." Amen.

—*CW* 434:1

"The voices of bride and bridegroom"

Jeremiah 33:1–13

The edges of the picture look faded now. Discolored lines cut through the black-and-white image. The sun has bleached the fringe. Yet despite its age, the vivid details of the photograph still shine through. Even after all these years, the fence running along the right side still shows its original lean. The grass appears remarkably defined. The dirt road still runs clearly down the left side. Of course, if you were looking at that picture now, these details would seem superfluous. Not one of these photographic aspects are the defining element of the picture. Strewn along that leaning fence, matting down the defined grass next to that dirt road, are bodies. Lots of bodies. Littered with holes, they lie mangled across the ground. Believe it or not, that is what the photographer originally wanted to capture. That is what he wanted you to see—with every detail preserved.

Alexander Gardner took photographs like these for a reason. Many in the North refused to believe the battles of the American Civil War could be so bloody. People still expected a swift Northern victory. Gardner saw it as his duty to bring the dead of the battlefields inside people's homes. For the first time in history, photographs detailed the horrors of death.

And people reacted. One writer memorably admitted, "The dead of the battle-field come up to us very rarely, even in dreams."[1] That was no longer the case. The real-life nightmare of the Civil War

---

[1] Mathew Brady, "Brady's Photographs; Pictures of the Dead at Antietam," *New York Times*, October 20, 1862, 5.

was manufacturing carnage at a frightening pace. Thanks to those photographs, everyone understood just how serious the national fighting had become.

The Lord holds a similarly horrifying photograph before Jeremiah's eyes. Still confined to the courtyard of the guard, Jeremiah possessed all the time in the world to view the pictures the Lord passed before his eyes. But unlike Gardner's Civil War photographs, the events captured in the pictures passing before the mind's eye of the prophet had yet to happen.

Crumbling city houses laid bare around the rubble of royal palaces. Their grandeur disintegrated. Ancient buildings collapsed while freshly constructed siege ramps stood tall, strongly supporting their ascending Babylonian soldiers. The sun glinted off iron swords as they swung through Jerusalem while Israelite gold fell, stained atop the muddy ground.

As awful as these moments appeared, the worst part of the Lord's picture was still to come. Frightening faces covered the dead strewn throughout Jerusalem. "[The houses] will be filled with the dead bodies of the men I will slay in my anger and wrath." Jeremiah beheld an uncanny picture from the Lord. So very rarely the dead of the battlefield approach us, but now the Lord brought their slaughtered carcasses right up to Jeremiah eyes.

But something was missing. One important face had been removed from the image. The Lord explained why to Jeremiah, "I will hide my face from this city because of all its wickedness." No punishment crushes more than when the Lord hides his face.

Yet not everyone wanted the Lord to hide his face. Jeremiah, horrified at the pictures his mind's eye beheld, must have wanted to cry out to his Lord for help. Could the Lord simultaneously hide his face from some in Jerusalem while still showing the face of his love to others? The Lord himself answers the question for his prophet, "Call to me and I will answer you."

At the very moment the Lord closes the door on many, he gives out his loving invitation to those who still believe. To those the law has cut to the heart, to those still bleeding from their sins comes God's healing promise. "I will bring health and healing to it; I will heal my people and will let them enjoy abundant peace and security."

As if these gospel promises appeared too small, the Lord continues to call out to the remnant soon heading away to captivity: "I will bring Judah and Israel back from captivity and will rebuild them as they were before." Emotional pain, physical loss, desertion, and punishment will all give way to God's gracious acts of love.

There remains no greater loving act than what the Lord promised next. "I will cleanse them from all the sin they have committed against me and will forgive all their sins of rebellion against me." Filthy acts cleansed. Forgiveness for sins. Even rebellion, that ancient awful sin against the Lord, is taken away by the shepherding Messiah promised to come. Sheep that rebelliously scattered themselves will be found again, saved by the willing death of their Good Shepherd.

It is remarkable that the Lord would choose to flash these pictures before Jeremiah as he stands confined in the courtyard. Jeremiah's low situation, his ministerial nadir, had probably left him feeling alone expecting judgment and destruction. The prophet was ready to die with his rebellious parishioners, the captors who wanted nothing to do with his message. Into this darkness shone God's gospel restoration. Promise after promise reminded Jeremiah that the Lord hears him, protects him, and most importantly, forgives him.

It is precisely when your ministry appears darkest that the Lord shines his gospel promises around you. When circumstances bind you, when members corner you, when no one seems to be listening to the word of the Lord you are faithfully proclaiming, God's love shines ever brighter. To the depressed pastor, to the overworked teacher, to the underappreciated worker, the Lord whispers "call to me in your day of trouble" (Jeremiah 50:15). Then just as quickly he promises: "I will indeed deliver you!"

Then there sits your long list of sins. Rebellions against differing opinions. Better-than-thou attitudes that pushed down those around you. Over-humiliations that refused to trust that the Lord is able to use you for the good of his ministry. All of them forgiven by the cleansing flood of blood your Savior poured down upon you from the cross.

This brings a new picture into focus. The edges remain crisp and new. No lines alter its technicolor brilliance. No detail is rendered superfluous. The black-and-white battlefield has been changed to the scene of a most wonderful wedding. The dead corpses have been transformed into perfect bodies. These timeless believers stand as a splendid bride looking lovingly at her groom. He's the one in the middle, the most important location. The scene is quite literally picture-perfect. And while this scene reveals events yet to happen, rest assured, dear believer in Christ, they will. Jesus promises.

"There will be heard once more the sounds of joy and gladness, the voices of bride and bridegroom, and the voices of those who bring thank offerings to the house of the LORD, saying, 'Give thanks to the LORD Almighty, for the LORD is good; his love endures forever.'"

Prayer

"Lord, when your glory I shall see
And taste your kingdom's pleasure,
Your blood my royal robe shall be,
My joy beyond all measure!
When I appear before your throne,
Your righteousness shall be my crown;
With these I need not hide me.
And there, in garments richly wrought,
As your own bride I shall be brought,
To stand in joy beside you." Amen.

—CW 219

"I will make a Righteous Branch sprout"

Jeremiah 33:14–26

If you have ever seen a solar eclipse, then you know just how awe-inspiring astronomical events can be. Peering through the appropriate eyewear, one can view the moon slowly passing across the face of the sun. As the total solar eclipse approaches, light begins to change. The view of the world appears as it would through sunglasses. Shadows begin to disappear. The descending darkness confuses animals. Birds roost. Dogs and cats wander. Nocturnal animals begin waking up.

Humans witnessing the event also act strangely. As the event culminates in a total solar eclipse, groups of people gather together. Office buildings unload their workers onto the streets below. Normally fractured individuals immersed within their own little worlds all look up together as one. Glasses come off. Naked eyes witness the rare event of the moon momentarily blotting out the sun. If you could gather the strength to look around (and refuse every inclination to look up), you would witness jaws opening into smiles releasing sounds of awe. You would notice children's fingers pointing to now-visible stars and planets. Eventually, you would hear hands clapping.

Then, as quickly as it comes, the event is over. Yet the smiles remain. People stay in their groups as long as they can. Office computers wait a little longer while their owners jointly reflect on the marvel they just beheld.

Why is that? Perhaps it is because so few things in this world get us to stop and look up anymore. Screens tightly hold our attention.

Work consumes our conscious thought. Play immerses us. And really, who has time anymore to look up and philosophically consider the heavens? Not many events can bring strangers together and leave them all with joy. But a total solar eclipse can.

One of the most marvelous aspects of an eclipse is its rarity. People can go their entire lives without witnessing one. When we are blessed to see it happen, it seems so unnatural. It feels as though an event like this isn't supposed to happen.

That is because we are used to God carrying out his covenant with the day and the night. After the flood waters receded, the Lord re-established that covenant when he promised Noah, "As long as the earth endures, seedtime and harvest, cold and heat, summer and winter, day and night will never cease" (Genesis 8:22). Some things will continue until the Lord returns. The last constant God listed may have been the most important. Day and night will never cease.

The Lord builds on that foundational covenant as he speaks to Jeremiah. "If you can break my covenant with the day and my covenant with the night, so that day and night no longer come at their appointed time, then my covenant with David my servant—and my covenant with the Levites who are priests ministering before me—can be broken and David will no longer have a descendant to reign on his throne." The understood meaning is that God's covenant with day and night will not cease. Therefore, God's covenant with David will also never cease.

This must have been a welcomed comfort to Jeremiah. After all, he knew the end was coming. The Lord had shown him how the Babylonians would soon burst through Jerusalem's old city walls. He saw every temple stone crumble. He watched as palaces fell. He stood helplessly in the vision as priests all around him perished. Worst of all, Jeremiah was about to see his king, Zedekiah, captured while attempting an escape with his family. This descendant of King David would helplessly watch as his own children were killed in front of him. It would be the final scene Judah's last king would see. Immediately, Nebuchadnezzar would blind him and carry him captive to Babylon.

Awaiting the brutal end of everything he held dear, Jeremiah desperately needed a comforting message from his Lord. While everyone else in Jerusalem bitterly cried out "The LORD has rejected the two kingdoms he chose," Jeremiah held on to God's gospel promise. It was as sure as day and night. It held fast as constantly as God's covenants with Abraham, Isaac and Jacob. "For I will restore their fortunes and have compassion on them." The Lord would fulfill that promise of compassion through a dead tree.

A few thousand years ago, in Oregon, a mountain erupted. After the plumes of smoke blew away and the dust settled, the top of the mountain revealed a massive crater. Periodically snow would fall, covering this mountaintop crater. The summer sun would methodically follow, melting the ice atop the isolated summit. Slowly, over the course of a few thousand years, a beautiful, crystal clear lake appeared.

Curiously, an old man has lived in the middle of this clear lake for over a century. Throughout the year, he slowly roams about the lake, and at a height of thirty feet, this old man towers over the secluded water. He was first seen in 1896, and if you are able to make the arduous climb to the summit of Crater Lake, you can still see him today.

As you may have guessed, this old man isn't really an old man at all. He is a tree—a dead one, to be exact. The locals call him "The Old Man of the Lake," and he continues to float lifelessly across the immaculate waters. As tranquil as it appears, this dead floating tree will eventually decay into nothing. When that happens, the Old Man will be no more.

Jeremiah must have been concerned about the stump that Judah had become at this point. The ax was at the root of David's family tree. Isaiah's words may have even come to mind: "As the terebinth and oak leave stumps when they are cut down, so the holy seed will be the stump in the land" (Isaiah 6:13). Nebuchadnezzar was swinging that ax. The once-strong oak was about to fall.

Such axes continue to instill fear in God's people today. Jeremiah's hopelessness and despair may periodically well up in your heart, too. Is the tree of Christianity about to fall to the double-sided ax of unbelief and false religion? Every day brings another swing. Every chop appears to be one cut closer to the ultimate demise of our churches. In such dark days, promises get forgotten. Covenants appear to crumble. It feels like God is impotent . . . or worse, uninterested.

The bitter thought of an uncaring God threatens to lead a called servant into all sorts of temptations. The sinful nature contends: "If God is ending this ministry, then why should I work hard at trying to preserve it?" Selfishness leads a pastor to work for his own good, or his own paycheck, rather than on behalf of those who called him. Without a confident trust in the Lord's loving kindness, teachers begin to educate for their own prominence rather than for the sake of the children sitting before them. Instead of an "us" mindset, a "me-versus-them" attitude rears its ugly head.

But the Lord had not abandoned Jeremiah. He will not abandon you either. He remains omnipotent. He continues to graciously care for you. And he will always help you during your struggles with sin. He promises to strengthen you when pain and sorrow threaten to drown your faith. And he will turn your selfish "me" into a selfless "we."

That "Old Man in the Lake" may be dead, but he isn't lifeless. Years after it was first discovered, a closer inspection revealed moss growing on the tree stump. The Old Man's lifeless wooden surface still provides a place for something else to grow.

The stump of Jesse's tree continued to do the same. Yes, Jeremiah could hear the Babylonian army surrounding the city of Jerusalem. Yes, the ax appeared to be at the base of King David's ancient family tree. Yes, everything was falling apart around him. Yet the promise remained: "In those days and at that time I will make a righteous Branch sprout from David's line." This wouldn't be just another sinful king of Judah. Quite the contrary! *This* king "will do what is just and right in the land." No army will withstand him, not even a Babylonian army. No commander will outflank him, not even Nebuchadnezzar. In fact, "In those days Judah will be saved and Jerusalem will live in safety."

How is such a future possible for a people nearly wiped out? It all has to do with his name. More than mere *kingly*, this righteous Branch is the *King* of kings. Far more powerful than *mighty*, he remains *almighty*. He bears a name you know, a name that is forever the object of your faith. This name has stood since before the creation of the world. And on the Last Day, when God's covenant with the sun and moon finally ends, all will bow at his name. This name forever remains your salvation, your comfort in strife, and your calm in every storm. "This is the name by which he will be called: The LORD Our Righteous Savior."

Prayer

"Hail to the Lord's Anointed, Great David's greater Son!
Hail, in the time appointed, His reign on earth begun!
He comes to break oppression, To set the captive free,
To take away transgression, And rule in equity.

"He comes with rescue speedy To those who suffer wrong,
To help the poor and needy And bid the weak be strong,
To give them songs for sighing, Their darkness turn to light
Whose souls, condemned and dying, Are precious in his sight." Amen.

—CW 93:1–2

"You will see the king"

Jeremiah 34:1–7

"We are watching for the fire-signals of Lachish . . . for we cannot see Azekah."[1]

A worried commander wrote those words on a piece of pottery and sent it to his Judean fortress city of Lachish. Those two cities, Azekah and Lachish, were the only ones King Zedekiah still controlled from his capital of Jerusalem. One by one the fires were snuffed out in Judah's last, strongest beacons of safety. As the pottery illustrates, Nebuchadnezzar and his insurmountable, multinational army would soon destroy the small fortress of Azekah. Lachish would be next. Then, at the end of it all, the flames would consume Jerusalem. By the time the fire petered out, nothing would be left.

These fires must have been on the minds of King Zedekiah. After all, he had been told that the fires of sacrifices that burned for centuries in Judah's capital would give way to a kingly funeral pyre. As Jerusalem was surrounded, as the fires were going out, as his capture and death appeared imminent, what was King Zedekiah to do?

Perhaps he dared to hope. Perhaps he thought a last-second miracle would save him and his city the way one did when King Hezekiah was besieged generations ago. That didn't seem likely.

---

[1] Joseph Naveh, *Encyclopedia Online*, https://www.encyclopedia.com/religion/encyclopedias-almanacs-transcripts-and-maps/lachish-ostraca (accessed January 12, 2018).

After all, the Lord had made it clear through Jeremiah that these grim, final days of Jerusalem would be her last. Zedekiah's hope in the Lord had come too late . . . if it ever truly came at all.

Zedekiah's personal future seemed hopeless, too. Chapter 34 implies that Zedekiah's worst fear would be realized as he would be forced to stand before King Nebuchadnezzar. His fear made sense. What defeated king would want to be summoned by the conqueror of the Middle East who brutally destroyed cities and whisked entire kingdoms into captivity? And if Nebuchadnezzar could be especially hard on leaders, what did he have in store for this final king of Judah?

But Zedekiah *could* have hope. The very king who locked up Jeremiah while his city was under siege now heard these heavenly words: "This is what the LORD says concerning you: You will not die by the sword; you will die peacefully."

The Lord actually promises this wicked king some dignity in death! Jeremiah may have wondered why. Maybe you do, too. After all, what had Zedekiah done to deserve a peaceful death? The answer, of course, is nothing. He had done everything to quicken his punishment of destruction. In his defiance, he had led his people away from the Lord. So why this blessing of an honorable death?

Because of David. For the sake of that servant king, his final descendant to sit upon Judah's throne would receive a portion of mercy from the Lord. His children, however, would not. "They killed the sons of Zedekiah before his eyes. Then they put out his eyes, bound him with bronze shackles and took him to Babylon" (2 Kings 25:7). Zedekiah's fate would be both a blessing and a curse. The final action his eyes would behold was the murder of his sons. At that point, a man wishes death on himself so his sons would live. Instead, their fire would be snuffed out, too. Like so many fathers on that day, Zedekiah would be forced to live in a world where the fires of the young are snuffed out and the flickering fires of the old burn on in sadness and despair.

The roaring flames of a youthful ministry can soon become a flicker, too. Teachers ready to set the world on fire face one cold bucket of water after another. Pastors wanting to turn their church and their people into the greatest of saints soon find their flame doused. Does the flame of your ministry appear to be going out? Do personal attacks, overwork, and volatile relationships threaten to extinguish your once strongly burning flame? Or perhaps your own shortcomings threaten your ministry even more. Pride and arrogance tempt the called worker to believe the flame of their service burns because of their own skill and effort rather than by the grace of God. Doubt in one's ability, or even all-out despair, threaten to snuff out ministry, too.

So what is left for you when your enemies have surrounded you and your sinful nature threatens your faith from within? Where is the hope? Take a lesson from Judah's last days. King Zedekiah's immediate family may have been extinguished, but the tribe to which they belonged burned on. Like a lone candle flame pushed by the wind, the tribe of Judah would endure their captivity by the grace of God. Hope endured.

Six hundred years and fourteen generations later, fires continued to burn in Jerusalem. These flames were not licking up the temple. No funeral pyre burned the memory of a recently dead king into the minds of the people. These were the harvest festival fires of ingathering. Towering over the people, these flames could be seen throughout the city of Jerusalem . . . and even beyond.

While everyone focused on these ancient festival celebrations, a man walked alone into Jerusalem. No one knew it yet, but his ancestors had once ruled this city. Their horses marched at the head of armies through the city gates, their heads were crowned in honor, and when their reigns ended, the funeral pyres burned their memory high into the sky.

It was this burning that the man would have noticed. He began teaching. Many started to listen. Others argued against him. The man talked about giving living water. Some called him a prophet. Others went so far as to label him the Messiah.

But as those four pillars burned brightly on that last day of the festival, as those fires reflected in the eyes of those looking upon this Messiah in the midst of his city, he spoke a message those people would have mulled over during their long, dark journey back home. "I am the light of the world. Whoever follows me will never walk in darkness, but will have the light of life" (John 8:12b).

What it must have been like to be a person in the crowd on that day! The promised Messiah had just revealed himself to be the Light of the world—the fulfillment of the very pillars of fire that had just been extinguished in Jerusalem. And more than that, as the sun set on the people walking home, as the thick darkness of their sins weighed heavy on their hearts, they realized that their light had dawned.

The fires of those ancient cities of Lachish and Azekah, and eventually even Jerusalem, had gone out so long ago. Yet another fire burned. The brilliance of this fire could not be outdone, even by the sun. This fire burned not only *for* people but *in* them.

Not long after the festival, this Light of the world would again journey to his ancestral city of Jerusalem. He entered his gates as the humble, peace-bringing king. Yet by the end of the week, he left his city carrying a cross. On that instrument of death, this Light of the world allowed himself to be snuffed out.

The darkness that followed must have been frightening to behold. The sun stopped shining. The earth shook. The rocks split. The dead who died in the Lord were raised. And Jesus' body was placed in a tomb. All hope appeared to be lost.

Then came the brilliance of Sunday. The tomb was open, the body gone. The Light of the world shone with a greater brilliance than anyone had ever seen. Jesus, the Light, revealed that darkness had been defeated.

The Babylonian fire that swept through Jerusalem so many centuries earlier, those countless funeral pyres, and the festive torches were all eventually extinguished. The harsh nature of those flames eventually gave way to the gentle brilliance of Christ.

Now his fire burns in you.

Jeremiah knew how that felt. "Is not my word like fire?" the Lord had once told him. The flames that burst forth from countless men and women in Christ's service now fuel you. That word of the Lord burns in your words and actions. Remain in it, even when you feel burned out. Look to the light of the word when the world turns dark around you.

And just you wait. The time is coming when we will see more than just a glimpse of the Light. Someday you will behold with your own eyes the brilliance of your eternal home: "There will be no more night. They will not need the light of a lamp or the light of the sun, for the Lord God will give them light" (Revelation 22:5).

Just you wait.

Prayer

"The Christ is ever with them; the daylight is serene.
The pastures of the blessed are ever rich and green.
There is the throne of David;
And there from care released,
The shout of them that triumph,
The song of them that feast.
To God enthroned in glory the church's voices blend,
The Lamb forever blessed, the light that knows no end." Amen.

—*CWS* 728:3

"I now proclaim freedom for you"

Jeremiah 34:8–22

Israel's emancipation from Egyptian slavery needed to begin with a washing away of the past. A god of a Pharaoh had rushed forward with hosts of soldiers speeding atop mighty chariots. So determined was this army that even the sight of the walling up of the Red Sea waters could not stop them. Chariots and horses flooded into the dry expanse, frantically chasing after their lost Israelite slaves. Then, all at once, the water walls came tumbling down. The true God crashed the Red Sea waters down upon them. Once-strong Egyptian men now floated lifelessly. Sharp, deadly iron began to rust. Chariots sped to the sea floor. And Egypt's godlike slave driver had been rendered a poor weakling.

Those destructive waters of the Red Sea not only washed away Israel's harsh slave past. They also served as a wall for the Israelites. They prevented backsliding Israel from returning to their Egyptian shackles. In perfect wisdom, the Lord had closed the backdoor to slavery. As illogical as it sounds, he knew the desolate wilderness would renew an Israelite yearning for Egyptian slavery.

Just days after their emancipation, that very yearning for slavery enticed the Israelites. Their Egyptian food had run out. So they cried out with empty bellies, "If only we had died by the LORD's hand in Egypt! There we sat around pots of meat and ate all the food we wanted, but you have brought us out into this desert to starve this entire assembly to death" (Exodus 16:3).

The people had already forgotten the hard slave work under the crack of those Egyptian whips. With sinful longing, God's people yearned to be enslaved once again. Backsliding ideals like this were a hallmark throughout Israel's history. Every time Israel turned back, slavery, in one form or another, remained the driving force.

Understanding Israel's affinity for sinful backsliding, the Lord established laws that safeguarded his people from themselves. In the wilderness, God commanded his people, "If you buy a Hebrew servant, he is to serve you for six years. But in the seventh year, he shall go free, without paying anything" (Exodus 21:2). One would think that as former slaves, the Israelites would welcome the opportunity to free one another from slavery every seventh year. Their motivation for emancipation was to stem from their own freedom God had won for them.

Yet this emancipation never seemed to come to fruition. Scour Israel's Old Testament history and you will fail to find any specific instance of masters releasing slaves in their seventh year of labor. It is not hard to surmise why. Masters thought they needed slaves to work their fields and serve in their homes. Everything looked as though it would fall apart if masters set slaves free arbitrarily.

Finally, after centuries of refusing to emancipate their slaves, the leaders of Judah relented. The scene Jeremiah witnessed must have appeared too phenomenal to be true. Walled up in Jerusalem, the wishy-washy King Zedekiah finally passed a positive, God-pleasing law. He "had made a covenant with all the people in Jerusalem to proclaim freedom for the slaves." Unlike many modern laws, this command of the king gave specifics. "Everyone was to free his Hebrew slaves, both male and female; no one was to hold a fellow Hebrew in bondage."

This year became the seventh year for every slave. However, the slaves themselves might have felt as skeptical about Zedekiah's motives as we do. The gesture of freedom seemed rather empty when they looked out beyond the walls of Jerusalem. The Babylonian army continued to enact their siege. These slaves were indeed free, but they had nowhere to go. Pessimistically, masters may have wanted to release their slaves so they did not have to feed them. Or perhaps Jerusalem's army needed more men to guard her walls. Needless to say, some of the slaves wondered how genuine their newfound emancipation was.

Yet the Lord shows through Jeremiah just how genuine the king's pronouncement of freedom was. "Recently you repented and did what is right in my sight: Each of you proclaimed freedom to your own people." There appeared to be no ulterior motives for Zedekiah's proclamation of freedom. In fact, the Lord tells us that the king "even made a covenant before me in the house that bears my Name."

This emancipation was legitimate. Jerusalem truly repented. Then came the backslide. "Afterward they changed their minds and took back the slaves they had freed and enslaved them again." The slaves had nowhere to run. Their masters forced them back into service. What could have been Jerusalem's "great year of freedom" had become their "year of the big backslide." And throughout all of it, King Zedekiah said nothing. His silence during Jerusalem's great "never-mind" to emancipation spoke volumes.

In reality, Zedekiah's Jerusalem had become just like Pharaoh's Egypt, chasing after the slaves they willingly freed, even in the midst of disaster. Pharaoh was willing to ride into walls of water to bring back his Israelite slaves. Zedekiah and Jerusalem's masters were willing to backslide on their emancipation even as Babylonian armies walled them up in their own city.

If the Lord's anger burned before, it was about to explode now. "This is what the LORD says: You have not obeyed me; you have not proclaimed freedom for your own people." Punishment now quickly approached. "So I now proclaim 'freedom' for you, declares the LORD—'freedom' to fall by the sword, plague and famine."

So who exactly *were* the slaves in Jerusalem? Looking through the eyes of the prophet Jeremiah, we see slaves everywhere. From King Zedekiah sitting on his royal throne to the masters who took their slaves back, and finally down to the lowliest slaves themselves, Jerusalem bustled with captives. Sin had enslaved the entire population. It was the worst kind of slavery because no one realized they were captured. And no seventh year could release Jerusalem from this bondage.

Is our backsliding any different? God had granted King Zedekiah and his Jerusalem leaders a wonderful opportunity to show love to those underneath them. Freedom to slaves illustrated a genuine repentance. But by revoking emancipation, the leaders exemplified a different type of leadership, a Pharaoh-like pursuit of selfish ideals.

Viewing slavery through the eyes of faith, Augustine once surmised, "He that is kind is free, though he is a slave; he that is evil is a slave, though he be a king."[1] As leaders in our community of believers, what are we exemplifying? Certainly each of us has fled back to slavery under sin. The words we use to speak out against our slavery to sin might sound genuine, but our actions speak even louder. Once Jerusalem's masters took back their slaves, the entire city saw their hearts clearly.

King Zedekiah witnessed the backsliding of the masters and said nothing. That temptation to silence ourselves when we see backsliding taking place can be difficult to avoid. But is that the loving action our Lord expects of us in the ministry? Are we to "live and let live" when we see others returning to sinful slavery? Here is what Paul forcefully reminds us: "For we know that our old self was crucified with him so that the body ruled by sin might be done away with, that we should no longer be slaves to sin" (Romans 6:6).

Freedom from sin means helping one another remain free from sin. As leaders and servants, we are given that blessedly arduous task of equipping God's people for works of service. This type of service in God's kingdom might feel like slavery. It might even *look* like slavery. Yet it is true freedom. "Live as free people, but do not use your freedom as a cover-up for evil; live as God's slaves" (1 Peter 2:16).

By the grace of God, that is exactly what Jeremiah did. Throughout this entire account, he faithfully continued to speak God's word to the people. He commended them when they repented. He warned them with God's law when they revoked their oaths. Through all of it, Jeremiah remained a captive of his own king. And yet, through all of it, Jeremiah remained a free man. He believed his Lord's promise to forgive his sins and set him free. And with that freedom in his Lord, he served.

By the grace of God, so do you. Do not let sinful backsliding become your hallmark. Instead, by virtue of your call, exemplify the freedom that enables you to serve. Your ministry will not always look like freedom. And it certainly will not always *feel* like freedom.

---

[1] Augustine, *The City of God*, translated by Marcus Dods (Overland Park: Digireads.com Publishing, 2017), 102.

Yet the humility that led Christ to the cross to set you free remains yours through the working of the Holy Spirit. Live that freedom, looking to the day when you will be free from your body of sin and raised up to the eternal freedom in heaven won for you by your great emancipator, Jesus Christ.

Prayer

"From thee I gladly all receive, And what is mine to thee I give; My heart, my soul, and all I own Let these be thine alone." Amen.

—CW 43:4

"Everything he ordered"

Jeremiah 35

What makes your family traditions so important? Were they seared into your heart at a young age? Did a certain tradition once anchor your ship at a time when everything else was sinking around you? If so, then you personally witnessed how family traditions have a way of reinforcing our foundations.

Human psychology seems to back up that assessment. Those who study how families function find a strong connection between unified families and those that follow traditions. I suppose that finding is pretty intuitive. The families that follow traditions together are usually stronger for it.

The importance of family traditions in Old Testament Israel also seemed intuitive. Israelite families gathered together at certain times of the year for a variety of reasons. Farmers planted and harvested at traditional times and in set ways.

Even death was treated traditionally. When an Israelite died, his family would surround him. Their subsequent wailing could compare to the cries of jackals (Micah 1:8). Some family members would even shave their heads (Micah 1:16), although the practice was forbidden by the Lord (Deuteronomy 14:1).

Family traditions like these wove the tapestry of Israelite families closer together. They brought about joy and engendered reminiscence. They aided families in grief. All in all, traditions usually *helped* families.

But not always. That Deuteronomy passage remains an important one. Knowing the strong pull of family traditions, the Lord warned his people against harmful traditions. "You are the children of the LORD your God. Do not cut yourselves or shave the front of your heads for the dead" (Deuteronomy 14:1). Certainly traditions had helped Israelite families, but there were times when they could also be harmful.

Jeremiah writes of one such Israelite family. Babylonian armies threatened the Rekabite tribal group's very existence. As many Israelite families did in those days, the Rekabites moved their families and homes within the protective walls of Jerusalem. In the midst of Judah's chaos, no one seemed to notice the fleeing family. No one, that is, except the Lord.

He commanded Jeremiah, "Go to the Rekabite family and invite them to come to one of the side rooms of the house of the LORD and give them wine to drink." Jeremiah had not hosted many gatherings, so this seemed to be a special occasion. Using a side room of the temple, Jeremiah invited this family to come and drink wine. That last part was an especially deliberate command of the Lord. He wanted Jeremiah to hear this family's response to the invitation.

"I set bowls full of wine and some cups before the men of the Rekabite family and said to them, 'Drink some wine.'" But the family refused. Such noncompliance might be construed as obstinance. At the very least their actions would probably cause offense. But it seems that the Rekabites were used to that possibility. They had refused wine before, and they were ready with their explanation. "We do not drink wine, because our forefather Jehonadab son of Rekab gave us this command: 'Neither you nor your descendants must ever drink wine.'"

That was quite a powerful command. One man, Jehonadab, who lived two and a half centuries before Jeremiah and these Rekabite descendants, commanded his entire family to not drink wine. And they obeyed! As if that command wasn't difficult enough, Jehonadab had given them another, even more difficult command to follow. "Also you must never build houses, sow seed or plant vineyards; you must never have any of these things, but must always live in tents." No wine, no buildings, no crops, always wandering.

Those family wanderings finally led the Rekabites to Jerusalem and Jeremiah. The prophet must have been amazed at the obedience of this family. After all, who of us have perfectly carried out the wishes of a loved one after their death?

Now the Lord wanted to show the rest of his people what that kind of commitment looked like. Speaking through Jeremiah, the Lord told the people of Jerusalem, "Jehonadab son of Rekab ordered his descendants not to drink wine and this command has been kept. To this day they do not drink wine."

This family tradition was not a bad one. It also was not mandatory. The Lord will not command Judah to become Rekabites and refuse wine while roaming as nomads. Instead, the focus is on their commitment to obedience. "I have spoken to you again and again, yet you have not obeyed me." God wanted the families of Judah to hold on to one important family tradition: obedience. "But you have not paid attention or listened to me." Disobedience had become Judah's longest-held tradition.

Families are not the only entities to hold on to traditions. Churches are families, too. The traditions found within the walls of your church can be found everywhere. They so permeate our worship experience that we hardly notice them at all. In fact, the only time we *do* notice traditions is when they are overlooked or removed. If a called worker removes a congregation's beloved tradition purposefully, their ensuing response might result in treating his actions as heresy.

That's what happened to me. I can still see the faces of my members who came to speak with me after the incident. I can still hear their angry words yelled into my face. I will always remember being told, "You will have to stand before God someday and tell him what you did here." My heinous crime, the action I will always be remembered for at that congregation, was daring to move our children's Christmas Eve service to the Sunday before Christmas Eve.

Silly, right? Why should such a thing matter? As a young pastor, I knew I was in the right. This tradition of my congregation could be changed just like any piece of adiaphora. But after hearing the emotionally charged responses from my members, I realized all too late that I had it all wrong. I had heartlessly ripped away a tradition my people cherished. I was thinking about *my* ministry instead of *our* ministry. I confess I have treaded on my members' consciences. I placed my wants above their needs. For those sins, and all of my ministerial shortcomings, I needed to once again flee to the cross of Christ, where his blood has mercifully washed them all away.

What about you? Have you mercilessly ripped away a piece of tradition firmly held by your congregation or school for your own sake? If you have, you probably met a similar resistance to what I faced. Perhaps you became bitter . . . maybe even vengeful. I certainly did. But remember, those are the wrong reactions. Previous called workers and their congregations developed those traditions for a good reason. If they do not go against scripture, and if they do not harm faith or set up road blocks to the gospel, then they have helped. Is there a better way you and your people could accomplish that portion of ministry? Probably. But your people have chosen this tradition, and they have grown to love it. Try not to mercilessly rip it away from them.

That is how the Lord treated his Rekabites. They had developed traditions for refusing wine, houses, and growing crops. The Lord's response to this was not a sermon on adiaphora. He refrained from explaining how Christian freedom can allow the family to throw out the rules they had been following. Instead, he used their obedience as an example for the rest of Jerusalem.

The Lord also blessed them for their obedience. "This is what the LORD Almighty, the God of Israel, says: 'Jehonadab son of Rekab will never fail to have a descendant to serve me.'" I sometimes wonder if that promise continues even today. Could there still be a Rekabite descendant somewhere in Christendom serving the Lord faithfully? Only the Lord knows.

Make faithful obedience your family tradition. Don't tread on the helpful traditions of your people. And if the Lord wills, through patient, prayerful consideration, perhaps he will allow you as a family of believers to begin new traditions founded on his word. Families of believers who place the word of the Lord at the center of their traditional daily life continue to hope for the Lord's Rekabite blessing, never failing to have a member to serve him.

Prayer

"You led our fathers to this land,
A land of beauty, bounty, pow'r;
You blessed the labors of their hands,
Upheld them in each trial hour.

You kept them faithful to your Word,
Were not ashamed their God to be.
So we, their children, gratefully
Now sing the hymn of jubilee." Amen.

—*CW* 535:2

"The king burned the scroll"

Jeremiah 36

A tardigrade is a *real* animal. Remember that, because its description sounds more like science fiction than scientific fact. Tardigrades are commonly known as "water bears." The name is deceptive, because they are quite tiny. The average size of these micro-animals stands equal to a letter on this page. But what they lack in size, they more than make up for in stamina.

If the existence of these little tardigrades threatened humanity (and thankfully, it does not), we would all be doomed. If we launched a tardigrade into the harsh, cold vacuum of space, it would live on. If we threw one in the oven and turned up the temperature as high as we could, the tardigrade would still be alive when we opened the door an hour later. We could sink them into the deepest, most pressurized trenches of the ocean and tardigrades would act as if nothing happened. Putting a tardigrade in the microwave wouldn't hurt it either. In fact, scientists are fairly certain that a nuclear bomb would not be able to kill one. The deadly radioactive fallout after the explosion would not hurt it either. We could try to starve them, but they can live without food or water for over thirty years.

Because of these almost omnipotent attributes, it might not surprise you that these animals have been found everywhere on earth, from active volcanoes to rainforests, from pressurized deep-sea trenches to the frozen mountains of Antarctica. But the most impressive tardigrade feature is its ability to survive what scientists call "mass-extinction events." An asteroid could hit the earth and wipe everything out, but not tardigrades. The sun could send a gamma-ray burst and push the world into chaos, but the tardigrade community would continue on as though nothing had happened. It is even theorized that if our sun would explode in a technicolor supernova, tardigrades could survive!

Science fiction has nothing on the water bear, which, as you may recall, is a *real* animal.

As frail and self-destructive as this world can be, the tardigrade proves there are some surprisingly durable creations in our Lord's earthly menagerie. The sun will continue to shine as long as humanity needs it. Earth's highest mountains stand as mighty, immovable fixtures on our horizons. The roaring waves of the seas continue to wash over our world and shape our coasts while rivers cut through dirt and rock. The wind constantly gusts over the plains as an unseen force.

But on one occasion, it looked as though every earthly constant became imbalanced. Noah witnessed this global upheaval firsthand. Within the safe confines of the ark, he heard the waters fall from the sky and burst out of the depths. He felt his boat rise above the highest mountains. He saw the sun blotted out by the falling water. Then, after a year on the ark, he heard the strong winds blow those destructive waters away.

By the grace of God, Noah and his family had survived this epic cataclysm with tardigrade-like resiliency! But that type of horrific experience can shake a man to his core. As Noah stepped out of the ark, he must have felt a little unnerved. Could he ever trust the constants of creation after what he lived through?

The Lord understood Noah's concerns. That is why he promised a physical foundation for Noah to stand on. "Never again will I destroy all living creatures, as I have done. As long as the earth endures, seedtime and harvest, cold and heat, summer and winter, day and night will never cease" (Genesis 8:21–22). In love, God established these earthly foundations for his traumatized Noah. Even today, thousands of years later, those blessings endure.

Jeremiah wasn't on that ark with Noah, but he had his moments of trauma, too. The only constant in his ministry was the pain of persecution and the frustration of rejection. He must have had his Noah moments of doubt, wondering if God's constants would really last. In a city doomed to destruction, under a king who wanted him dead, surrounded by people who hated him, Jeremiah may have wondered if the words he wrote would even last beyond his own life. Can God's word really be indestructible when the entire world is trying to destroy it?

The Lord brought this question into sharp focus when Jeremiah sent Baruch with his word to King Jehoiakim. The Lord had dictated the words to Jeremiah, who in turn recited them to his scribe, Baruch. Baruch, in turn, had written them down. It was now Baruch's duty to carefully carry those very words of God all the way to the king. Even though it was winter, by the time this scroll reached the king, it probably still looked to be in mint condition.

The Lord's entire purpose of sending Baruch centered on his gospel message. He even shared that purpose with his servants: "Perhaps when the people of Judah hear about every disaster I plan to inflict on them, each of them will turn from his wicked way; then I will forgive their wickedness and their sin." Even when wicked Jerusalem stood on the precipice of a disaster of their own making, the Lord yearned to lead them to repentance. He desired with all of his heart to grant them forgiveness.

Upon his arrival, Baruch first needed to read these words of the Lord to the king's officials. As Baruch recited God's words, concerned faces of the officials met one another in fear. By the end, they ominously stated, "We must report all these words to the king." Of course, that was the idea, but on this occasion neither Baruch nor Jeremiah would be the spokesperson. Instead, Jehudi stood before the king in his winter apartment. With the fire crackling in the foreground, Jehudi read one verse after another. After each set of verses, the king took his knife and coldly cut through the scroll, tossing it into the fire. Section after section burned before the king's gleeful eyes.

Grim and deliberate, the king continued this charade until the entire scroll was read, then cut, and then burned. Most in the room silently approved of the king's defiant actions. In fact, "the king and all his attendants who heard all these words showed no fear, nor did they tear their clothes." How the devil must have delighted in watching God's word burn. He knows how powerful that word can be, and as he haunts this earth, he wants nothing more than to rid himself of it. After all, these are the words that promise his demise and sentence him to the fires of hell for all eternity. Because he cannot avoid his own destruction, he continues to attempt the next best thing. He endeavors to destroy the words that remind him of his impending punishment.

Sinful humankind carries that same motivation. Why do you think the king would defiantly burn God's word? The physical ink and paper were harmless. Why should a powerful king worry about the scribbles of a sad, lonely prophet? The answer is pretty simple: those powerful words of the Lord struck the king's conscience. In a futile attempt to silence his internal objections, the king burned Jeremiah's scroll. Little did he realize that neither his conscience nor God's word could ever completely be destroyed.

Humankind's futile attempt to silence their consciences by destroying God's word continues today. The worst part of these attempts is that they *seem* to be working. Persecution of Christians and the silencing of biblical messages march on today as strong as ever. And there you are, a called worker of the Lord, wondering when it will all end. Perhaps you feel like Baruch, looking on the destruction of your faithful work and wondering what the point of all of it was. If they boldly destroy God's word, what is keeping them from ferociously hunting you down?

Is this how Noah felt before the flood—surrounded by the wicked violence of unbelief? Did he feel any safer after the floodwaters receded? Perhaps not. No wonder God blessed him with a solid promise upon which he could hold for the rest of his life. "Never again . . ."

The few believers standing around the king that day needed a solid promise like that. So did Baruch. And with the still, calm voice of one who is in complete control, the Lord spoke again to his prophet and his scribe. "Take another scroll and write on it all the words that were on the first scroll, which Jehoiakim king of Judah burned up." The Lord could dictate his word all day, every day, for all eternity. Try burning all *those* words up.

How the heart of the Lord must have broken that day. He had hoped for genuine repentance, only to be met with defiant obstinance. The account might have been one of those miraculous conversion chapters of scripture, like King Manasseh or the city of Nineveh or the apostle Paul. Instead, a greater message rises from the pages of

God's unburned verses. In the face of angry kings and cold officials, false prophets and defiant peoples, audacious indifference and blatant ignorance, the word of the Lord endures forever.

The Lord really created animals like the tardigrade. Nearly indestructible and almost unable to die, these animals might just outlive all of us today. But the tardigrade has nothing on the word of the Lord. Tardigrades live a long time, but the word of the Lord endures forever.

Prayer

"We have a sure prophetic Word By inspiration of the Lord,
And, though assailed on ev'ry hand, Jehovah's Word shall ever stand.
"By pow'rs of empire banned and burned, By pagan pride rejected, spurned,
The Word still stands, the Christian's trust, While haughty empires lie in
    dust.
"Whate'er the Word in times of old Of future days and deeds foretold
Is all fulfilled while ages roll, As traced on the prophetic scroll.
"Abiding, steadfast, firm, and sure, The teachings of the Word endure.
Blest all who trust this steadfast Word; Their anchor holds in Christ, the
    Lord." Amen.

—CW 291

"What crime have I committed?"

Jeremiah 37

Fyodor Dostoevsky might just be the most Russian of all Russian authors. His father was murdered. His mother died when he was fifteen. At the age of twenty-four, he published his first novel. Then he published his next one fifteen days later. After that, Dostoevsky's rise among Russian novelists was nothing short of meteoric. Then, just as quickly, Dostoevsky fell. He developed a gambling addiction and lost everything. Soon admirers found him begging for money on the streets.

Yet it was Dostoevsky's personal connections that led to his most harrowing experience. He had belonged to a literary group that was critical of the Russian tsar. When the authorities found him out, they sentenced him to death. Miraculously, at the last moment, Dostoevsky's sentence was commuted. He was then shown "mercy" by being banished to a Siberian prison camp, where he probably spent his days wishing he *had* been executed.

The experience was not wasted on Dostoevsky. In that prison, he realized a profound truth: "You can judge a society by how well it treats its prisoners."[1] Having been thrown into the confines of a brutal, murderous clan of criminals, the sensitive Dostoevsky judged his society harshly. He saw guards delightfully beating and murdering prisoners. He witnessed convicts coldly attacking and killing one another without a hint of remorse. In the midst of it all, Dostoevsky

---

[1] Fred R. Shapiro, *The Yale Book of Quotations* (New Haven: Yale University Press, 2006), 210.

felt he actually lived in a land of horrors. He called it the "house of the dead."

Dostoevsky's profound truth wasn't uniquely Russian. It continues to ring true throughout every culture and in every age. "You can judge a society by how well it treats its prisoners." The theory is that a truly selfless society will try to help its prisoners change their lives. On the other hand, a society that mistreats its prisoners, or doesn't care about them at all, is a society that doesn't really care about anyone.

This also true of individuals. You can peer deep into people's character by witnessing how they treat those under themselves. How does your date treat the waitress? If he derides her because of a small mistake during your dinner, you might not want to plan a second one. If she gets angry at the store clerk for an innocent error, it might be best for you to find a different companion.

Jeremiah had become Judah's Dostoevsky. After the Babylonian siege left Jerusalem, King Zedekiah and his people thought they were saved. The Lord promptly told Jeremiah that they were not. In a world where wars and rumors of wars often merged, God explained to Jeremiah where Nebuchadnezzar's army was actually marching. Egypt had once again rebelled, so they turned to first break Pharaoh's reed of an army and then vowed to return to Jerusalem to finish their conquest.

The Lord summarized Judah's situation with these memorable words: "Even if you were to defeat the entire Babylonian army that is attacking you and only wounded men were left in their tents, they would come out and burn this city down." Even if the Babylonian army consisted of one man, he alone could win the victory over Jerusalem. When the Lord stands behind an army, even an enemy army, victory is already won.

Knowing all of this, Jeremiah needed to act quickly. Back in chapter 32, the Lord had told Jeremiah to purchase his relative's field. This was his last opportunity to accomplish that transaction. But while Jeremiah walked through the Benjamin Gate, the captain of the guard noticed him. He had heard Jeremiah's "pro-Babylonian" prophecies and now saw him leaving the city after the Babylonians. He yelled at Jeremiah, "You are deserting to the Babylonians!" He arrested Jeremiah on the spot.

The guards prodded Jeremiah down into the dark recesses of Jerusalem's dungeons. Jeremiah was thrown into this "house of the cistern" with only his thoughts to keep him company. What might have passed by his mind's eye as he sat in the blackness of his cell? Perhaps he thought about how his obedience to the Lord's command had once again incurred persecution. Maybe he wondered how long his unjust imprisonment would last.

Then again, perhaps his thoughts led him to a Dostoevskian conclusion. After all, a person can find out quite a bit about a country by how he is treated as a prisoner. If Jeremiah's treatment as a prisoner indicated Judah's spiritual condition, then the hearts of God's people were as dark as the prophet's cell.

What dark secrets do you hold down in the hidden cell of your heart? What would it take for those true emotions and raw feelings to rise up and reveal the real self you have meticulously hidden away all these years? If a country can be evaluated by its prisoners, then what do the thoughts you hold hostage reveal about you?

Persecution has a way of setting that hidden anger in the cauldron of our hearts to a hot boil, bubbling over and burning everyone around us. Secret thoughts burst forth into vocal attacks. After our hearts finally cool down to a simmer, we realize all too late that we deserve imprisonment in the deepest, darkest cell.

If the persecutions we face seem harsh, just remember Jeremiah's situation. After preaching a Babylonian victory, the Lord commanded him to purchase a worthless piece of property, and while he was on his way to buy the land, he was captured. Jeremiah never seemed to catch a break!

But if Jeremiah's persecutions appear brutal, Jesus' suffering remained infinitely worse. You can tell a lot about a people by how they treat their prisoners. Riding into that same capital city of Jerusalem that once imprisoned Jeremiah, Jesus willingly allowed himself to be made our prisoner. Seeing everything grow dark around him, Jesus said to his captors: "But this is your hour—when darkness reigns" (Luke 22:53).

After a show trial, he let soldiers mock him and brutalize him. With his own people yelling at him, nails pierced the Savior's perfect flesh. As his cross rose up, he was spiritually cast down to the fires of hell. On top of a mountain, your Savior visibly endured the punishment for your secret sins. Nothing could be hidden from him so he in turn could wash away everything.

Where Jesus displayed perfect resiliency, his ancestor, King Zedekiah, epitomized perfect indecision. Sending for Jeremiah, the king asked his prophetic prisoner a remarkably selfish question: "Is there any word from the LORD?" He didn't care about how he had mistreated the prophet. He didn't care about the rest of his people. He wanted to make sure his own life was safe.

Jeremiah's answer was less than comforting: "Yes . . . you will be handed over to the king of Babylon." Zedekiah must have feared that fate more than any other. The king's silent contemplation gave Jeremiah the opportunity to speak about Jerusalem's lack of justice. "What crime have I committed against you or your attendants or this people, that you have put me in prison?" His next words might very well have been a final plea to Zedekiah—the kind of parting words you give when you realize you may never see a person again. "Where are your prophets who prophesied to you, 'The king of Babylon will not attack you or this land'?"

For the first time in his reign, King Zedekiah listened to Jeremiah. Jeremiah's prison cell opened up to the courtyard of the guard. Like Dostoevsky's transfer from death row to his Siberian prison, Zedekiah's measure hardly freed Jeremiah. But it didn't seem to matter. The storm clouds of a Babylonian siege were returning soon anyway.

Ministry can feel that way. Once-opportune offices soon feel like holding cells. Classrooms can make prisoners of teachers. When darkness descends, emotions run high. At those moments, a change of perspective is in order. View your ministry the way your Lord sees it. Feelings need to give way to faith.

You can tell a lot about your Lord by the way he treats those weaker than himself. Having sacrificed his one and only Son on your behalf, he now promises to strengthen you with his word, even when the iron bars of this world imprison you. He daily reminds you that your shackles have fallen. Your eternal sentence has been served. And the very One who took your punishment away will be with you always, just as he promised when he first read these words from the prophet Isaiah in his hometown synagogue: "The Spirit of the Sovereign LORD is on me, because the LORD has anointed me to proclaim good news to the poor. He has sent me to bind up the brokenhearted, to proclaim freedom for the captives and release from darkness for the prisoners" (Isaiah 61:1).

Jesus promised it: "good news . . . freedom . . . release." His fulfillment made you forever free.

Prayer

"Oh, how blest are they whose toils are ended,
Who through death have unto God ascended!
They have arisen From the cares which keep us still in prison.
"We are still as in a dungeon living,
Still oppressed with sorrow and misgiving;
Our undertakings Are but toils and troubles and heartbreakings.
"Come, O Christ, and loose the chains that bind us;
Lead us forth and cast this world behind us.
With you, th' Anointed, Finds the soul its joy and rest appointed." Amen.

—*CW* 554:1–2, 5

"The good of these people"

Jeremiah 38:1-13

How many lives have "greater good" arguments taken throughout the years? Local Roman authorities tortured and executed Christians for the greater good of their emperor-worshiping communities. Roman emperors Trajan and Domitian took the argument one step further. Both men ordered the execution of Christians throughout the empire, once again claiming their murderous actions supported the greater good.

Although historically on the receiving end of "greater good" persecutions, Christians too have succumbed to these cold, calculating arguments. Perhaps no one did more harm within Christianity under the guise of "greater good" principles than Pope Gregory VII. In a historically important conflict between church and state called the Investiture Controversy, Gregory claimed the title of God's chief representative on earth for the good of the church. This newfound papal supremacy led Gregory to demand other changes, too. He established the College of Cardinals to ensure the church elected popes instead of the state. Gregory went even further, forcing every active priest, married or single, to become celibate.

If the greater good remained the ultimate goal, then Pope Gregory VII could claim to be the most successful leader in church history. Yet the results of his "good" work reveal a very bad picture. With his claim of complete supremacy on earth, Gregory had created great rifts with state leaders. He had forced all of his priests to divorce from their families. And perhaps most unnerving of all, he had established a dangerous papal precedent of using the "greater good" to fulfill his own power-filled desires.

The wisest king of all, King Solomon, realized how dangerous well-intentioned individuals could be. He once wrote, "All a person's ways seem pure to them, but motives are weighed by the Lord" (Proverbs 16:2). The Lord has always been more concerned about our hidden motives than our outward show of actions. After all, believers can look very similar to unbelievers on the outside. However, on the inside, their motives for speaking and living could not be more different. The world allows the end to justify the means. Believers are to see their situations in an entirely different light. "Better a little with righteousness than much gain with injustice" (Proverbs 16:8).

Jeremiah's Jerusalem often desired much gain, and their last prophet always seemed to receive the consequent injustice that came with it. While under house arrest in the courtyard of the guard, Jeremiah refused to silently sulk. Anyone who walked through the area—and there must have been quite a few traversing through—would hear a mini sermon courtesy of the prophet. "This is what the LORD says: 'Whoever stays in this city will die by the sword, famine or plague, but whoever goes over to the Babylonians will live. They will escape with their lives; they will live.'"

No wonder why Jerusalem considered Jeremiah a Babylonian sympathizer! He promised life to those who fled to the Babylonians and a gruesome death to those who held fast to the walls of Jerusalem. Now death once again threatened Jeremiah. "The officials said to the king, 'This man should be put to death.'" One might wonder why the officials would even care about the words of a prophet they considered to be a raving lunatic. With Nebuchadnezzar slowly choking their city, perhaps Jeremiah was the only enemy they could defeat.

"He is discouraging the soldiers who are left in this city, as well as all the people, by the things he is saying to them." True, Jeremiah's words would discourage the loyal soldiers protecting the city—but that was the point. Jeremiah was telling these soldiers that they *should* be discouraged to fight against an army for which God had already declared victory.

But there was one other age-old argument these officials had to make to their king—and it would prove to be the most convincing. "This man is not seeking the good of these people but their ruin."

There it is, that ancient and dangerous "greater good" argument. Caught in the swirling storm of misperceptions, these officials, their soldiers, their people, even the enemy commander Nebuchadnezzar and his Babylonian army all thought their actions were leading to a greater good.

In the middle of that storm sat the calm, indomitable prophet Jeremiah. Of all the words that were spoken, of all the actions that were being undertaken in Jerusalem, only Jeremiah's could be considered "good." And his actions are labeled "good" only because they came from the Lord himself.

Upon hearing the treasonous charges against Jeremiah, King Zedekiah does what we have come to expect from him: nothing. "'He is in your hands' King Zedekiah answered. 'The king can do nothing to oppose you.'" Quite honestly, the king could have done whatever he wanted. The problem was that he did not want to do anything. He feared his officials, and his ensuing silence sentenced Jeremiah.

The guards grabbed the prophet and lowered him down into the base of a dried-up cistern. Upon reaching the bottom, Jeremiah slowly sank into the muddy floor. The confines of that sludge-filled dungeon may have been his worst punishment yet. Perhaps in those dark, dreary confines, the prophet considered how the word of the Lord had once again brought him personal punishment and grief. His words in the book of Lamentations seem to reveal what was going through his mind: "They tried to end my life in a pit and threw stones at me" (Lamentations 3:53).

Not every official approved of Jeremiah's silencing. A man named Ebed-Melech, a palace official, boldly approached King Zedekiah as he sat in the public forum of the Benjamin Gate. The location would afford this servant of the king an honest audience for his good intentions. "My lord the king, these men have acted wickedly in all they have done to Jeremiah the prophet. They have thrown him into a cistern, where he will starve to death when there is no longer any bread in the city."

The plea worked. The king ordered thirty men to lift Jeremiah back out of the pit. Carefully they sent ropes down covered with rags. Delicately they lifted the prophet back up into the land of the living. As Jeremiah's eyes adjusted to the streaming sun, he must have thanked the Lord for once again preserving him in the wake of his enemies' good intentions.

I know *you* have good intentions. As a follower of Christ, how can you not? But acting with good intentions can be a subtle poison. As we drink it down, we convince ourselves of its merit, its usefulness, and its effectiveness. Then, when the contamination becomes apparent, we learn all too late that our desire for the greater good came at too high a price.

What is the price of your good intentions? A pastor can start a new ministry in his church, making it sound effective through positive words and encouraging tones. But if it harms the souls he was called to care for, then he has done his people a grave disservice. The greater good claims another victim.

The teacher decides to change her approach in the classroom halfway through the first semester. This new design promises to educate children, wow parents, and illustrate just how great of a teacher he is. Then, as often happens in ministry, the plans flop. Children struggle. Parents become frustrated. But the teacher marches on, convinced her new approach will work. Good intentions have poisoned that ministry, sending innocent Jeremiahs careening down into the sludge of cisterns unseen.

To be clear, pastors and teachers *must* have good intentions. But we also must realize the difference between good intentions and the actual reason the Lord called us. Certainly we have all been guilty of using greater good arguments for personal gain. But it is precisely because of these ministerial shortcomings, these failures, these sinful desires for personal glory that our Lord descended from heaven. His good intentions perfectly fulfilled that first gospel promise in the garden of Eden. He humbly set aside his glory and gave himself up to eternal pain, torment, and death to win for you the *greatest good*.

That is what honest and good intentions look like. They show themselves in actions that glorify God even while humbling yourself. They live for building others up even to your own detriment. They give freely and never ask in return. They look outside of yourself.

You know what this greater good looks like. You've seen it before. It looks like Christ.

Prayer

"I come, O Savior, to your table, For weak and weary is my soul;
O Jesus, you alone are able To satisfy and make me whole.
Lord, may your body and your blood Be for my soul the highest good!
"Oh, let me loathe all sin forever As death and poison to my soul,
That I through willful sinning never May see your judgment take its toll!
Lord, may your body and your blood Be for my soul the highest good!
"Your heart is filled with fervent yearning That sinners may salvation see
Who, Lord, to you in faith are turning; So let me, too, come trustingly.
Lord, may your body and your blood Be for my soul the highest good!"
  Amen.

—CW 310:1, 4–5

"Do not hide anything from me"

Jeremiah 38:14–28

Recognizing the close of a literary circle can feel so fulfilling. When the final chapter of a long book ends, we often search for allusions to the book's beginning. Whether we realize it or not, we yearn to watch the narrative wrap around itself. A good author sentimentally taps into that desire. Emotions flood our senses as the conclusion draws on the almost-forgotten tidbits in the first chapter. It does not take much—just one word, one discarded item, or the memory of one individual for the ending to draw you back to the beginning with tears of joy.

Amazingly, history closes circles, too. The first major battle of the American Civil War, the First Battle of Bull Run, took place on a piece of land owned by a man named Wilmer McLean. The battle forced Wilmer and his family to move away to a small, out-of-the-way town called Appomattox. Owning no land, they found the town's courthouse to be a suitable living space where they could wait out the rest of the war. Then, on April 9, 1865, the war found the McLean family again. Robert E. Lee's Confederate army surrendered to General Grant's northern army there in the town of Appomattox. To make everything official, Lee and Grant met to discuss the terms of surrender in the Appomattox courthouse, the very building where Wilmer McLean was living. Noticing history's circle closing around him, Wilmer McLean later recalled, "The war began in my front yard and ended in my front parlor."[1]

---

[1] Joy Halkim, *War, Terrible War, 1855–1865*. (Oxford, UK: Oxford University Press, 2002), 139.

In scripture these literary and historical narratives fuse together into grand circles. Not only does the Lord delight to bring the beginning into the end of a historical event, but he also delights in writing down the account with a literary closed loop. As Moses and the Israelites marched toward the Promised Land, the Lord gave them an odd-sounding command: "In the seventh year the land is to have a year of sabbath rest, a sabbath to the LORD. Do not sow your fields or prune your vineyards" (Leviticus 25:4). The Lord attached a stern warning to this seemingly innocuous order. If the Israelites did not obey this command and leave the land fallow every seven years, then the Lord himself would make it happen. "Then the land will enjoy its sabbath years all the time that it lies desolate and you are in the country of your enemies" (Leviticus 26:34). Sadly, we never hear of any Israelite obeying this command.

Hundreds of years later, after Joshua conquered the Promised Land, after David defended it, after Solomon increased its wealth, the entire kingdom disobeyed God's command. So the Lord punished his people as he promised. Assyria and Babylon carried everyone off into captivity. And at the end of it all, the Lord uses one of the final verses of the book of 2 Chronicles to close the circle. "He carried into exile to Babylon the remnant . . . The land enjoyed its sabbath rests" (2 Chronicles 36:20–21).

Jeremiah and the rest of Jerusalem stood at the end of that loop. With destruction and captivity the Lord was about to close the circle. King Zedekiah must have seen that coming because he had Jeremiah secretly brought to an entrance of the temple. He needed a question answered. Somewhat surprisingly, the king added, "Do not hide anything from me."

Jeremiah saw the contradiction. "If I give you an answer, will you not kill me? Even if I did give you counsel, you would not listen to me." It was true. King Zedekiah had never listened to Jeremiah. All he ever seemed to want for Jeremiah was punishment and death. Perhaps enduring threats and contradictions like these had finally jaded Jeremiah. No one listened. Everyone threatened.

Ministry can often feel that way. A delinquent can pull you aside after coming to church for the first time in years, only to ask for a favor—or to tell you what you did wrong in the service. King

Zedekiah was that sort of a man. Now, at the end of his people and his kingdom, he needed to hear God's warning more than ever.

The historical circle surrounding God's people continued to turn in on itself. Jeremiah spoke God's word to the king of God's people at the very temple of God. How many prophets and priests and kings had gathered around God's word to accomplish God's will at that sacred location over the past centuries?

The scene where Jeremiah and Zedekiah stood had begun in a flourish of silent construction. King David had built her altar. Solomon finished the project, leading the ark of the covenant into the sanctuary. The people witnessed the fire and smoke that represented God's presence in his temple. King Jehoshaphat led his people in prayer at the temple gates when enemies marched toward them.

As the years passed, the temple's magnificence faded. Her altar fell into disrepair. David's descendant, King Hezekiah, brought God's people back to his temple. Then Josiah reformed them again.

At that ancient place, filled with historicity, stood Jerusalem's last prophet speaking with Judah's last king. And yet, the scene carried no pomp or grandeur. The crowds were gone. The enemy had come. And for the last time, God's prophet would speak God's word to God's king at the temple.

"If you surrender to the officers of the king of Babylon, your life will be spared and this city will not be burned down; you and your family will live. But if you will not surrender to the officers of the king of Babylon, this city will be handed over to the Babylonians and they will burn it down; you yourself will not escape from them."

King Zedekiah was afraid, but not for the reasons he should have been. He feared what his own people were capable of. If his own Jews could get their hands on him, they would mistreat him or even kill him. Jeremiah calmed his king one last time. "They will not hand you over."

Honestly, none of it mattered. Jeremiah needed to remind King Zedekiah what *did* matter: "Obey the LORD by doing what I tell you." It all harkened back to Moses' parting words to the Israelites as they were about to enter the Promised Land. After the Lord reaffirmed his covenant with his people, Moses reminded them: "When such a person hears the words of this oath and they invoke a blessing on themselves, thinking, 'I will be safe, even though I persist in going my own way"' (Deuteronomy 29:19). King Zedekiah had made that same mistake.

Now, because of Zedekiah's refusal to obey, God's earliest warning to his people was about to be fulfilled. Destruction approached. "All the nations will ask: 'Why has the LORD done this to the land? Why this fierce, burning anger?' And the answer will be: 'It is because this people abandoned the covenant of the LORD'" (Deuteronomy 29:24–25). It was all coming full circle.

In response to Jeremiah's final warning, King Zedekiah gave a final warning of his own to the prophet. "Do not let anyone know about this conversation, or you may die." In the face of God's spiritual warning, the king still threw out his physical threats. Zedekiah still cared more about what others thought rather than the desires of his Lord. In the end, it meant his undoing and Jerusalem's destruction.

Did all of this enter Jesus' mind when he arrived at the temple? Did he consider Moses' warnings or the history of David's altar or Solomon's beautiful words at the completion of the temple? Did Jesus think back to those final words between the much-maligned prophet Jeremiah and King Zedekiah? After all, if anyone understands the importance of completing circles and fulfilling promises, it is Jesus.

As the Prophet, Jesus entered his ancient capital, preaching God's word to his same old obstinate people. As Israel's Great High Priest, Jesus came to that temple and then hung on our cross as our perfect Lamb of sacrifice. As Israel's King, our risen and ascended Lord now reigns over all things for the good of those who love him. He reigns in you.

The end calls back to the beginning. Jeremiah would watch his Jerusalem burned and obliterated. He would see his people scattered. Pain and sadness and misery and death would continue to reign . . . until the return of the King.

This is what his perfect reign looks like: "He who was seated on the throne said, 'I am making everything new!'" (Revelation 21:5). No more distance, no more pain, no more sadness, no more death. "God's dwelling place is now among the people, and he will dwell with them. They will be his people, and God himself will be with them and be their God. He will wipe every tear from their eyes. There will be no more death or mourning or crying or pain, for the old order of things has passed away" (Revelation 21:4).

It does not take much, just one word or phrase, one discarded item—"sabbath rest, tears wiped away, a new Jerusalem"—and the ending draws you back to the beginning with tears of joy. Recognizing the close of a literary circle, especially when Jesus is the one closing it, can feel so fulfilling.

Prayer

"There is a higher throne than all this world has known,
Where faithful ones from every tongue will one day come.
Before the Son we'll stand, made faultless by the Lamb;
Believing hearts find promised grace; salvation comes.
Hear heaven's voices sing; their thunderous anthem rings.
Through emerald courts and sapphire skies their praises rise.
All glory, wisdom, power, strength, thanks, and honor are
To God our King who reigns on high forevermore." Amen.

—*CWS* 727:1

"Because you trust in me"

Jeremiah 39

After thirty months under the Babylonian siege, after ten years, four months, and nine days under King Zedekiah's governance, after 424 years of rule under King David's descendants, and after 820 years of living in the Promised Land, everything finally came crashing down. On July 18, 586 BC, Nebuchadnezzar's army finally broke through the thick walls of Jerusalem that had turned away so many other invaders. The Hebrew poet Asaph describes the infamous scene as one who witnessed it firsthand: "They have defiled your holy temple, they have reduced Jerusalem to rubble" (Psalm 79:1). The dead carpeted the streets: "left . . . as food for the birds of the sky" (79:2). Blood saturated Jerusalem's ground: "poured out blood like water all around Jerusalem" (79:3).

When Jerusalem needed their kingly descendant of David the most, Zedekiah had abandoned them. The very sight of Nebuchadnezzar's officers had frightened him even more than death, so he and his soldiers "left the city at night by way of the king's garden." Swiftly and quietly they headed toward the Arabah, hoping they could live to fight another day.

They never made it. "The Babylonian army pursued them and overtook Zedekiah in the plains of Jericho." Bound in the chains he so dreaded, Zedekiah now faced the man he feared so much. Nebuchadnezzar pronounced his sentence to him and then swiftly carried it out. Zedekiah's sons were killed before his own eyes. That murderous act would be the last Zedekiah ever saw as the Babylonians blinded Judah's last king and pulled him in shackles to Babylon.

Fire destroyed the rest of Jerusalem. As the flames burned through farms and palaces, as walls crashed down and screams rang off the rubble, the prophet Jeremiah found himself in the midst of a hell on earth. There God's servant stood, still bound to the courtyard of the guard.

But Jeremiah was not forgotten. Nebuchadnezzar had given a command about him: "Take him and look after him; don't harm him but do for him whatever he asks." For the first time in a long time, Jeremiah was allowed to return home.

The Lord had prophesied all of it. Just before the walls gave way to the invading army, the Lord told his bound and battered prophet, "I will save you; you will not fall by the sword but will escape with your life." Then he told Jeremiah why: "Because you trust in me."

Armed with the Lord's promise of protection, Jeremiah stood tall while the rest of Judah was bowed low. He remained one of the few the Babylonians allowed to return home. The chapter adds, "So he remained among his own people." Whether their poor circumstances kept Jeremiah's kin at home or it was the mercy of Nebuchadnezzar, the entire extended family was allowed to stay home.

Was this what Jeremiah wanted? The prophet seemed to be silent. Certainly he had much to think about. Having witnessed his king's blatant disregard for God's warning, having seen the walls come down and the Babylonian swords swinging through his countrymen, Jeremiah may have sat silent in deep grief. Who could blame him? Like Cassandra in Troy, Jeremiah had warned his people for years that this destruction was coming and no one listened. Even his own family had rejected him and his message.

Jeremiah's trip back home seems to have been a difficult one. As one of the sole survivors of the worst day in the history of his people, Jeremiah's guilt might have taken hold at that point. The grief he felt over the destruction he witnessed finally burst forth in the longest series of laments in scripture. "Is it nothing to you, all you who pass by? Look around and see. Is any suffering like my suffering that was inflicted on me, that the LORD brought on me in the day of his fierce anger? From on high he sent fire, sent it down into my bones" (Lamentations 1:12–13).

These are the cries of a survivor who feels as though he died anyway. Perhaps in a way he did. Jeremiah's Jerusalem ministry had ceased. Some might ask the Lord at that point "What now?" Jeremiah's grief would not even allow him to ask the question. "See, LORD, how distressed I am! I am in torment within, and in my heart I am disturbed, for I have been most rebellious. Outside, the sword bereaves; inside, there is only death" (Lamentations 1:20).

How is a minister supposed to feel when he outlives the very place where he ministered and the people he shepherded? A sort of ministerial survivor's guilt seems to be a natural conclusion in such circumstances. Guilt living that deep within a person often defiantly remains until death itself dislodges it.

In 1987, Northwest Airlines flight 255, a large passenger plane, crashed shortly after takeoff from an airport in Michigan. Newspapers around the world labeled it one of the deadliest airplane tragedies in history. Everyone on board, 154 people, died in the crash . . . except for one little four-year-old girl. A rescuer had been frantically digging through the burning wreckage when he heard her whimper. Apparently, her mother had covered the girl during the crash, using her own body as a shield to protect her daughter.

That little girl is now an adult. Every day she lives with what psychologists call "survivor guilt." Her mind asks the question every day, "Why me?" Jeremiah knew exactly how she felt. "I am in torment within; my heart is poured out on the ground because my people are destroyed, because children and infants faint in the streets of the city" (Lamentations 2:11).

Perhaps you know how that feels, too. Christians today see spiritual destruction everywhere. When the Lord calls faithful, longtime members home to heaven, a hole in the church is left. Pastors see empty pews where families once happily sat hearing the word. Many of those families have become busy with other priorities. Teachers who remember their school rooms bursting to the seams now have too many desks and too few students.

After the frustration over the situation subsides, guilt always seems to remain. So many have been called home to heaven or have fallen away, yet there you stand, a ministerial survivor. Go ahead, ask the question: "Why me?" But be honest about the answer. If left to your own devices, you too would be long gone. Jeremiah added honesty to his lamentations by admitting who he was by nature. "The crown has fallen from our head. Woe to us, for we have sinned!" (Lamentations 5:16).

The guilt of his sins hung heavy around Jeremiah's neck. The Lord had allowed him to survive the destruction of his people, but Jeremiah knew he did not deserve his rescue. That added more guilt, increasing the spiritual weight yoked to him.

But perhaps dying inside helped dislodge the weight of that guilt living deep within the prophet. In the middle of that rubble and smoke and death, Jeremiah once again looked up to his Lord in faith. God had not rescued him to make him feel guilty. He was not meant to live in perpetual lamentation. Quite the contrary. In the middle of Jeremiah's lamentations stood his sure and certain hope. "For no one is cast off by the Lord forever. Though he brings grief, he will show compassion, so great is his unfailing love" (Lamentations 3:31–32).

Further tragedy was on the horizon for Jeremiah and his fellow survivors. Tragedy hovers above your horizon, too. But as you lament this wicked world and the loss of fellow believers, make sure to not weep as those who have no hope. Like Jeremiah, your hope rises out of the dust of your lamentations. The rubble of the old Jerusalem will give way to the strong walls of your New Jerusalem. Ashes will rise to perfection. Temporary tears of sadness will turn to eternal tears of joy.

Prayer

"Oh, come, oh, come, Emmanuel, And ransom captive Israel
That mourns in lonely exile here Until the Son of God appear.
Rejoice! Rejoice! Emmanuel Shall come to you, O Israel!

"Oh, come, O Root of Jesse, free Your own from Satan's tyranny;
From depths of hell your people save, And bring them vict'ry o'er the grave.
Rejoice! Rejoice! Emmanuel Shall come to you, O Israel!" Amen.

—CW 23:1–2

"Today I am freeing you"

Jeremiah 40

Sometimes the Lord packages a familiar message in an unlikely container, and the effect can be jarring. In the God-forsaken city of Tyre, a Gentile woman desperately pleaded with Israel's Savior to help her demon-possessed daughter. She probably never expected to actually see the Savior in her town. She certainly did not expect to see this side of the Savior. When the distressed woman begged Jesus for help, Jesus feigned refusal. The heartless appearance might have shocked some—but not Jesus' disciples. They piled on. The cries of the frantic woman were starting to annoy them. They wanted Jesus to dismiss her like some disinterested earthly king might dismiss a beggar.

But Jesus held back. Sometimes all the lights need to turn off before we can see what truly shines. "It is not right to take the children's bread and toss it to the dogs" (Matthew 15:26). Jesus just called this loving mother and her dying daughter "dogs"! He insinuated that they did not deserve the life-giving food he possessed. And if all of this was not harsh enough, Jesus told her that he was not sent to this world for her kind of people. Do you see the light dimming? Can you hear the switch click off?

Now see what really shines.

"Even the dogs eat the crumbs that fall from their master's table" (Matthew 15:27). Her Savior must have smiled. This undeterred, Gentile mother just let the light of her faith shine in her completely darkened world. The Light of the world could now chase her darkness away. "Woman, you have great faith! Your request is granted"

(Matthew 15:28). Sometimes the Lord packages a familiar message in an unlikely container.

The Lord had just turned off the lights in Jerusalem. The spreading darkness of bondage and captivity awaited those sad Jewish survivors. Palaces, homes, and even God's temple lay broken along Jerusalem's ancient streets. Empty altars stood silent. Ash replaced incense, rising from the rubble.

Nebuzaradan, the commander of Babylon's imperial guard, marched Jewish captives out of this desolate picture. Chained with the rest, the prophet Jeremiah stood with his people at the Babylonian staging ground in Ramah. They all awaited their fate.

Then a message came for Jeremiah. It was wrapped in the most unlikely container. The commander Nebuzaradan found Jeremiah and said, "The LORD your God decreed this disaster for this place. And now the LORD has brought it about; he has done just as he said he would. All this happened because you people sinned against the LORD and did not obey him." Jeremiah heard the word of the Lord echoed back to himself from this heathen commander!

Although he knew the word better than anyone, he also needed to hear it. Chained and bound for Babylon, Jeremiah might have wondered if these were the final days of his ministry. So his loving Lord repeated his message through Nebuzaradan.

Better news followed. The commander told Jeremiah, "Today I am freeing you from the chains on your wrists. Come with me to Babylon, if you like, and I will look after you; but if you do not want to, then don't come." Of all God's people, from those carried off to those killed off, not one of them was granted a release like Nebuzaradan had just granted to Jeremiah. No one in Judah could have known how Jeremiah felt at that moment.

But you do. Do you remember hearing the phone ring on a Sunday afternoon? The number did not look familiar. Your spouse quickly shot you a knowing look. In the moment, both of you knew the person on the other line would either be Grandma calling from a new cell phone or the chairman of a faraway congregation. And sure enough, the male voice on the other line instantly indicated the latter. As you heard the details, your heart probably skipped from excitement to uncertainty to fear and perhaps ultimately ending in dread.

The Lord blessed you with a call to serve another congregation! But it perhaps did not feel like a blessing at that point. What would you decide? Your people probably came to you with a lot of advice—some worthwhile, others well-intentioned. By the end of the three to four weeks of deliberation, you probably learned quite a bit about yourself, about your people, and about the congregation or school that sent you the call.

Then again, perhaps you still felt lost. Calls do that to a servant. They force you to look at situations and circumstances that you otherwise would never even glance at. Your sinful nature becomes exceedingly active at those times, too. Selfishly, it pushes you to take the easier-looking call, or the school with less conflict, or the congregation without any perceived problems.

Which choice would have led Jeremiah to an easier future? Journeying into captivity in Babylon may actually have led to more pleasant prospects. Nebuzaradan implied as much when he told Jeremiah, "I will look after you." But it seemed the Lord had other plans for Jeremiah. Then again, it seems that Nebuzaradan did, too. "Before Jeremiah turned to go, Nebuzaradan added, 'Go back to Gedaliah . . . and live with him among the people, or go anywhere else you please." Jeremiah's path seemed to lay itself out before him.

The Lord knew which path Jeremiah would choose before he even created the world. Yet in love, he allowed Jeremiah to wrestle with the decision himself. Eleven years earlier, when other Jews were being carried off into captivity, the Lord had his prophet write a loving promise down in a letter for the exiles. It included this passage: "'I know the plans I have for you,' declares the Lord, 'plans to prosper you and not to harm you, plans to give you hope and a future'" (Jeremiah 29:11).

The Lord had encouraged Jeremiah through the unlikely words of Babylonian commanders and even his own writings. The Lord does that more than we might think. Sometimes the Lord packages a familiar message in an unlikely container.

When that call comes your way, you need not look for hidden messages or wait for God's voice to tell you from heaven which choice you ought to make. In his wisdom, he gives you family members and friends who know you well enough to give you appropriate encouragements as you deliberate the calls he has blessed you with.

Most loving of all, God still gives you the choice. And in the end, your decision cannot be wrong. Now certainly, a call decision can be made with the wrong motives. Called workers have even been known to renege on their decision after making it. One memorable servant of the Lord even fled the decision completely, climbing aboard a boat only to be washed into the belly of a fish and spit out toward his destination anyway.

We have every reason to believe Jeremiah took these choices seriously. No doubt he prayed to the Lord for guidance, strength, wisdom, and humility. In the end, Jeremiah chose to stay, and the Lord's will was accomplished.

The Lord continues to accomplish his will in your ministerial decisions as well. When the call comes your way, when the important life decisions arrive at your doorstep, wrestle with them seriously, consider them prayerfully, and thank the Lord for his continuing grace humbly. Remember that your Lord plans to prosper you, not to harm you. He gives you a sure and certain hope, a future both here and in eternity. For the faithful servant of the Lord who honestly considers his call, the answer is always God-pleasing.

Prayer

"O Christ, who sent the Twelve
On roads they'd never trod
To serve, to suffer, teach, proclaim
The nearer reign of God:
Send us on ways where faith
Transcends timidity,
Where love informs and hope sustains
Both life and ministry." Amen.

—CWS 770:3

"Do not be afraid to serve"

Jeremiah 40:7–41:15

Jerusalem's prophet had decided to stay back with his people. The Babylonian commander Nebuzaradan must have been happy about that. He had just appointed Gedaliah to be the governor of the poor souls left behind in Judah, and the position was not an enviable one. Enemies of Judah and foes of Babylon lurked everywhere in the wake of Jerusalem's destruction. Babylon needed a strong, faithful leader to stabilize the entire region. Gedaliah was to be that man, but he needed help.

From King Josiah to King Jehoahaz to King Jehoiakim to King Jehoiachin and finally to King Zedekiah, the prophet Jeremiah had served as God's mouthpiece to more rulers than most. Now, amid the rubble of Jerusalem's collapsed monarchy, the Lord once again called upon his prophet to assist a leader of Judah. This time, however, the situation appeared entirely different. This man seemed far different from his kingly predecessors.

At the beginning of his service, the governor Gedaliah introduced himself to his people with these words: "Do not be afraid to serve the Babylonians." Needless to say, no king of Judah ever uttered words like those—especially not while taking his oath of office! "Settle down in the land and serve the king of Babylon, and it will go well with you."

If his encouragement sounds familiar, it is because you have heard it before. Jeremiah wrote a similar encouragement to the exiles: "Seek the peace and prosperity of the city to which I have carried you into exile. Pray to the LORD for it, because if it prospers, you too will prosper" (29:7). Seeking peace and prosperity for your conqueror was easier said than done for God's people. Remember, Judah's world-view had just irrevocably changed. Everything they knew, and most of the people they loved, had been destroyed right in front of their eyes. The physical foundations of their culture that had existed for hundreds of years—their king, their kingdom, their sacrifices, their temple—had disintegrated at the hands of the Babylonians. For the first time in their lives, they would grapple with what it meant to serve a foreign ruler who believed in false gods.

To a certain extent, Jeremiah already knew what that felt like. For years he served as God's spiritual emissary to the kings of Judah. One by one, he warned them to cease their idolatry. He pointed them back to the true God. He even prayed on their behalf. Now idolatrous Babylon ruled in place of Jerusalem's idolatrous kings. The names were different, but the command remained the same. God expected his people to serve their rulers faithfully.

However, a shift in worldview can prove too much for many. The dark days of Jerusalem's destruction would grow darker still, with some individuals deciding to take matters into their own hands. As Jews streamed back into the region of Judah, bad news accompanied them. A man named Johanan, an army officer still operating in the region, brought the shocking information: "Don't you know that Baalis king of the Ammonites has sent Ishmael son of Nethaniah to take your life?"

The message was unbelievable—or at least, Gedaliah did not believe it. Even when Ishmael and his ten men arrived to eat with Gedaliah, Judah's new governor remained skeptical of evil intent. Then, all at once, Ishmael and his men stood up, drew their swords, and killed Gedaliah. Then they fanned out and killed every Jew associated with Gedaliah, even those bringing offerings.

Those Ishmael kept alive probably wished they had died. Jeremiah tells us that "Ishmael made captives of all the rest of the people." The army officers who had warned Gedaliah about Ishmael's intentions caught the group and freed the families. Although Ishmael escaped, justice was momentarily restored.

What was the prophet Jeremiah to think about all of this? No sooner had Judah lost her king than the entire region devolved into chaos. Would a wise, God-fearing leader ever arise?

We continue to ask that question today. If you wait for good earthly leaders to arise, you may be waiting forever. The political streams, for the most part, continue to powerfully flow away from God's word. Betrayal, back-stabbing, and fear are considered worthy instruments to use in the pursuit of power. Perhaps that is why the phrase "Christian politician" has become more of an oxymoron than a reality.

What is a called worker to think about all of this? The ancient wisdom both Gedaliah and Jeremiah expressed continues to stand: "Seek the peace and prosperity of the city to which I have carried you into exile. Pray to the LORD for it, because if it prospers, you too will prosper" (29:7). The message is as clear today as it was when Jeremiah first spoke it. Settle down and serve your rulers, even when you disagree with their policies and rhetoric. Jeremiah and Gedaliah hardly walked in spiritual lockstep with their Babylonian conquerors. Yet Gedaliah rightly commanded the few remaining Jews to live faithfully. As the next chapters indicate, if conquered peoples walk the road to rebellion, there is no turning back.

Rebellion seems to mar many American establishments. No sooner do we unite under one banner than divisions and factions form. And yet, through all of these political and social battles, most consider rebellion a worthy ideology! The world has come to expect rebellion. God expects quite the opposite: "Whoever rebels against the authority is rebelling against what God has instituted, and those who do so will bring judgment on themselves" (Romans 13:2).

Christians can become quite adept at spotting secular rebellion and avoiding it. But hidden, deceptive rebellions within a church can be far more difficult see, and much more enticing. What do you feel like doing when a member of your church openly criticizes something you have done? In the heat of the moment, our sinful nature wants to fire back an even worse accusation. After days of considering his words, the cold, calculating retributions begin to form. We consider how to remove this thorn of a person. Ostracization, malicious gossip, and removal from the church all become enticing means to this end.

Families in your school are capable of these same criticisms. Some will be founded, others fabricated. Your sinful nature urges you to find a reason to remove the children of difficult families under the guise of some disciplinary loophole.

These are not the responses of faithful called workers. Pastors and teachers do not remove members they refuse to get along with.

Ministry is not a zero sum game marked by the charred ground of your scorched-earth policies. You have not been called to divide the sheep how you see fit. The Lord called you to serve your sheep, whether they faithfully follow or brazenly bellow. To attempt to reform your church and school in your own image soon becomes akin to Ishmael's audacious assassination of Gedaliah. How many spiritual removals will it take before your ministry becomes like Jerusalem—a smoking husk of division, destruction, and emptiness?

You have been called to serve faithfully in the midst of this increasingly divisive world. And you have been called by increasingly divisive congregations and schools. But do not use these divisions as an excuse to act out in kind. Use God's word to mend these divisions so that you and your flock can live in the unity the Holy Spirit desires.

Jeremiah knew exactly how it felt to serve in the midst of rifts like these. The Lord had him speak patiently, but boldly, to kings who refused to listen and priests who wanted him dead. The Lord's prophet listened to false prophets attack his message and his character. It all could have been enough to make Jeremiah lash out against them with the type of carefully selected words that assassinate character and destroy individuals. It also could have led him into despair and the temptation of giving up altogether.

Thanks be to God, Jeremiah remained faithful. After seeing his own family betray him, his city destroyed, and his last leader assassinated, Jeremiah continued to speak God's word. In a way, it made him the calm in the middle of Judah's storm. The Lord promises to help you become that calm in the midst of your ministerial storms, too. When words cut you down and your character is attacked, when your family is threatened and hostile divisions rekindle among your people, flee to the word. Don't get caught up in the storm. Listen to the calm voice of the One who always remains in control: "Be still, and know that I am God" (Psalm 46:10).

Prayer

"How good it is and how pleasant to live in unity and peace.
How good it is and how pleasant to live together in one Lord." Amen.

—*CWS* 773:1

"Destined for death"

Jeremiah 41:16–43:13

The narrator of the classical work *Moby Dick* begins his story by asking the reader to call him "Ishmael." If you know the ending, you might simply call him "doomed." Throughout the book, the intelligent Ishmael struggles as a worker aboard the *Pequod* who is surrounded by a superstitious crew under the leadership of their obsessed captain, Ahab.

The novel immerses Ishmael and the reader into a world weighed down heavily by death. The bones of whales adorn Ahab's ship. A man aboard another ship prophesies doom for those on the *Pequod*. And the darkest cloud of all arrives when Ahab ominously declares his intent to kill Moby Dick, the famous white whale responsible for the deaths of countless sailors. It seems Ahab's very fanaticism is cursed. Men start accidentally falling off the ship. A hurricane nearly sinks the *Pequod*. Some go crazy. Fear grips others.

As Ahab sails his crew closer to the ocean swells of Moby Dick's territory, he meets ships sailing the other way. Each one had recently run into Moby Dick, barely escaping with their lives. Undeterred, Ahab sails on. Finally, he and his crew meet the great white whale. Over the course of two days, Ahab and his men grapple with the large beast. On the third day, the whale rams the boat, sending it to the depths of the ocean. Ahab strikes back, hitting the beast with his harpoon. However, in the midst of the battle, Ahab becomes caught in the line. Moby Dick drags the obsessed captain by his own harpoon down to the depths of the sea. At the end of it all, the entire ship and her crew are lost, except Ishmael. Having been thrown from the ship, he stayed afloat on top of his crewman's coffin.

Captain Ahab's obsession had led him and his crew into certain death. Countless warnings indicated their fate, yet the unquestioning crew sailed on behind their defiant leader. And there was poor Ishmael, caught with the crowd in their doomed battle against that white whale.

Jeremiah must have felt like Ishmael. The Ishmael of Jeremiah's day appeared more like the vengeful Captain Ahab. He had assassinated Judah's governor, Gedaliah, and captured an entire group of people. It took an army officer, Johanan, and his men days to find and defeat the assassin, Ishmael, and free the people he captured.

Now death hung heavy in the air. Who wanted to explain to the Babylonians that their handpicked leader had just been assassinated? Fearing the worst, the group called upon their aging, weather-beaten prophet Jeremiah for advice. "Pray that the LORD your God will tell us where we should go and what we should do."

Jeremiah agreed. However, the group's prayers for guidance were met with heavenly silence. Ten whole days passed without a message from the Lord. Finally, the word of the Lord came to the prophet Jeremiah: "If you stay in this land, I will build you up and not tear you down; I will plant you and not uproot you, for I have relented concerning the disaster I have inflicted on you." No one expected to hear these words from the Lord. In the wake of Jerusalem's disaster and Gedaliah's murder came the Lord's promises of strength and comfort. "Do not be afraid of the king of Babylon, whom you now fear . . . for I am with you and will save you and deliver you from his hands." Even at this late date in Jeremiah's ministry, these words may have sounded familiar to him. The Lord gave a similar promise to Jeremiah the day he called the young man to be his prophet. Now in these dark days, everyone needed that firm promise of the Lord.

The Lord knew his people needed his help. He understood the situation. He saw the families packing their bags, ready to make an exodus to Egypt. So he added a strong warning. "However, if you say, 'We will not stay in this land,' and so disobey the Lord your God . . . 'If you are determined to go to Egypt and you do go to settle there, then the sword you fear will overtake you there, and the famine you dread will follow you into Egypt, and there you will die." The Lord's words could not have been clearer. Stay and live or leave and die.

"You are lying!" came the defiant response of the arrogant leaders. As God's people had threatened for nearly a thousand years, so Johanan now led his people back to the perceived safety of Egypt. The Egyptian strength Johanan expected would prove to be a mirage. Once again, Jeremiah's ministry would appear to be driven by the arrogant and the disobedient.

This time, however, Jeremiah and his scribe, Baruch, could not walk away from Judah's sinful consequences. "They took Jeremiah the prophet and Baruch son of Neriah along with them." Like Ahab pulling Ishmael into his cataclysmic battle against the white whale, Moby Dick, so Johanan forced Jeremiah and his scribe to make the journey to Egypt, too.

Ominous reminders of death appeared everywhere. The Lord had Jeremiah take large stones and bury them at Pharaoh's palace as a sign for Nebuchadnezzar. "He will come and attack Egypt, bringing death to those destined for death, captivity to those destined for captivity, and the sword to those destined for the sword." Even Egypt's monumental preoccupation with death should have been a reminder to God's people of the death their defiance was leading them into.

If some of the group were destined for death, and others were headed for captivity, then what was Jeremiah's destiny? He was simply a hostage forced on this death march out of Johanan's superstitious presuppositions. Why should he get dragged down to death?

Ministry sometimes feels like Jeremiah's hostage situation. The prideful and arrogant rule the day and pull you along, refusing to heed your warnings. Even previous failings no longer deter them. Jeremiah's group had just witnessed the destruction of their people, their city, and their temple at the hands of the Babylonians *because* Judah had refused to listen to God's warnings. Now, just three months later, they once again refused to listen to God's warnings in order to flee into Egypt!

So why would the Lord let this defiant group take Jeremiah and Baruch? Once again we remember that the Lord can use one situation for the benefit of all involved. The group needed Jeremiah to speak God's law faithfully. They needed Baruch to write down that word for them, both as a reminder and as an indictment. And in a strange way, Jeremiah needed the situation as well. Looking at the entirety of Jeremiah's ministry, one gets the impression that Jeremiah could have been lost in the temptations of an easy ministry. The Lord used the difficulty of Jeremiah's surroundings to focus him back on the Lord and the efficacy of his word.

We need those reminders as well. Ministry is messy and maddening and heartbreaking. Preaching God's word to sinners can be fierce and frustrating and depressing. Teaching sinful students can feel like Jeremiah's hostage situation as arrogant and defiant parents and students throw up roadblocks to your ministry. Every one of these hardships makes ministry difficult on an almost-daily basis.

But if we honestly describe our people, we should also honestly characterize their called workers. In the midst of messy ministry, servants of the word can become arrogant and pharisaical too. Like a doctor looking down on his sick patients, pastors and teachers can easily forget just how sick with sin they are too. Is your spiritual life really any cleaner than your members? Perhaps you hide it better. But secret sins do not make for a perfect minister.

You are not a hostage of the brothers and sisters in Christ who called you. You are a servant of the Lord. You are called to be a servant to your people—even those who struggle with arrogance and defiance. Sin and temptation may drag your ministry into the ominous, death-filled shadows of Egypt. Jeremiah experienced that physically. Yet the Lord of Judah remained the Lord over Egypt as well. And while the defiant brought death and captivity and the sword on themselves, God's first promise remained his everlasting promise for his prophet. In the face of the beasts of this world and the earthly obsessions that captain our enemies, this is God's everlasting promise for you, too: "Do not be afraid of him, declares the LORD, for I am with you and will save you and deliver you."

Prayer

"You, O Lord, yourself have called them
For your precious lambs to care;
But to prosper in their calling,
They the Spirit's gifts must share.
Grant them wisdom from above;
Fill their hearts with holy love.
In their weakness, Lord, be near them;
In their prayers, Good Shepherd, hear them." Amen.

—CW 545:2

"Stop burning incense to other gods"

Jeremiah 44

"I call to you, Lord, come quickly to me; hear me when I call to you. May my prayer be set before you like incense; may the lifting up of my hands be like the evening sacrifice" (Psalm 141:1–2). King David's petition to the Lord transcends time. His prayer, accompanied by the incense rising to the heavens, has remained the prayer of believers ever since he wrote it. With his beautiful word picture, David was specifically requesting a familiar petition from the Lord: "Lead me not into temptation, but deliver me from evil."

It is almost as if he had been standing in Egypt with Jeremiah, smelling the incense and watching the smoke rise above the people of Judah. Had David actually been in Migdol, Tahpanhes, and Memphis, he probably would have cried out to God's people, desperate to halt their blatant idolatry. No doubt he would have first called out to the Lord: "I call to you, Lord, come quickly to me" (Psalm 141:1).

While David was long gone, God's people still held another spiritual guide hostage—the prophet Jeremiah. While the malodorous incense of idols rose up before the Lord, the Lord himself spoke his word to Jeremiah, "This is what the Lord Almighty, the God of Israel, says: You saw the great disaster I brought on Jerusalem and on all the towns of Judah. Today they lie deserted and in ruins because of the evil they have done." Why hadn't God's people learned their lesson? They had seen the fatal consequences of sin firsthand.

But God's people had not learned anything. So the Lord employed an extended history lesson to detail what went wrong.

Their past would inform their future. "Again and again I sent my servants the prophets, who said, 'Do not do this detestable thing that I
hate!' But they did not listen or pay attention; they did not turn from
their wickedness or stop burning incense to other gods." On and
on the cycle of sin continued in Israel and Judah.

The situation remained far worse than any Jew in Egypt realized. The remnants of God's faithful people continued to be scattered
throughout Babylon and Egypt. Believers numbered fewer every
day. Time was running out. "Why bring such great disaster on yourselves by cutting off from Judah the men and women, the children
and infants, and so leave yourselves without a remnant?"

Hundreds of years earlier, when Egypt had enslaved the
Israelites, the Lord commanded Pharaoh to let his people go into
the wilderness. The Lord had a specific reason for this: worship. At
one point, after the plague of hail, Pharaoh became surprisingly
acquiescent. But he added a caveat. "Have only the men go and worship the LORD" (Exodus 10:11). The women and children were to
stay behind in Egypt as hostages to make sure the Israelite men came
back. Moses stood his ground. "We will go with our young and our
old, with our sons and our daughters, and with our flocks and herds,
because we are to celebrate a festival to the LORD" (Exodus 10:9).
What Pharaoh and the Israelites needed to understand was that worship remains a blessing for the entire family, led by the father.

By the time of Jeremiah's ministry, Israelite families were once
again worshiping together in Egypt. Sadly, they had become as idolatrous and stubborn as Pharaoh had. Jewish wives and mothers
burned incense to "the Queen of Heaven." They poured out drink
offerings to her and baked cakes in her image. Their husbands and
fathers remained as silent as Adam before the Tree of the Knowledge
of Good and Evil when the devil spoke to Eve. The silence and disin-
terest of husbands regarding their headship role spiritually destroyed
their households.

When these Jewish families heard the Lord's warning through
Jeremiah, they defied his word as strongly as their people ever had:
"We will not listen to the message you have spoken to us in the name
of the LORD!"

King David would not have remained silent: "Set a guard over
my mouth, LORD; keep watch over the door of my lips" (Psalm

141:3). While the women poured out their drink offerings, while they pressed their cakes with images of idols, David would have poured out his heart and pressed the matter further: "Do not let my heart be drawn to what is evil so that I take part in wicked deeds along with those who are evildoers; do not let me eat their delicacies" (Psalm 141:4).

Jeremiah remained firmly founded on David's words.

Jeremiah revealed the error of their superstitious beliefs with a word of warning. "Because you have burned incense and have sinned against the LORD and have not obeyed him or followed his law or his decrees or his stipulations, this disaster has come upon you, as you now see." We all struggle to graciously accept discipline. While these Egyptian Jews seem unnaturally blatant in their idolatry, similar defiance can threaten to take hold of us, too.

Throughout his ministry Jesus emphasized the importance of genuine repentance and grace-filled forgiveness. "If your brother or sister sins, go and point out their fault, just between the two of you. If they listen to you, you have won them over" (Matthew 18:15). The encouragement sounds so simple. Yet our sinful nature recoils at any prospect of correction and discipline. If my brother shows me my sin, I want to return in kind: "Who are *you* to show me my fault?" If my brother sins, I'm tempted to either look the other way or hammer him with his sin in front of everyone.

David's approach to repentance mirrors Jesus' sermon on the matter. "Let a righteous man strike me—that is a kindness; let him rebuke me—that is oil on my head. My head will not refuse it, for my prayer will still be against the deeds of evildoers" (Psalm 141:5). If the wrongdoing of evil ones unjustly harms you, the Lord promises to use it for your good. If I deserve the punishment that comes my way, I am to accept it gladly.

I do not need to tell you how difficult Jesus' command can be. The devil constantly works against the selfless attitude of called workers, convincing them to consider themselves above *any* reproach. When members rightly reprimand their pastor, the devil works on the sinful nature's high self-perception. When students point out a teacher's error, the devil whispers to her that she need not take correction from these lowly children.

The Jews refused to accept the Lord's correction. One again, repentance would not be found in Egypt. And because they had hardened their hearts like Pharaoh a thousand years earlier, the Lord responded in the same way. "Go ahead then, do what you promised! Keep your vows!"

David also understood idolatry's destructive outcome: "Their rulers will be thrown down from the cliffs, and the wicked will learn that my words were well spoken. They will say, 'As one plows and breaks up the earth, so our bones have been scattered at the mouth of the grave'" (Psalm 141:6–7).

History was about to repeat itself. God's warning became very specific. Pharaoh Hophra would become just like King Zedekiah: defeated and imprisoned by Nebuchadnezzar. The Jews living under the Pharaoh's protection would meet the same fate. "I am watching over them for harm, not for good; the Jews in Egypt will perish by sword and famine until they are all destroyed."

Looking back on their impenitent history, the Jews should have finally learned from the wicked examples of their predecessors. Yet in their defiance lay the worst sin of all: the refusal to accept correction from the Holy Spirit. How does a servant of the Lord respond to correction? When your brother or sister shows you your sin, repent. Private confession can greatly aid the pastor or teacher in this admonition of guilt. Just as importantly, private absolution greatly consoles and comforts the sinful worker by pointing him to Christ, his Savior from sin.

King David knew the importance of repentance and forgiveness as well as anyone. Having been caught in sin himself, he finally acknowledged: "I have sinned against the LORD" (2 Samuel 12:13a). Then came the Lord's beautiful absolution, made possible by David's promised descendant: "The LORD has taken away your sin. You are not going to die" (2 Samuel 12:13b).

May David's words of confession daily be on your lips, and the lips of the family of believers who called you. May Nathan's proclamation from Jesus himself be confidently proclaimed to you and your flock also. Then you too, in the peace of that forgiveness, can boldly proclaim with fellow forgiven servants like Jeremiah and David: "My eyes are fixed on you, Sovereign LORD; in you I take refuge" (Psalm 141:8).

Prayer

"'As surely as I live,' God said, 'I would not have the sinner dead,
But that he turn from error's ways, Repent, and live through endless days.'

"To us, therefore, Christ gave command: 'Go forth and preach in ev'ry land;
Bestow on all my pard'ning grace Who will repent of sinful ways.'

"The words which absolution give Are his who died that we might live;
The minister whom Christ has sent Is but his humble instrument.

"When ministers lay on their hands, Absolved by Christ the sinner stands;
He who by grace the Word believes Forgiveness, sure and sweet, receives."
    Amen.

—*CW* 308:1–2, 5–6

"Seek them not"

Jeremiah 45

By 605 BC, the prophet Jeremiah's scribe, Baruch, had had enough. And who could blame him? He had faithfully remained with Jeremiah while the rest of the world castigated the prophet. He stood up for Jeremiah when the king's officials threw the prophet down into a cistern. He devoutly wrote the prophet's words, only to have them burned by his own king. Then he resolutely wrote them again. Along with his master Jeremiah, Baruch had been despised, ostracized, and persecuted.

A career assessment wouldn't have provided any solace either. Baruch had spent his life working for the least-"successful" prophet in the history of God's people! But if Baruch thought the worst was behind them in 605 BC, he was horribly mistaken. Things were only going to get worse. Jerusalem was about to fall, and Baruch and Jeremiah would be there to see it.

Whether it was one of these specific hardships that troubled Baruch or the entire pile of them, Baruch had had enough. He felt broken. He couldn't go on any further. So he says something to the Lord that people say when they have had enough: "Woe to me! The LORD has added sorrow to my pain; I am worn out with groaning and find no rest."

How could we argue with him? Persecuted, hated, cast off—it is a list of woes no person would ever want to endure. Baruch had given an ancient complaint that sounds so very modern: "I didn't sign up for this!"

So what *had* Baruch signed up for? If Jeremiah 45 didn't exist, we might always wonder. But in this chapter—the only chapter dedicated specifically to the scribe of Jeremiah—God reveals to us the real motives Baruch harbored in his heart. "This is what the LORD says: I will overthrow what I have built and uproot what I have planted, throughout the earth. Should you then seek great things for yourself? Do not seek them."

Little did we know Baruch secretly wanted fame and recognition for being the scribe of the prophet Jeremiah! By this point Baruch must have known all too well that no helper of Jeremiah was ever going to be revered by the people of Judah. Kings weren't promoting him; they were threatening him. Priests weren't supporting him; they were imprisoning him. To pick up and work for any other prophet would mean serving a false prophet. Baruch couldn't do that. He felt stuck.

Baruch's words ring true for us, don't they? "The Lord has added sorrow to my pain." Have you ever felt that way? Pain comes in a variety of ways in this sinful world. When heartbreaking sorrow is added to that pain, we might feel broken too.

When Baruch says, "I am worn out," he isn't talking about being tired after a good day's work. He is talking about not wanting to get up in the morning to face the evils of each day. That type of "worn out" expects a fresh taste of hell in every new and agonizing job done for the Lord. Certainly you understand that type of ministerial "worn out." Some days have probably made you feel like you literally couldn't walk another step. To do so would only bring more sorrow and pain and persecution.

Baruch says he could "find no rest." To the human eye there was no safe place in Israel. If they weren't being hunted by their own king, their own priests, and their own people, they were fearing the Babylonians, who could come at any moment to destroy them.

"The fear of the LORD leads to life; then one rests content, untouched by trouble." (Proverbs 19:23). Baruch might have known that proverb by heart. But he had his doubts. His service to the Lord seemed to *cause* all the trouble in his life. Untouched by trouble? Baruch felt tortured by trouble.

Maybe you do, too. Maybe you know what Baruch was going through. Sorrow is added to your pain. You feel "worn out . . . and find no rest." You consider giving up, crying out like Baruch, "Woe to me!" Or even, "I didn't sign up for this."

We would expect that when the Lord hears us cry those words out, he would fly down like a concerned counselor. But he doesn't come to coddle. He refreshes and gives strength. And with Baruch, he adds a strong reprimand. "This is what the LORD says: I will overthrow what I have built and uproot what I have planted, throughout the earth. Should you then seek great things for yourself? Do not seek them."

Seeking great things for ourselves comes so naturally. It is built into our culture to achieve great positions of renown. We are told to climb ever higher on the rungs of society. Worldly success builds on self-promotion and offers self-gratification.

On the other hand, what is the world's view of failure? Wouldn't it be Baruch's very position and job? The world calls out to Baruch: "You don't have to stand for that! Why fight a losing battle? Leave on your own terms and achieve something greater!"

The temptation might sound odd, but it continues today. Satan entices us to give up these crazy beliefs to make our lives a little easier. "Compromise here, give in there, and no one will bother you at all!"

"Should you then seek great things for yourself?" God asks you. While you wonder how to answer, the Lord firmly answers his own question: "Seek them not."

Somewhere in the wilderness, Satan offered the best-sounding earthly deal Jesus would ever hear. Taking him to the top of a very high mountain, Satan showed Jesus all the kingdoms of the world. "'All this I will give you,' he said, 'if you will bow down and worship me'" (Matthew 4:9). Had the devil made the offer to anyone else, the answer would have eventually led to, "Yes!" But not Jesus. "Away from me, Satan! For it is written: 'Worship the LORD your God, and serve him only'" (Matthew 4:10).

Every day we find ourselves with Baruch-type problems. I want to seek great things for *myself*. I want to make a name for *me*. I want the power and the riches of those people who have sought great things.

Seek them not, Baruch. In fact, listen to King David's description of all of these worldly treasures: "Do not fret because of those who are evil or be envious of those who do wrong; for like the grass they will soon wither, like green plants they will soon die away" (Psalm 37:1–2). The power, prestige, and possessions of this world only serve to pull you away from the one who really gives power, who gives eternal worth, and who has won your eternal possession. Don't get the good stuff and thereby give up the best possession you have ever been given.

In mercy the Lord reprimanded Baruch. Then he said something that only he would say to a whining believer who was unhappy with his momentary struggles and suffering. "I will bring disaster on all people, declares the LORD, but wherever you go I will let you escape with your life."

While the Lord let Baruch escape with his life, he didn't allow an escape for his one and only Son, Jesus. The persecution he faced, the pain and sorrow he went through, and his death far outweighed any troubles we will ever experience. And his resurrection means heaven belongs to you. That is where pain and sorrow and sin will no longer plague you.

Troubles? They have always afflicted believers in this world. Baruch knew that well. And troubles will torment our lives, too. Feelings of pain and sorrow exist because we struggle with sin in a darkened world. Yet these pains are momentary. In each and every hardship, look to Christ. He promises strength through his word, forgiveness through his sacraments, and help in your sufferings. There is no more experienced helper for the battered believer than Christ. After all, he experienced every hardship *for* you. *Of course* he knows how best to end them.

In the end, "The fear of the LORD leads to life; then one rests content, untouched by trouble" (Proverbs 19:23).

Prayer

"Preach you the Word and plant it home
To those who like or like it not,
The Word that shall endure and stand
When flo'rs and mortals are forgot.

"We know how hard, O Lord, the task
Your Servant bids us undertake:
To preach your Word and never ask
What prideful profit it may make." Amen.

—CW 544:1–2

"Egypt rises like the Nile"

Jeremiah 46

There is an old Egyptian proverb: "One who drinks from the Nile is destined to return." For four hundred years, the Israelites slaves drank from those waters. Once the Lord freed them, they found themselves trapped all over again between the waters of the Red Sea and Pharaoh's pursuing chariots. Just days after miraculously crossing those Red Sea waters, God's people looked like they would die from a lack of water in the wilderness. Then, soon after, hunger threatened to starve the million-person exodus.

Every one of these problems led to the same Israelite refrain: "It would have been better for us to serve the Egyptians than to die in the desert!" (Exodus 14:12). Even though the Lord made a point to close the road back to Egypt by the Red Sea, the Israelites always seemed to look longingly back on the better parts of their slavery in Egypt. Perhaps the proverb was right: "One who drinks from the Nile is destined to return." For years Israel sang their song of yearning for Egypt. Finally, the Lord needed to sound his own refrain in response: "Don't look back to Egypt."

When the battle looked lost as Pharaoh and his army approached the Red Sea, the Israelites thought back to their safe, Egyptian slave lives. The Lord reminded them: "Don't look back to Egypt."

When their desert battle against hunger and thirst seemed to be lost, the Israelites recalled the plentiful food of Egypt and those cool, constant waters of the Nile. "Don't look back to Egypt."

When an Amalekite attack at Rephidim threatened the traveling Israelite families, God's people had precious little time to yearn for Egyptian peace. The Lord miraculously won the battle for his people, once again reminding them: "Don't look back to Egypt."

Long after Moses had ascended Mount Sinai, the Israelites wondered if he had abandoned them altogether. When they gathered around his older brother, Aaron, the Israelites requested an image that represented Egyptian strength and ceremony. "Come, make us gods who will go before us." Aaron acquiesced. He formed a golden calf similar to the Egyptian bull-god Apis. When Moses came down the mountain and witnessed the godless revelry around this idol, he disciplined the people. Then he asked the Lord for forgiveness on their behalf. Moses had looked to the Lord. The Israelites had returned to Egyptian gods. "Don't look back to Egypt."

When the Israelites stood at the gates to the Promised Land, hearing the spies' report of fortress towns and giant peoples, the song remained the same: "We should choose a leader and go back to Egypt" (Numbers 14:4). Once again, the patient refrain of the Lord followed: "Don't look back to Egypt."

The kings of Judah continued the song, making alliances with the pharaohs rather than allying their hearts with the Lord. In response, the prophets of the Lord continued the Lord's refrain: "Woe to the obstinate children . . . who go down to Egypt" (Isaiah 30:1–2). Egypt enticed Israel for centuries with their mirage of power and protection. The Lord continually showed his people what these Egyptian mirages really were: "Don't look back to Egypt."

In the days of remnants and scattered tribes, God's people once again yearned for the waters of the Nile. Jeremiah walked with his people, an unwilling participant in their journey back to Egypt. He could not escape Egypt, but he could speak the Lord's final Egyptian warning to his people.

Jeremiah's Egyptian prophecy really divides into two prophecies. The first detailed Egypt's loss to Babylon at the epic battle of Carchemish in 605 BC. Egypt thought victory was in hand. Rarely had they lost a battle in the Middle East. They considered their troops superior, their tactics well-prepared, and their chariots the swiftest killing machines on any battlefield.

Egypt thought she could rise up against the entire world like the flooding waters of the Nile River. Yet the battle of Carchemish crushed those Egyptian notions. Jeremiah's prophecy recounted just how badly Nebuchadnezzar defeated the haughty Egyptian army.

Jeremiah's second Egyptian prophecy points to a future Egyptian defeat at the hands of Nebuchadnezzar. Although the battle sounds similar, one important difference stands out. The exiled Jews would witness this second Egyptian defeat from the within Egypt. The irony may have been lost on Judah, but not on Jeremiah. God's people would become trapped by the very Egyptians they had trust in.

As always, the Lord reveals nations for what they really are. "They will exclaim, 'Pharaoh king of Egypt is only a loud noise.'" The historically mighty kingdom of Egypt had become a broken reed. "Daughter Egypt will be put to shame, given into the hands of the people of the north." The Babylonians would finish her off, and she would never again rule over that part of the world.

In responses to Jeremiah's prophetic warnings, the exiles from Judah defiantly sang the song of their ancestors, putting the last of their trust in the failing power of Egypt. Jeremiah faithfully sang back his poetic refrain. Does it sound familiar yet? "Don't look back to Egypt."

In all of this, Jeremiah epitomizes what it feels like to be a believer of the Christian church in every age. No one in Jerusalem listened when he warned of Babylonian victory. The city walls crumbled. Countless died. Palaces burned. The temple fell. In the wake of Jerusalem's worst day, Jeremiah was whisked away by his fellow countrymen into Egypt against the Lord's warning. Once again, he had warned them not to go. Once again the people refused to listen. Now, held captive by his own people in Egypt, Jeremiah saw the Babylonian army coming all over again. He was caught between the victorious Babylonians and his own defiant people.

If a scenario could ever be labeled a no-win, this was it. Sadly, situations like these were nothing new for the prophet. Jeremiah always seemed to find himself in defeated situations like these. So does the church. Nicolai F. S. Grundtvig captured this picture of defeat perfectly in his hymn "Built on the Rock." Looking around and assessing the church's situation, Grundtvig wrote:

> Built on the Rock the Church shall stand
> Even when steeples are falling.

Crumbled have spires in ev'ry land;
Bells still are chiming and calling.

The church has always looked like this. Enemies from without have displaced Christians. Enemies from within have ransacked churches, stealing away the treasure of the gospel and replacing it with manmade laws. Rubble has always seemed to surround crosses; bells are broken amid war. By every sight and sound, defeat seems to follow the gospel everywhere.

And yet, God's word remains. The everlasting nature of the word, seemingly always on the brink of destruction, is a miracle we often take for granted. Nowhere was that rubble and destruction more apparent than Warsaw, Poland, during World War II. The German attacks had left the center of the once-thriving city a ruinous crater. In the middle of the rock and brick stood a single wall. Before the war, it had been part of the headquarters of the British and Foreign Bible Society. Miraculously, it still stood, surrounded by debris. On this last standing wall these still legible words had been etched: "Heaven and earth will pass away, but my words will never pass away."

Jesus' words in Matthew 24:35 had become a rallying point for the city's defeated Christians. Their homes and churches and businesses had become scattered debris. Their loved ones had died. Their world was gone. And yet . . . God's word remained.

Was it any different for Christ on the cross? Defeat reigned as the Son of God suffered. His disciples had scattered. His enemies thought they had won. And yet . . . Jesus himself declared from that instrument of death: "It is finished." Death, the ultimate victor, had been defeated.

That is what victory looks like in God's kingdom, dear Christian. A cross, a broken church, bells falling, and Christians dying. The world stands with Egypt, claiming victory in every battle. And yet . . . your Lord has already won your victory.

Don't look back to Egypt. Don't return to trusting in your own wits and wisdom or in your own strength in crisis. The things of this world that seem so powerful and trustworthy are fading away. "The grass withers and the flowers fall, but the word of our God endures forever" (Isaiah 40:8). And so the Lord delights to place you in the paradox, promising strength in weakness, victory in defeat, and even life from death.

Prayer

"Built on the Rock the Church shall stand Even when steeples are falling. Crumbled have spires in ev'ry land; Bells still are chiming and calling, Calling the young and old to rest, But above all the soul distressed, Longing for rest everlasting.

"Here stands the font before our eyes, Telling how God did receive us. Th' altar recalls Christ's sacrifice And what the sacrament gives us. Here sound the scriptures that proclaim Christ yesterday, today, the same, And evermore, our Redeemer." Amen.

—CW 529:1, 4

"Alas, the sword of the Lord"

Jeremiah 47

In the dead of the night, two men snuck deep into enemy territory. Quietly they walked by sleeping guards and crept around pitched tents. Miraculously, the entire camp of the army of Israel was sound asleep. They should have known better. Saul and his men had been looking for the wily fugitive David. Up until this night, David had outmaneuvered Saul's army at every turn. Now he and Abishai smuggled themselves right through Saul's encampment. The ghostly silence may have unnerved the two warriors. Not a soul awoke.

In the middle of everything stood Saul's tent. The two slipped inside and discovered Saul's spear stuck in the ground. Next to the tip of the spear rested the head of Israel's first anointed king, Saul. Murder had never seemed so simple. Under the cover of darkness, surrounded by the snores of the enemy, the spear would instantly mute the king, promptly ending his prideful reign.

Feeling prophetic, Abishai saw the entire scene unfolding in his mind's eye. "Today God has delivered your enemy into your hands. Now let me pin him to the ground with one thrust of my spear; I won't strike him twice" (1 Samuel 26:8). The signs could not have been clearer. This would be Saul's last night on earth, run through by his own spear in the middle of his own camp, by the man already anointed to be Israel's next king.

David viewed the same scene quite differently. Indeed, the Lord had laid the army down into a deep sleep. Yes, Saul's spear stood in the ground next to his head. But this would not be Saul's last night on earth. David knew the lesson tonight would not be vengeance. It was to be mercy.

"'As surely as the LORD lives,' he said, 'the LORD himself will strike him, or his time will come and he will die, or he will go into battle and perish'" (1 Samuel 26:10). Quickly, the two men grabbed Saul's spear and water jug, leaving as silently as they had approached.

The ensuing conversation between David and Saul would be their last. Immediately following this final show of mercy, David would escape to the Philistine army while Saul would go on to fight them. The old, complicated relationship of Israel's first two kings would now be trumped by Israel's ancient foe.

In the end, the Philistines fulfilled David's prophetic, midnight words. Saul did march into battle. His time had arrived. Israel's king died while the Philistine onslaught swept over Israel's army.

Saul's demise was not the first Philistine victory in Israel. The Philistines always seemed to have the upper hand. From Ashkelon to Gaza, from Ashdod to Ekron in the north and Gath with their mighty Goliath, the Philistines always seemed to be Israel's living, breathing thorn. Always mightier, always more numerous, always better equipped, they relished every perceived superiority they held.

By the days of the prophet Jeremiah, Philistia's glory had faded. Like Judah, her cities lay broken. Her people remained a husk of their former selves. No giants remained to hold back the coming armies. Even the historically defiant northern cities of Tyre and Sidon could not withstand the flood from the north. "They will overflow the land and everything in it, the towns and those who live in them."

The defeat of Israel's ancient foe must have felt like a bitter-sweet victory. Finally, the insolent pentapolis would receive justice. Finally, "Gaza will shave her head in mourning" and "Ashkelon will be silenced." Yet Abishai knew exactly how empty victories like these felt. His face must have looked flabbergasted as his leader, David, told him to pick up Saul's spear and jug to leave. You can probably hear his thoughts: *What are we doing, David? If you weren't going to kill Saul, then why did we sneak into his tent in the first place!*

Shouldn't victory feel triumphant? Why did the Lord, who could have eliminated the Philistines before Joshua ever marched through the Promised Land, leave the enemy at the gates for so long? Like Israel and Judah, we struggle with the appearances of defeat. We refuse to listen to David's faithful whispers about our enemies: "His time will come and he will die, or he will go into battle and perish" (1 Samuel 26:10). I want the Goliaths in my life to perish *now*. My heart desires to obliterate this world's Philistias in *my* time and on *my* terms.

The truth is, once the sword of the Lord begins swinging, we often cry out for it to stop. Certainly the Philistines had. "Alas, sword of the Lord, how long till you rest? Return to your sheath; cease and be still." Our deep desire for vengeance melts away when we see fathers refusing to turn and help their children. Anger bleeds away when hands of our enemies become limp. Yes, they had destruction coming. Yes, we wanted to see that destruction with our own eyes. But in the end, we realize that we deserve that destruction, too.

The swift recourse of vengeance brings fleeting elation. How much more so in your ministry? Feelings of retribution sweep over New Testament hearts as much as they filled hearts in the Old Testament. Remember those poisonous words your member poured over your head? How could you forget! Deep down, you may have vowed *never* to forget. So you wait. As your heart grows cold, the opportunity for recourse soon comes. Then what? A second helping of poison poured over the poor soul who dared to strike you first.

The assassination of your member's character never seemed so simple. Like Abishai desired, you grabbed the spear of your enemy resting next to his head and put an end to him right then and there. However, soon the victory becomes hollow. You realize quickly that your act of vengeance was not really a victory at all. It was a resounding defeat for everyone. And there's no way to turn back time and return the spear you used to the tent you took it from.

These are the battles the devil delights to pull you into. Like the Philistine Goliath, he entices you into the fray against your brothers and sisters in Christ. What is a pastor to do? How should a teacher react? Listen to the boy who walked up to Goliath when no one else dared defy him. He knew the Philistines better than anyone. More importantly, he understood how a faithful servant of the Lord ought to respond.

In the Valley of Elah, David launched his first faithful volley. There was no poison in those words—just heavenly justice. "You come against me with sword and spear and javelin, but I come against you in the name of the Lord Almighty, the God of the armies of Israel, whom you have defied" (1 Samuel 17:45). By the time David slung that stone, victory was already won.

The Philistines of the world stand defeated already. Those within the church who act like Philistines toward you and your ministry need mercy and patient instruction, not vengeance. Among believers, slings and stones must give way to spears and water jugs. These are the sheep of the flock the Lord called you to serve. These fellow believers, bought with the blood of Christ, stand together with you facing the altar, confessing their sins with you before the Lord. And these are the sinners to which you are blessed to recount the Lord's very words of forgiveness.

If one of them has sinned against you, go and show him what he has done. Speak about it just between you two. If he listens, praise the Lord! You have won him over. If he speaks to you about your sin, listen to him. If you are led to repentance, praise the Lord! He has won you over.

David knew how that felt, too. "How good and pleasant it is when God's people live together in unity!" (Psalm 133:1). Victory never tasted so sweet.

Prayer

"Sheep that from the fold did stray Are not by the Lord forsaken;
Weary souls who lost their way Are by Christ, the shepherd, taken
In his arms that they may live Jesus sinners does receive.

"Come, O sinners, one and all, Come, accept his invitation.
Come, obey his gracious call; Come and take his free salvation!
Firmly in these words believe Jesus sinners does receive." Amen.

—CW 304:3–4

"Put salt on Moab"

Jeremiah 48

A French folktale places a princess before her father, the king. In her novice attempt at metaphor, she tells her father: "I love you like salt." The king becomes offended. How could he, the king of the land, be compared to something so lowly, so *quelconque*, as salt! It was as if his very own daughter wounded him—and then rubbed salt into it.

As the days went by, the king slowly realized just how often the people of his palace, indeed his very kingdom, needed to use salt. His servants worked with salt in immense quantities, curing meat and eating food. They traded tidy sums to acquire salt. When they were unable to purchase salt, they would patiently evaporate seawater and collect the salt the water left behind.

In the end, the king realized salt's vital importance to his kingdom. More importantly to the folktale, the king realized the wisdom behind his daughter's loving comparison. In the Middle Ages, a salt-like love could be considered the strongest of all.

Recently, salt scientists have been concurring with Medieval princesses. Research shows just how important salt can be. Your body needs it just as much as it needs water. Like that French king realized, salt continues to hold its position as an important commodity. In fact, from the beginning of civilization until about a hundred years ago, salt was one of the most-desired commodities on earth.

However, too much of a good thing can have bad consequences. Too much salt in your diet will lead to death. Then again, too little salt can kill you also. In a way, the very core of salt remains a paradox.

Two very dangerous substances by themselves, sodium and chloride, combine to produce this much-needed product of salt.

In chapter 48, Jeremiah places you right on top of that salt paradox. As the Lord continues to turn his attention to Israel's ancient enemies, he fixes his gaze on Moab, promising to use something good as a method of complete annihilation. "Put salt on Moab, for she will be laid waste; her towns will become desolate, with no one to live in them."

To empty the Middle East of her wicked nations, the Lord promises to "send men who pour from pitchers." The tipping of this pitcher of soldiers would be surprisingly gentle to leave the sediment in the base. Yet the amount of men coming from the north would be staggering. No amount of Moabite warriors, valiant though they were, could stop the flow of the Lord's Babylonian army.

This flood of destruction swirled around Moab all because of her worship. Because shame was not a common Moabite sentiment, the Lord's discipline would need to instill Moabite humility. This had been a problem for these people ever since their conception. In the wake of the destruction of their home and the death of their mother, Lot's older daughter made her father drunk and slept with him. She named the son she bore, "Moab." Genesis tells us, "He is the father of the Moabites of today" (Genesis 19:37).

Moab was not the first nation to face the Lord's degradation. He had held a mirror to a nation's shame before. "Moab will be ashamed of Chemosh, as Israel was ashamed when they trusted in Bethel." By the date of Jeremiah's writing, the Lord had already sent the northern kingdom of Israel into captivity because of their godless worship. Salt tells the tale. The offerings the Lord had prescribed for his people needed to be salted. "Season all your grain offerings with salt. Do not leave the salt of the covenant of your God out of your grain offerings; add salt to all your offerings" (Leviticus 2:13). In fact, the Lord described his entire sacrificial code, which Israel rejected, as "an everlasting covenant of salt before the LORD" (Numbers 18:19).

Abijah took this salt metaphor even further. When he spoke to the usurper, Jeroboam, he emphatically reminded him that David's kingly line, and therefore Rehoboam, belonged to the Lord "forever by a covenant of salt" (2 Chronicles 13:5). Salt protected the important objects of Jewish everyday life, too. On Friday evening, before the Sabbath, the Jews still dip their bread into salt. The Lord promised daily bread, and he preserved that bread with salt.

How a family used salt revealed their priorities. Would their salt sprinkle a sacrifice meant for an idol? Did their salt lazily sit during the Sabbath rather than faithfully covering their Sabbath bread as the Lord expected? Needless to say, Israel had broken that covenant of salt.

Moab never wanted God's sacrificial salt in the first place. Retribution loomed. As Lot's daughter made her father drunk to establish an entire shameful nation, so now the Lord promises to end that nation through the same method: "Make her drunk, for she has defied the LORD."

Beware when you start to see the sprinkles of salt falling around you. Fire and destruction always seem to follow. So does sacrifice. One descendant of the Israelite, Boaz, and the Moabite, Ruth, experienced that personally. As the Son of God, Jesus allowed himself to enter our world as your sacrifice, salted to perfection. That salt, meant as a death sentence to any animal, should have marked our eternal sentence of hell. Like Old Testament Israel, we have broken God's covenant of salt, too.

Then came that perfectly salted sacrificial Lamb. His one sacrifice fulfilled every salted animal sacrifice that came before him. It was not an army of retribution that poured forth from heaven at the cross. It was Jesus' blood. That cleansing flood washed away every sinful miss-step you have made. It purified you from every insolent remark and every sinful desire to misuse the salt in your life.

By Jesus' day, salt had become even more important. Roman soldiers received their pay in salt. Jewish families bartered for it. Salt continued to drive important aspects of the world's economy. So when Jesus used salt as a metaphor for faithful living, the crowd sitting on the mountainside instantly realized the importance of the comparison. "You are the salt of the earth. But if the salt loses its saltiness, how can it be made salty again? It is no longer good for anything, except to be thrown out and trampled underfoot" (Matthew 5:13).

Salt remains quite a paradox. Too much salt kills; too little harms. Here Jesus compares your life, your ministry, to salt. Sprinkled by the Holy Spirit, you have been salted for the sake of the world around you. In fact, Jesus calls *you* salt. The long list of indictments aimed at Moab continue to threatens our salty servitude. The Moabites trusted in their deeds and riches, a temptation that hits close to our hearts as well. The Lord associates the Moabites with drunkenness, a sin that can easily seize called workers today. Moab ridiculed the other nations with selfish pride and misplaced arrogance, two common sins that seduce pastors and teachers in positions of trusted authority. Finally, the Lord numbers the Moabites with thieves, the allure of which continues to draw servants of the Lord to the things of this world.

The feet of so many sinful temptations threaten to trample us down. The devil hastens to infect us with a sort of spiritual hyponatremia, squelching our faithful saltiness. Where does a called worker turn when his saltiness becomes threatened by his sinful nature within and the world without?

Flee to your salt-providing Savior. Run back to his word, which strengthens your spiritual saltiness. Daily confession and absolution remain paramount for the pastors and teachers to humbly serve their Lord. We are blessed to hear those life-giving and life-preserving words: "I forgive you all your sins." Then we remember the name by which it was all made possible, the perfectly salted sacrifice killed for you, Jesus Christ.

Realize just how important salt is. Understand by faith just how gracious your Savior remains. And daily remember that your Lord, Jesus, loves you . . . even more than salt.

Prayer

Lord keep me now from sinful pride
That humbly I always confide
In your grace and in your voice
Salted by love your name rejoice. Amen.

"The pride of your heart"

Jeremiah 49:1–22

Saint Augustine once wrote: "It was pride that changed angels into devils; it is humility that makes men as angels."[1] It seemed that pride had turned the Ammonites into a kingdom of devils. No other nation had become more of a stumbling block to Israel than the descendants of Ammon. From the days of the Exodus through the period of the Judges and well after the reign of King David, the Ammonites continued to methodically flood the eastern tribes of Israel.

Given the origin of these people, perhaps their actions shouldn't surprise us. The night after Lot's older daughter made her father drunk to sleep with him, her younger sister followed suit. Like her older sister, she also conceived and gave birth to a boy. She named her son "Ammon." The Bible tells us, "He is the father of the Ammonites of today" (Genesis 19:38). His descendants continued to live with the same audacity his mother exhibited.

After Tiglath-Pileser's Assyrian invasion of the tribes east of the Jordan River, the Ammonites swept in and reconquered the area for themselves. The Lord addressed the Ammonites' actions by using an inheritance metaphor. "Has Israel no sons? Has Israel no heir? Why then has Molek taken possession of Gad? Why do his people live in its towns?"

---

[1] Hialmer Day Gould, *Best Thoughts Of Best Thinkers: Amplified, Classified, Exemplified And Arranged As A Key To Unlock The Literature Of All Ages* (Cleveland: Best Thoughts Publishing Company, 1904), 356.

The Lord refers to Ammon by the name of the god she worshiped: Molek. If pride had turned the Ammonites into a nation of devils, their god Molek had become the king of devils. In the Ancient Near East, there existed no more despicable false deity than Molek. Worship of this false god meant sacrifice. However, unlike most foreign deity worship, the god of the Ammonites demanded more than just animal sacrifice. He commanded the sacrifice of children.

Apparently, Ammon faithfully carried out these despicable sacrifices. Soon these sacrifices enticed Israel into idolatry as well. Already in the book of Leviticus the Lord warned his people against these godless actions: "Any Israelite or any foreigner residing in Israel who sacrifices any of his children to Molek is to be put to death" (Leviticus 20:2). Then, because sacrifices became so tempting, God actually needed to explain *why* infanticide was so wrong: "By sacrificing his children to Molek, he has defiled my sanctuary and profaned my holy name" (Leviticus 20:3).

Israel got caught up in sacrificing children anyway. This worship began in Israel already under the reign of the once-wise king, Solomon (1 Kings 11:5). It spread during the wicked reign of King Manasseh (2 Chronicles 33:6). The Lord stated through the prophet Isaiah, "You went to Molek with olive oil and increased your perfumes" (Isaiah 57:9a). In following Ammon's path of idolatry the Lord labeled Israel's actions for what they were: "you descended to the very realm of the dead!" (Isaiah 57:9b).

In comparison to Ammon's foolish worship, the nation of Edom had been known for her wisdom. However, this was not always the case. Continuing the family theme that began so many Middle East kingdoms, Edom also dated back to Abraham's extended family. After Jacob tricked his twin brother, Esau, into giving him their family's birthright for a hot meal, Esau yelled, "Quick, let me have some of that red stew! I'm famished!" Scripture tells us "That is why he was also called Edom" (Genesis 25:30).

Like the famished Esau coming in from the open country, it appeared that Edom had lost their wits as well. "Has counsel perished from the prudent? Has their wisdom decayed?" (Jeremiah 49:7). Like Moab's "overweening pride and conceit," like Ammon's boasting of her fruitful valleys and her "trust in riches," so the Edomites also held great pride. Their pride rested in their weapons and fortresses.

Like he accomplished for every other nation, the Lord shows what pride actually brought Edom. "The terror you inspire and the pride of your heart have deceived you." While the Lord promises to restore the fortunes of Moab (48:47) and Ammon (49:6), he makes no such promise to Edom. Quite the contrary, the Lord promises to drag Edom away like a young flock and "completely destroy their pasture because of them."

"It was pride that changed angels into devils." With these words Augustine looks back at the devil's original reason for rebellion. Pride led Satan to fight against his Creator. Ultimately, it also led to his fall, along with all "the angels who did not keep their positions of authority but abandoned their proper dwelling" (Jude 6). If God's prophecy against the king of Tyre in Ezekiel 28 is also aimed at Satan, then we see just how damning pride really is. "In the pride of your heart you say, 'I am a god'" (Ezekiel 28:2). For everyone enslaved by pride, from the king of Tyre to Ammon and Edom and to the devil himself, the Lord warns what those arrogant assumptions lead to. "Because you think you are wise, as wise as a god' . . . They will bring you down to the pit, and you will die a violent death" (Ezekiel 28:6, 8).

If pride could change angels into devils, what could it do to pastors and teachers? Throughout the book of Jeremiah, we have seen what pride accomplished in the hearts of Jerusalem's prophets as they poisoned their listeners' minds with lies. We witnessed priestly pride as they audaciously viewed God's temple to be a superstitious charm. And we witnessed the most concentrated examples of pride in the Davidic dynasty as wicked kings arrogantly considered themselves God, using his throne to enact their personal sins.

Pride rests like a sleeping giant in our hearts, too. Pastors are always one word of praise away from waking the prideful beast within themselves. Teachers witness the strides their students make and soon feel pride coiling around themselves. How quickly pride turns the genuine gratitude of others into the food that arrogance loves to devour. After years of praise and piles of pride, a called worker eventually views himself as the foundation of his ministry.

For as powerful and presumptuous as pride can be, it also can exhibit surprising subtlety. Moab's pride began with arrogance in conceit. Perhaps that is the type of pride your sinful nature latches onto—the selfish desire to turn the world toward yourself. Ammon's pride rested in her riches. Maybe that form of pride lures your sinful nature more frequently as you secretly desire more money, a better house, and more possessions. Edom's pride gloried in her strength and wisdom. Perhaps pride takes that approach with you, appealing to the physical gifts the Lord has given you. Or maybe pride appeals to your mind, reminding you just how intelligent you are, with or without the Lord.

Pride swirled around our Lord when he stood in Jerusalem. Pharisees, teachers, disciples, and crowds of people all exhibited various forms of pride. One by one, Jesus turned away the prideful hearts with his law. Pride cannot hope to view God's law seriously and remain arrogant. The law shows us as we are. So Jesus showed us who he is—our perfect, humble Savior. He very clearly explained that he came *not* to be served, but to serve. That dutiful humility led Jesus to suffer in our place for all of our prideful sins and arrogant thoughts.

"It was pride that changed angels into devils; it is humility that makes men as angels." Christ's humility saved us. Now the sanctifying work of the Holy Spirit enables us to live that humility. "In your relationships with one another, have the same mindset as Christ Jesus," Paul wrote (Philippians 2:5). Then he summarized that work of Christ by adding, "He humbled himself" (Philippians 2:8).

We humble ourselves, too. Pastors and teachers, elected leaders in the church, mothers and children, we all place ourselves last out of love for him who placed us first in his heart.

Prayer

"The King is born in poverty, His chariot is humility,
His kingly crown is holiness, His scepter, pity in distress.
The end of all our woe he brings; Therefore the earth is glad and sings.
To Christ the Savior raise Your grateful hymns of praise." Amen.

—CW 3:2

"Arise and attack a nation at ease"

Jeremiah 49:23–39

All the way back in chapter 25, the Lord told Jeremiah that he was going to pour out his wrath on an entire list of nations. In these final chapters, we have seen that same list detailed in an almost identical order. The Lord prophesied Egypt's destruction (46), followed by the downfall of the Philistines (47), the Moabites (48), the Ammonites (49), and the Edomites (49).

Now the Lord continues his prophetic pouring on the second half of his list. "All the kings of Tyre and Sidon; the kings of the coastlands across the sea; Dedan, Tema, Buz and all who are in distant places; all the kings of Arabia and all the kings of the foreign people who live in the wilderness; all the kings of Zimri, Elam and Media; and all the kings of the north, near and far, one after the other—all the kingdoms on the face of the earth" (Jeremiah 25:22–26). These lands stood quite a distance away from Judah. Yet the Lord cared about these nations, too, even if his people knew little about them.

Jerusalem was not the only city wrestling with terror. Although the inhabitants of Jerusalem often walked under the cloud of disaster, the city of Damascus perpetually danced with death. As one of the earliest cities ever to be established on earth, the ancient grandeur of Damascus has drawn the envious gaze of countless conquerors.

Today, the city still stands as the capital of Syria. Before Syria controlled the city, the French held it following the First World War. Four hundred years before the French marched in, the Ottoman Empire had taken control of the city during the same month Martin

Luther nailed his 95 Theses in Wittenberg. Prior to the Ottoman's lengthy reign, the Mongols besieged the city, taking it away from the Muslim rulers who controlled it during the Crusades. They in turn had stolen Damascus away from the Romans, who had taken the city from the Greeks. The leopard-like Greeks had swiftly seized the city from the Persians.

The Lord chose not to show Jeremiah all of these future storms headed for Damascus. Instead, he revealed the empire that would begin the city's two-and-a-half-millennia dance with death. The Babylonian conquest was coming for Damascus, too. The emotions Jeremiah describes would plant themselves forever in this ancient city. Her inhabitants would be "dismayed" and "disheartened, troubled like the restless sea." Panic would grip her fleeing people. An unquenchable fire would melt her ancient walls.

Damascus would not face her prophetic ruin alone. Kedar and Hazor, perhaps settlements of Ishmaelite origin, would also incur Nebuchadnezzar's wrath. "Their tents and their flocks will be taken; their shelters will be carried off with all their goods and camels." Desolation would mark their demise.

The final name on the Lord's list of destruction lived the farthest away from his people. The Elamites lived far off in the eastern reaches beyond Babylon. They made their prowess with the bow known throughout the world. Yet mighty as they were, the Elamites would also buckle and break under the weight of the Babylonian army. The Lord says, "I will break the bow of Elam . . . I will shatter Elam before their foes." The Lord would send disaster to pursue them, turning her arrows on her own kings and officials.

At first glance, these nations appear in an almost random list. And really, who cares about the Elamites? We don't even know exactly where Kedar and Hazor existed. Why bother warning nations that will never hear the word in the first place?

Somewhat surprisingly, these nations and peoples do have something in common. Like Ammon, Moab, and Edom, these areas of Damascus, Kedar, Hazor, and Elam all have connections to Abraham's life. Soon after Abraham and Lot separated from each other, the first recorded world war swept over the kingdoms of the world. The king of Elam and Kedorlaomer united with three other kings and attacked the kings of Sodom, Gomorrah, Admah, Zeboiim, and Zoar. The war consumed much of the known world.

The king of Elam's allied armies won. In their conquest, they captured Abraham's nephew, Lot, and his family. When a servant escaped to tell Abraham the news, the patriarch gathered 318 of his trained men and chased after the army of the united kingdoms. During the night, Abraham divided his men into three groups and routed the king of Elam, pursuing them beyond Damascus.

Not long before he had his first son, Ishmael, the ancestor of Kedar and Hazor, Abraham might have been the first man to conquer both the king of Elam and the area of Damascus. In a much different way, Nebuchadnezzar was making his own conquest through the same territory. Every timeworn site Abraham visited, each of his old allies and every ancient foe he faced, was now being swallowed up by the Babylonian army.

Yet this would not end with Damascus' ultimate destruction. The people of Kedar and Hazor would once again have their victories. Perhaps more than any other nation, Elam would see future success. The Lord himself declared, "I will restore the fortunes of Elam in days to come."

The history of nations bears these prophecies out. Damascus still stands today. Kedar and Hazor may very well still survive among the Arab peoples. And the area of Elam continues to thrive amid the deserts and wars of the Middle East. Yet the Lord was not just looking at the physical nature of countries. Nations would continue to rise and fall. Cities suffer defeat. Peoples continue to be scattered. The Lord had a far greater blessing in store for these conquered nations.

A week and a half after Christ ascended into heaven, having completed his perfect work of innocent sacrifice and triumphant resurrection, he sent the Holy Spirit. His timing was impeccable. The festival of Pentecost brought into Jerusalem "God-fearing Jews from every nation under heaven" (Acts 2:5). These peoples included Medes and Elamites (Acts 2:9), residents from Mesopotamia (Acts 2:9), which probably included some from Damascus, and Arabs (Acts 2:11), who probably came from the desert areas of Dedan, Tema, and Buz.

Restoration for these people arrived in the form of the Holy Spirit. The violent sound of wind, tongues of fire above the disciples' heads, and the many languages bursting forth among the thousands illustrated a new conquering campaign. On that day the Lord captured hearts through his word. The law cut the crowds "to the heart" (Acts 2:37). Repentance prepared those hearts for the water and the word. And the waters of baptism washed those multinational hearts with God's gospel.

Defeat preceded victory on the battlefields of our hearts as well. The Lord has conquered our souls as he did with those thousands on Pentecost. Bathed in those same baptismal waters, you now stand among a list of fellow-conquered souls. You are a child of paradise. Listen to Paul's beautiful description of the scene: "Don't you know that all of us who were baptized into Christ Jesus were baptized into his death? We were therefore buried with him through baptism into death in order that, just as Christ was raised from the dead through the glory of the Father, we too may live a new life" (Romans 6:3–4).

Your new life in Christ exhibits itself in faithful service to the Lord in his kingdom. This service will often be difficult. Work in the kingdom often takes place out of the spotlight, back in humble corners and dirty alleyways. Kingdom work serves the weak and the helpless, expecting nothing in return. Only the Holy Spirit, working in your heart since those baptismal waters covered you, can produce such selfless service in your life and ministry.

Ancient cities fall. Empires collapse. The Lord orchestrates it all. His list of promised destruction transformed into his list of fulfillment. But then came another list, an eternal record God had prepared since the beginning of the world. "'Yet I will restore the fortunes of Elam in days to come,' declares the LORD." And if God promised that for Elam, he certainly promises to bring you to your eternal glory as well. That is the list that bears your name, etched in the book of life by the blood of Christ for all eternity.

Prayer

"Death, you cannot end my gladness:
I am baptized into Christ!
When I die, I leave all sadness
To inherit paradise!

Though I lie in dust and ashes
Faith's assurance brightly flashes:
Baptism has the strength divine
To make life immortal mine." Amen.

—CWS 737:4

"Your day has come"

Jeremiah 50–51

Job needed answers. After losing everything and everyone he held dear, he had a long list of questions for the Lord. One by one, his friends attempted to answer those questions with their philosophical perspectives. In reality, they were attempting to read the mind of the Lord. They didn't do a very good job. After days of listening to his companions' theological drivel, Job finally came to the conclusion that tragedy strikes all people, whether they are rich or poor, powerful or weak. "He makes nations great, and destroys them; he enlarges nations, and disperses them" (Job 12:23).

As far as we know, the Lord never revealed to Job the reasons behind the disasters that so afflicted him. And yet, Job still confidently declared that the Lord "reveals the deep things of darkness and brings utter darkness into the light" (Job 12:22). These last chapters of the book of Jeremiah reveal exactly those deep, hidden plans of the Lord. What Job's words prophesy, Jeremiah's words fulfill.

Year after year, nations rose and fell. For a time, the Lord allowed his people of Israel to stand on top under the faithful reign of King David. Then, when Israel's faithfulness waned, so did their national power. Other nations took their place, from Philistia to Moab to Edom and Ammon. Soon other, greater nations started building empires. The Assyrians swept down from the north, conquering much of the Middle East. Then the mighty Babylonians took their place. From the vantage point of Jeremiah's Jerusalem, Babylon appeared to be a great power for centuries to come. Nebuchadnezzar's dynasty looked resilient. The city of Babylon seemed eternal.

Jeremiah's own prophetic words bolstered such a view. In fact, the book of Jeremiah talks about the Babylonians more often than the rest of the Bible combined! According to the book of Jeremiah, Babylon was the "boiling pot, tilting away from the north" (1:13), the "lion" that "has come out of his lair" and a "destroyer of nations" (4:7). Jeremiah stated that Nebuchadnezzar "advances like the clouds, his chariots come like a whirlwind, his horses are swifter than eagles" (4:13). The Lord had Jeremiah call Babylon "a great nation" (6:22) that will be "cruel and show no mercy" (6:23). All of Judah would "be carried into exile" (13:19) by the mighty Babylonians for "seventy years" (25:12).

Now, at the end of the book of Jeremiah, everything has changed. The great Babylonian Empire and her fearless commander, Nebuchadnezzar, would finally see their demise. The Lord would make Babylon another powerful example of how "He makes nations great, and destroys them."

Babylon's disastrous details sound as stunning as her rise to glory had been. "Babylon will be captured . . . A nation from the north will attack her and lay waste her land." This alliance of great nations will plunder Babylon's wealth, turning her into "the least of nations."

God summarizes his punishing actions with one concise phrase. He tells the Babylonians: "Your day has come." Babylon would be given her time of dominance and glory, just as Assyria possessed great power before her. But this worldly dominance would be fleeting. Only seventy years of sovereignty and the mighty city of Babylon would forever crumble.

Yet for all of the ink Jeremiah spilled describing Babylon's rise and fall, the entire affair still remained secondary to God's ultimate purpose. "'In those days, at that time,' declares the LORD, 'the people of Israel and the people of Judah together will go in tears to seek the LORD their God.'" It was the fulfillment of these plans that led the Lord to orchestrate the movement of peoples and the rise and fall of nations. The repentance of his people was so vitally important that the Lord moved heaven and earth to accomplish it! The Lord unleashed the full measure of the law when he told Babylon: "Your day has come." Now, the Lord revealed the greatest depths of his gospel when he tells his people: "Your day has come."

Four centuries after the return of the exiles, Judah's day had come. The Lord himself, the King of kings, the mover of mountains, the Creator of the universe, had arrived in Jerusalem. Very few recognized him. Veiled in flesh, the Lord humbled himself like no other king ever had. He took upon himself the death of the worst of criminals and the punishment of hell for every sin. He gave everything up to earn everything for us. When he declared from the cross, "It is finished" (John 19:30), he said in essence: "The day of your salvation has come." Then he affirmed that eternal statement through his resurrection three days later.

Great leaders come and go. Empires rise from humble beginnings. Nations eventually crumble and cease to exist. Napoleon Bonaparte declared himself to be one of those great emperors. Yet for all of his bravado and megalomania ideals, Bonaparte revealed moments of superb insight. Looking back on history, he once said, "I know men and I tell you, Jesus Christ is no mere man. Between him and every other person in the world there is no possible term of comparison. Alexander, Caesar, Charlemagne, and I have founded empires. But on what did we rest the creations of our genius? Upon force. Jesus Christ founded his empire upon love; and at this hour, millions would die for him."[1]

The kingdom of God remains infinitely different from the worldly nations around us. Our Messianic leader defines loving servitude such as no other leader can claim or fulfill. And you belong to that kingdom. You have the privilege of serving your perfect ruler—the one willing to die for your salvation.

Like Nebuchadnezzar and King Zedekiah, you also work in a position of power. And while you probably lack an army and a throne, your Lord has entrusted you with a possession far more powerful: his word. It is a great responsibility. Do not take it lightly. Instead, hold it fiercely, share it lovingly, and stand on it resolutely.

Like he did with Israel of old, his word will send you "in tears to seek the Lord" when you need to repent. He will remind you, as he

---

[1] H. P. Liddon, *The Divinity of Our Lord and Saviour Jesus Christ; Eight Lectures Preached Before the University of Oxford in the Year 1866,* 4th ed. (New York: Scribner, Welford, and Armstrong, 1873), 147.

reminded his remnant in Babylon, that your "Redeemer is strong." "He will vigorously defend" your cause. And ultimately, he will bring you rest as well—eternal rest.

Let that eternal truth remain your comfort, even as nations rise and fall around you. Perhaps someday the country in which you dwell will see her decline and fall. As those days approach, keep your leaders in your prayers, as Jeremiah and his fellow believers did under Babylonian rule. Don't be surprised when their worldly interests pull them away from God's expectations. After all, "He makes nations great, and destroys them; he enlarges nations, and disperses them" (Job 12:23).

Prayer

"Rejoice, rejoice, believers, And let your lights appear;
The evening is advancing, And darker night is near.
The Bridegroom is arising And soon is drawing nigh.
Up, pray and watch and wrestle; At midnight comes the cry.

"You saints who here in patience Your cross and suff'rings bore,
Shall live and reign forever When sorrow is no more.
Around the throne of glory The Lamb you shall behold;
In triumph lay before him Your shining crowns of gold.

"Arise, Desire of nations; O Jesus, now appear,
The Hope and Expectation Of ev'ry Christian here.
With hearts and hands uplifted We plead, O Lord, to see
The day of earth's redemption That sets your people free." Amen.

—*CW* 7:1, 3–4

"As long as he lived"

Jeremiah 52

Before the "twenties" roared in America and nations warred in Europe, New York City witnessed the construction of a modern-day temple. Designed by the Pennsylvania Railroad Company, her grandiose facades and ascending columns would soon invite New Yorkers, and the rest of the nation, into the most magnificent train station the world had ever seen. Passing through the towering entrances, riders awed as natural light glistened through ornate windows. Stately eagles perched atop her summits as swift, state-of-the-art electric trains sped through her tunnels, effortlessly carrying passengers through earth and water to their destinations. Even New York citizens admitted they had never been in the presence of such grandeur.

Most amazing of all, Penn Station stood as a cathedral for the masses themselves. To pass through those stately pillars and to be bathed by the descending sunlight made even the humblest riders feel like kings.

Then came the advent of the automobile. The age of air travel followed, and New York once again underwent a transformation. Trains screeched to a halt. Stations shut down. Tracks went silent. Eventually, even Penn Station herself, in all of her magnificence, closed her elegant doors forever.

The city was shocked. As jackhammers ripped apart the station's concrete and her opulent, high-flying eagles descended, writers began to sing her memory through the written word. The greatest of these laments came from the timeless writer Vincent Scully. He wrote, "One entered the city like a god; one scuttles in now like a rat."[1]

Was the ancient city of Jerusalem any less majestic? Her sturdy stone walls rose high around the perimeter, safely surrounding her people. Her ornate, golden palaces housed kings great and small. Her streets echoed with the bustle of business. Merchants marveled as they passed through from one side of the world to the other.

Greatest of all, the golden temple of the Lord adorned the heights of the majestic city—the brightest jewel in Jerusalem's crown. Floating above Judah, the house of the Lord appeared to ascend her priests into heaven itself. The words of the psalmists hold our hands, carrying us ever higher into her ceremonious realms. "Those who trust in the LORD are like Mount Zion, which cannot be shaken but endures forever" (Psalm 125:1).

Like a daily commuter strolling through Penn Station's hallowed halls, most of Jeremiah's life passed behind Jerusalem's sturdy walls. He readily recognized every step around her golden palaces. His heart daily drew him into the reaches of her holy temple.

From little on Jeremiah personally looked upon the hallowed confines of the house of the Lord. Priests circumcised him within her walls on his eighth day. His mother would have returned with him thirty-three days later to be purified and to sacrifice a year-old lamb. Every Passover drew Jeremiah back into the city where he celebrated the ancient meal under the shadow of the temple. Yearly sacrifices returned the prophet to her magnificence.

Then, at the end of the age, Jeremiah watched the storm clouds of God's fulfillment thunder in the distance, finally moving in to pour down a flood of heavenly judgment. Those ancient stone walls that had protected generations of families crashed down. Those golden palaces burned with the fiery wrath of the Lord. Their ostentatious adornments melted alongside their inhabitants. The bustling streets now echoed the screams of the dying.

At the center of destruction's chaos stood Jeremiah's temple. Powerlessly he watched his spiritual home collapse. Babylonian

---

[1] Herbert Muschamp, "Architecture View; In This Dream Station Future and Past Collide," *The New York Times*, June 20, 1993.

soldiers streamed through her broken buildings, whisking away the Lord's golden articles. Smoke poured from the city. Tears streamed down Jeremiah's face. Where Israel once joyously entered the city of God, they now scuttled away like rats.

Jeremiah's heart plucked the strings of his lamentation:

How the gold has lost its luster,
the fine gold become dull!
The sacred gems are scattered
at every street corner. (Lamentations 4:1)

The Lord had finally fulfilled what he had been promising for generations. He had "kindled a fire in Zion that consumed her foundations" (Lamentations 4:11b). The descent of death had become more than anyone could handle . . . even Jeremiah. He would never forget the loss he suffered. He didn't want his Lord to forget it either. "Remember, LORD, what has happened to us; look, and see our disgrace" (Lamentations 5:1).

Yet there was more to Jeremiah than anyone realized. All the way back at the beginning of his ministry, the Lord explained to Jeremiah where the true walls stand. He pointed out to his newly minted prophet that some temples stand forever. "Today I have made you a fortified city, an iron pillar and a bronze wall" (1:18a). City walls had failed. Precious stones vanished. Yet the prophet remained. He remained because his Lord had made *him* an impenetrable city. The temple had been destroyed. And yet the Lord remained. He remained because the Lord ruled in the hearts of his people.

The Babylonians had fought against God's people and won. The Lord of lords had bequeathed victory to them on that day . . . but Nebuchadnezzar's reign would eventually run out. Kings and kingdoms would follow, rising and falling in turn. The Lord outlasted them all.

As you picture this worst day for the people of Jerusalem, who can you most identify with? Perhaps the prophet himself reminds you of the disasters you have faced and the loss of loved ones both physically and spiritually. Maybe you see yourself as one of those poor farmers granted land by the grace of the Lord through the Babylonian commanders. After all, you own very little, and what you have, God has given you. Perhaps you feel like one of those captives, bound to a place that does not feel like your own, serving a people you do not understand or recognize.

Then again, maybe none of them quite compare to the ministry in which the Lord has called you. There are three men who might just resemble you more than any others in this destroyed city. They were the three guards, holding fast at the doors of the temple until the very end. Long after kings and officials fled the city, while citizens were being cut down and bound for captivity, these doorkeepers remained steadfast, holding their positions until the very end.

It is possible these men were the descendants of Korah. According to 1 Chronicles 9, this family had guarded the gates to the tabernacle and then the doors to the temple from the very beginning. Even to the last day of Jerusalem, these men faithfully carried out their duty at the doors. They were living the words of Psalm 84: "Better is one day in your courts than a thousand elsewhere; I would rather be a doorkeeper in the house of my God than dwell in the tents of the wicked" (Psalm 84:10).

Throughout the centuries, God's workers have continued the heritage of exercising faithful service in the face of persecution and destruction. From patriarchs to leaders to judges to prophets and priests and kings, to disciples and apostles, the Holy Spirit has continually breathed through men and women. Humble service, against astounding earthly odds, continues today in your ministry.

The Lord knit you together in your mother's womb with every bit as much care as he used to form Jeremiah. The Lord walked with you during your formative ministerial years, protecting you from unseen temptations and enemies. Your God strengthened you when you felt too weak to continue serving in the public ministry he granted you. And your Lord will continue to walk with you, even to the end, just like he stood by Jeremiah, making him a fortress and an iron pillar and a bronze wall. The world fought against Jerusalem's final prophet, up through her final days. Yet, by the grace of God, the prophet remained.

Augustine was thinking specifically about these circumstances in Jeremiah's ministry when he wrote: "This calling, which works through the opportune circumstances of history, whether this calling is in individuals or in peoples or in humankind itself, comes from a decree both lofty and profound."[2] Indeed, what fitting descriptions for your ministry—lofty and profound! The world surrounding you will always appear strong. Yet your Lord remains ever stronger.

Like Augustine, Martin Luther understood what it felt like to view a strong-looking world. At a time when the Lord looked especially weak, Luther wrote:

> No one should become worried when God allows himself to appear as weak, while the world boasts and struts around. The same is true for all Christians, especially preachers. They are often weak and timid, while their powerful adversaries stomp their feet and threaten. This is nothing new. We have to get used to it. It doesn't only happen to us. It happened to all the prophets and apostles. They appeared weak compared to their oppressors. Yet it was in their weakness that they were the strongest.[3]

Luther's words could stand as an epitaph for the prophet Jeremiah. A prophet so weak he seemingly faced persecution every day. A man so broken he embodied lamentation. A ministry so tragic it ended with the destruction of the very people God called him to serve. The world was not worthy of him.

Luther's words could stand as an epitaph for your ministry as well. A called worker so weak others wonder if you are capable at all. An individual so sad at times that ministry mixes with tragedy. A calling that may one day end with the fading away of those who called him.

Jeremiah's Jerusalem crumbled, yet the word and the Lord remained. When the walls around you crumble, while the world tears down temples, persecutes pastors, and throws trials on teachers, look to the walls of Jeremiah's city. She is a new Jerusalem. Her architect is God himself. She bathes her believers in the eternal light

---

[2] Augustine, *On Eighty-Three Varied Questions, Fathers of the Church: A New Translation*, trans David L. Mosher (Washington, D.C.: Catholic University of America Press, 1947), 165.

[3] Martin Luther, *By Faith Alone*, ed. James C. Galvin (Iowa Falls: World Bible Publishers, 1998), 38.

of Christ. Her stream flows from the Lamb at the center, washing those with her perfect baptismal waters.

There, at the center of your heavenly home, will stand your Savior, Jesus. He will wipe every tear from your eyes. In fact, "There will be no more death or mourning or crying or pain" (Revelation 21:4). And if he sacrificed himself to lovingly give you all of this, surely he will be with you always. Remember? "'I am with you and will rescue you,' declares the LORD" (1:19).

Prayer

"Oh, sweet and blessed country, the home of God's elect
Oh, sweet and blessed country that eager hearts expect
Where they who with their leader
Have conquered in the fight
Forever and forever are clad in robes of white.
Jesus in mercy bring us to that dear land of rest
Where sings the host of heaven
your glorious name to bless." Amen.

—*CWS* 728:2

CPSIA information can be obtained
at www.ICGtesting.com
Printed in the USA
BVHW032258120520
579587BV00001BA/2/J